Law Enforcement—
Perpetrated Homicides

Policing Perspectives and Challenges in the Twenty-First Century

Series Editor: Jonathon A. Cooper,
Indiana University of Pennsylvania

In many respects, policing has evolved over the last two centuries; yet issues that concerned policing in the nineteenth and twentieth centuries continue to be salient to contemporary law enforcement. But how these challenges are manifest to the police today are distinct, as society and politics, too, have evolved. And so understanding the role of police in society, the behavior and organization of law enforcement, the relationship between officers and civilians, and the intersection of theory and praxis remain important to the study of police. To this end, volumes in this series will consider policing perspectives and challenges in the twenty-first century, around the world, and through a variety of disciplinary lenses. Ultimately, this series "takes stock" of policing today, considers how it got here, and projects where it might be going. *Policing Perspectives and Challenges in the Twenty-First Century* will be of interest and use to a variety of policing scholars, including academics, police executives, and others who study law enforcement.

Titles in the series

Law Enforcement—Perpetrated Homicides

Accidents to Murder

Tom Barker

LEXINGTON BOOKS
Lanham • Boulder • New York • London

Published by Lexington Books
An imprint of The Rowman & Littlefield Publishing Group, Inc.
4501 Forbes Boulevard, Suite 200, Lanham, Maryland 20706
www.rowman.com

6 Tinworth Street, London SE11 5AL, United Kingdom

British Library Cataloguing in Publication Information Available

The hardback edition of this book was previously catalogued by the Library of Congress as follows:

Library of Congress Cataloging-in-Publication Data Available

ISBN 978-1-7936-0190-2 (cloth : alk. paper)
ISBN 978-1-7936-0192-6 (pbk. : alk. paper)
ISBN 978-1-7936-0191-9 (electronic)

Contents

Acknowledgments

Most of those who helped me on this book will remain anonymous. They are former law enforcement that shared my desire to cut past the professional rhetoric of police apologists to describe the dark secret of law enforcement–perpetuated homicides. Until the law enforcement community comes to grips with this social justice issue and rids the police occupation of these minority trouble-makers, the Morally Dangerous Occupation will never be recognized as a profession. I once again acknowledge the special help of BSJ who made it all possible.

Chapter 1

Policework Occupation and Police-Perpetrated Homicides

INTRODUCTION: POLICE LEO HOMICIDES

The term "police homicides" is used in the popular and academic literature to describe two views of police homicides. The first view presents law enforcement officers (LEOs) as *victims* who die at the hands of a felon. A second view sees LEOs as the *perpetrators* of homicides. The latter police homicides result from accidents, justified legal interventions, or criminal action by LEOs on-duty or off-duty when facilitated and related to their official position as defined by law. These homicides with LEOs as perpetrators are the focus of this inquiry.

LEOs Defined

LEOs aka police officers are paid *public officials* with the *extraordinary powers of arrest* who perform *public safety functions of patrol, traffic control, investigation and detention* at the local, county, state, federal, or special district levels. The operation of the U.S. policing system is historically defined by its foundation in our English heritage and the current definition of the dangerous classes by the elites. Our English heritage served as a model for a policing system that resulted in limited authority circumscribed by law. The fragmented system would be largely local. The inherent fragmentation allowed "police" or law enforcement agencies to expand by legislative definition at the local, state, federal, and special district (Walker, 1983; Barker, 2011).

Police violence by these LEOs includes a variety of violent behaviors against others, including police-perpetrated homicides—a subset of the larger category of police violence. To identify police-perpetrated homicides as a part of police violence we first define homicide.

1

HOMICIDE

Homicide is the killing of a human being by another human being, and depending on the circumstances, the act may be accidental, justified, or criminal. The definitions of accidental, justified, and criminal homicides are important for the classification of police homicides (Harmon, 2008). Police *accidental homicides* not the result of reckless or negligent actions are generally ruled excusable and not subject to criminal sanctions, depending on the circumstances. Accidental—no criminal intent by the slayer—homicides that involve reckless or negligent actions by the slayer are prosecuted as criminal homicides. *Justifiable homicides* are commanded—executions after trail—or authorized by law such as the legal use of deadly force by LEOs. Homicides in the necessary act of self-defense to protect oneself from death or serious bodily injury or death *may* be deemed justified or excusable depending on the circumstances. Any police homicide that is not excusable or justified is a *criminal homicide*—manslaughter or murder. The killing of a human with malice aforethought—intent—is the most serious type of criminal homicide and is prosecuted as murder. Although LEOs homicides are rare events; their rarity provides little comfort or solace to the victims and their survivors. There are other terms used that need explication.

POLICEWORK OCCUPATION

Policework—one word—is an occupation performed by paid public LEOs at all levels of government. These paid public employees have general or limited arrest powers, depending on state and federal statutes, and case law. The workers—LEOs—in the policework occupation perform one or more of the public safety services of traffic, patrol, investigation, and detention/custody. These public officials have the power to detain, arrest, search, and use deadly force—the ultimate force granted by any society. The LEO definition includes publicly paid LEOs in local, county, state, federal, and special district agencies such as campus police agencies, park police, Indian police, and airport police. Detention/custody officials in lockups and jails are included; however, private security personnel are not (Barker, 2019, see Barker, Hunter & Rush, 1994 for an earlier definition).

Unequal Power Relationship

Police-citizen contacts—individually and in groups—are touchstone examples of unequal power settings between parties. LEOs have the legal authority to force compliance with their legal duties. Detention and correctional officers are granted the legal authority to use force in self-defense and the enforcement of rules, regulations, and laws against those remanded into their custody (Bittner, 1990). The legal use of force in these settings includes a wide range of force techniques and can result in police abuse of power.

Police violence against citizens, especially minority and marginalized groups without political power, is a perennial problem in a society with a formal system of social control based on public LEOs. This is especially true for paid public police forces based on the 1829 London Metropolitan Model and democratic policing. The United States exacerbated the police violence problem with the establishment of an alphabet soup creation of law enforcement agencies at all levels of government—ABC, ATF, BART, DEA, DIA, DART, FBI, ICE, IRS, ISDP, MARTA, TSA, USMP, USSS, ad infinitum (Barker, 2020). The legal use of force by these agencies includes a wide range of force techniques from verbal commands to the use of deadly force in individual or collective protest settings. The most severe use of deadly force is police homicides.

LEO-PERPETRATED HOMICIDES

LEOs-Perpetrated Homicides are deaths resulting from acts or omissions by LEOs acting in or related to their official position. Police-perpetrated homicides result from law enforcement actions-direct or proximate—and range from accidents to murder. In defining police-caused homicides, a modified version of law enforcement homicides suggested by Barber and her colleagues was used (Barber, 2016). The Barber study used three criteria in their definition. The first criterion was the *manner of death* that they defined as homicide, not suicide, accident, or natural. Their criterion was modified to include accidental LEO homicides that are the result of reckless or negligent acts regardless of intent. There is a long history of these accidental homicides in U.S. law enforcement activities. The modified definition included suicide by a cop where a person wishing to die provokes a cop into killing them. Murder-suicides were included when a LEO murders a domestic partner and then commits suicide. Their second criterion was that the suspect must be a *LEO* in some level of government—local, state, tribal, special district, or federal. This definition includes correction officers because correction officers like all LEOs are sworn public officers with authority to use lethal force. Last, Barber and her colleagues said police homicides had to occur in the *line of duty*. That is not true in LEO police homicide cases such as murders committed by LEOs for personal reasons while using their police position to facilitate or conceal their criminal acts. Therefore, police homicides occur on- and off-duty.

Historical empirical evidence reveals that a disproportionate number of police homicides result from police interactions with members and groups labeled the *dangerous classes* by the political or economic elite. The current debate over police homicides suggests that the majority to the victims are minority and marginalized victims of the *dangerous classes*. This is not the whole story. However, America's history provides evidence that members of the *dangerous classes* have been singular and multiple victims of police violence, including homicide, during protests and demonstrations. The definition of who is or is not a member of the *dangerous classes* is constantly in flux.

THE DANGEROUS CLASSES

Public police work evolved in England from a need by the political and economic elites to control the lives of the *dangerous classes*—the poor and the disorderly working class who migrated to the crowded cities because of the disruptions resulting from the Industrial Revolution. The Metropolitan Police Act of 1829 created the modern occupation of policing, but the poor and working class thought the New Police as public order police would enforce a moral code that would destroy or disrupt their recreations and lifestyles (Rawlings, 2002).

Their fears were accurate. The newly created paid public police occupation was a means for the "elite" to constrain the activities of the dangerous/marginalized classes in England because "Crime, illegitimacy, idleness, irreligion, poaching, dancing, drinking, the playing of games and so forth were believed to be linked" (Rawlings, 2002). The proactive policing model of the time is what is known as "quality of life" policing today. That is arrests for petty offenses in the streets (drunkenness, gaming, and other social-order offenses), and other acts that are not inherently evil. The new policework occupation was transported to the United States, where the *dangerous classes* were defined by race and ethnicity through the actions of the politically and economic elite.

America's Dangerous Classes in Brief

The treatment of the *dangerous classes* in American history have had tragic civil rights results on the disenfranchised and marginalized groups and stimulated what some consider the current racial based police agencies and a biased American criminal and civil justice system (Williams & Murphy, 1990, Davis, 2017, Slaughter-Johnson, April 13, 2019). The American *dangerous class* groups at various points in our history have included indigenous populations (American Indians), slaves (African, American Indians), and a variety of ethnic and nonwhite racial groups ranging from the Irish, Italians, Chinese, African Americans, Mexicans, to today's illegal immigrants.

Following the bloody removal of the American Indians from their lands, blacks were labeled the *dangerous class* during slavery when the large slave population at the bottom of America's caste system threatened the elite white minority (Reichel, 2013). However, other racial and ethnic groups were viewed as dangerous. The first federal law excluding immigrants based on race was the 1882 Chinese Exclusion law that barred Chinese immigrants—the despised Mongolians and this country's first illegal immigrants—from becoming U.S. citizens (Campbell, 2014). Mexicans in the Southwest, particularly the border states of Texas, California, New Mexico, and Arizona, became the *dangerous class* when the United States seized half of Mexico following the 1848 U.S. Mexican War and the Treaty of Guadalupe Hidalgo. Juan Crow laws—Jim Crow in the Southern states—in the Southwestern states prohibited Latinos and American Indians designated as non-whites from participating without restrictions in the public sphere (Campbell, 2014). American Indians residing in Arizona would not have the right to vote until 1948.

Radicalized miners, steelworkers, and other industrial workers joined the *dangerous classes* when they challenged the elite owner/worker status quo and had the temerity to join unions. The possibility of members of the *dangerous classes* combining and engaging in strikes and insurrections in the manufacturing districts was recognized in the early 1800s (Silver, October 7, 1965). For example, the second mission of the 1829 London Metropolitan Police Force against the *dangerous classes* was to suppress political agitation in the form of mobs and riots—social protest (Silver, October 7, 1965). The key to this control of the *dangerous classes* is the legal use of deadly force.

POLICE LEGAL USE OF DEADLY FORCE

Every community in history has used physical force as a means to secure the effective observance of laws and achieve justice (Reith, 1952). Deadly force has always been allowed if there is credible evidence to believe that the suspect(s) presents a threat of serious physical injury to the officer(s) or the public. However, there are long-standing limitations on the discretionary decisions to use deadly force. The typical restrictions include the following: (1) Deadly force may not be used if the offense is a misdemeanor crime, not a felony; (2) police officers can only use deadly force, in the performance of professional duties and not to advance their own personal reasons or the personal reasons of others; and, (3) police officers may not use deadly force maliciously, frivolously, negligently, or recklessly (Bittner, 1990).

As communities and modern societies evolved, they attempted to remove unnecessary and wanton deadly violence from the use of force in the administration of justice (Bittner, 1990). For example, the outdated common law use of deadly force to apprehend any "fleeing felon" is no longer applicable in modern societies such as the United States—1985 U.S. Supreme Court decision *Tennessee v. Garner* (Blumberg, 1991).

Fleeing Felon Doctrine

The "fleeing felony doctrine" as the legal use of deadly force developed in eleventh-century England and was transported to colonial United States and used against the defined *dangerous classes.* The English common law fleeing felon doctrine was necessary for early societies where (1) there were no weapons available that could kill at a distance—guns and rifles; (2) felonies were punishable by death; and (3) there was little, if any communication among law enforcement agencies in different communities—felons who escaped were lost forever (Sherman, 1980).

Although various states had removed the "fleeing felon" rule from their statutes, the first national action against police violence was the 1985 U.S. Supreme Court decision—*Tennessee v. Garner.* This ruling declared that the use of deadly force to stop all fleeing felons was unconstitutional. If the suspect poses no immediate threat to the officer or others, the use of deadly force was not justified. In the decision, the court pointed out that the officer who shot Garner was "reasonably sure" that he was an unarmed teenager running away from him. This decision had a profound effect on police homicides. The "fleeing felon doctrine" is gone; however, it was an accepted American police technique until 1985. At the time, it was difficult to get some police chiefs to accept that "the fleeing felon" laws were illegal, especially when it was legal in state statute—personal experience. However, an in-depth examination of the U.S. police use of deadly force when it was in effect provides empirical evidence that American *dangerous classes* groups, however defined, have been disproportionally the victims of civil rights violations and legal and extralegal police homicides

LAW ENFORCEMENT VIOLENCE AGAINST AMERICAN DANGEROUS CLASSES

Historical antecedents of Law enforcement violence and homicides against the *dangerous classes* mentioned earlier are essential to an understanding of the political and social context of this complex social justice issue. Race, economic, and political issues have always impacted the American system of justice. Members of the labeled *dangerous classes* are traditionally the victims of physical abuse, including legal and illegal violence. After the violent expulsion of Native Americans from their lands, the new white European immigrants and their police forces engaged in mass homicides against the unwilling immigrants—African slaves.

The Southern Slave Patrols

The first police agencies based on the London Metropolitan Police Model of a paid public police force developed in the northeastern cities in the mid to late 1840s. However, some argue that the Southern Slave Patrols were the first state-sponsored U.S. police agencies (Williams & Murphy, 1990; Ritchie & Mogul, 2008). This is subject to debate; however, it is true that rural white police agencies were in existence in the Colonial States of South Carolina, North Carolina, Virginia, and Georgia to control the American *dangerous class*—slaves—in the early to mid-1700s (Reichel, 1988). The slaves were dangerous because they ran away, committed criminal acts, including poisoning their masters, and engaged in revolts and insurrections. The most massive slave uprising in American history took place in 1739 in the South Carolina colony (Reichel, 1988). Fifty Negroes and thirty-five whites were killed. In the developing Southern cities of this early period, black slaves were the majority race, increasing the perceived and real threat to the white majority.

The slave patrols, at first voluntary and then compulsory by law, were formed to visit any plantation having slaves to look for arms, to find and punish runaway slaves, or to identify slaves off their plantation without permission (Hadden, 2001). The punishment included whippings and execution. After the demise of the slave patrols and the Civil War, the legacy behind the identification of freed blacks as a *dangerous class* continued. The early laws restricting the civil rights of black slaves and their freedom of movement segued into the "Black Codes." The codes were imposed on freedmen and freedwomen until they were dismantled by Reconstruction (Cooper, 2015). Then the codes morphed into the Jim Crow laws in the South and Juan Crow laws in the Southwest that formally separated the whites and people of color into unequal worlds. However, the division of American society into color and ethnic categories was not confined to any one region of the United States. LEO-caused homicides and violence were the norms against designated *dangerous classes* in the northeast United States before and after the establishment of police agencies modeled after the London Metropolitan Police Model.

NINETEENTH-CENTURY POLICE-PERPETRATED HOMICIDES AND VIOLENCE IN NEW YORK CITY

1834 Race Riot aka Anti-abolition Riots

Manumitted slaves were persecuted outside the Southern states and in supposedly free states. According to Kerber (1967), a freed female slave was stoned to death in Philadelphia in 1819. In 1829, 1,000 freed slaves were forced to leave Cincinnati, and manumitted slaves were not allowed to settle in Ohio. Controversy over the slavery decision and the amalgamation of the races was a hotly debated issue. This was especially true in nineteenth-century New York City.

Segregation laws were alive and functioning in New York City before a three-day Race Riot occurred in the summer of 1834 (Kerber, 1967). At the time, free Negroes were segregated by law and custom. Negroes had separate seating in churches, courtrooms, and theatres. They were denied the vote. Negroes could not attend public schools or sit in the horse-drawn streetcars, but they could ride on the exposed decks of steamers. The white residents of NYC believed that "God himself separated the white from the black" (Kerber, 1967: 28). The burgeoning abolitionist movement and their fiery speakers reminded the NYC residents that they had a race problem and called for reform, setting up an open conflict between Abolitionists and Amalgamators. This conflict resonated in fiery debates and violence for decades.

The integrationist ideas of the Amalgamators created a real fear of unfair competition between the white labor forces and the free blacks that competed with each other for the lowest-wage jobs. The competition was exacerbated by Irish immigration. In 1827 the British ended the legislation restricting Irish immigration and 30,000 Irish immigrants arrived in New York annually. These conditions created a series of riots between the whites and the blacks that had to be put down by the police—watchmen—and the militia. During the riots, the homes, businesses, and other buildings belonging to abolitionists and Negroes were burned. The militia was called out to support the police watch, and the riots ceased. The 1834 Riot and the 1849 Astor Place Riot foreshadowed the bloody 1863 New York Draft Riot.

1849 Astor Place Riot

The 1849 Astor Place Riot demonstrates how supposedly trivial events have violent outcomes when social classes conflict. The riot shows the distinct class divisions in play in nineteenth-century America. The hatred between two actors—William Macready, an English thespian who represented the

New York upper class, and Edwin Forrest, who was the hero of the lower-class and recent immigrants—erupted into a full-scale riot that led to the police and the militia firing into an angry crowd killing twenty-two persons and injuring forty-eight others (McNamara, February 17, 2019). Forrest supporters interrupted Macready's performance at the upscale Astor Opera House triggering the riot.

The violence between distinct groups continued. Six years later, twelve New Yorkers were killed in July 1857 in a battle between Catholic and Protestant gangs (Vodrey, 2010).

1863 New York City Draft Riots

Although the Draft Riots were initially intended as a protest against the newly created Civil War draft laws, the riots had a more sinister racial objective. The consensus is that the NYC 1963 Draft riot that resulted in from 1,000 to 1,500 white deaths and an unknown number of Negro deaths had its origin in the fear that the city's Irish workers would lose their jobs to an influx of freed Southern black slaves (Albon, 1951).

The Emancipation Proclamation and the fear of an influx of Southern freemen threatened the social status and economic position of the white Irish immigrants. Taking advantage of this proclamation, slavery supporters pressed the rumors that emancipation would create the business of importing freed blacks to the North to supply cheap labor. The Irish immigrant's fears were buttressed by the common practice of employers hiring free Southern blacks when the labor supply was low, or when workers complained about employment conditions or wages (Olzak, 1989).

When the riots first started the New York Metropolitan Police Department was the only "official" force available to stop it. The New York State Militia was at Gettysburg assisting Union troops. Until federal troops could be sent to the city, blacks were lynched, and homes were destroyed as the Metro Police beat the mobs with nightsticks and fired into the crowds in futile attempts to stop the violence (Vodrey, 2010; Johnson, 2003). The 1870–1871 religious riots followed these riots.

Orange Riots of 1870–1871

Irish Catholics protested parades held by Irish Protestants—Orange Men—commemorating the Battle of the Boyne—the battle between Catholic and Protestants in Ireland. The brutal NYPD suppressed this riot that killed over sixty people, including women and children, and left over a hundred injured. Once again, the police fired into the mobs (Johnson, 2003).

STATE VIOLENCE IN LABOR DISPUTES:
THE NEW DANGEROUS CLASSES,
RADICALIZED WORKERS, AND UNIONS

Taft (1966) opines that U.S. labor/management disagreements have turned violent when unorganized strikes occur or when labor union recognition is disputed. In these incidents, the *dangerous classes* are radicalized workers of no particular racial or ethnic group. The only common factor in these disputes is that one group—radicalized workers or union members—have tried to change the terms of employment and that has been resisted by the other groups—management and owners. These disputes resulted in state-sponsored violence by the police, the militia and federal troops. The police of that time were conventional in their thinking and were antagonist to labor unions, radical groups, and racial minorities (Fogelson, 1977). The worst-case scenario of their contempt is the Great Strike of 1877.

The Great Strike of 1877

The Great Strike of 1877 is considered the most extensive, most destructive, and most frightening use of state power against citizens since the New York City 1863 Draft Riots (Stowell, 2008). What began as a nationwide strike in July 1877 against railroads pay cuts lasted several weeks. The strike spread to sympathetic wageworkers throughout the country as working-class consciousness recognized its struggle against the capitalist classes (Harring, 1983). The elite owners used the police as a weapon against working-class wage earners to break strikes and end protests (DeMichele, 2008). Although the Great Strike took place throughout the country, police violence against peaceful crowds was most evident in Chicago and Pittsburg. In Chicago, the police fired into crowds of protesters until they ran out of ammunition (Schneiroy, 2008). Thirty-five men and boys were killed, and several hundreds were wounded. In Pittsburg, combined police and militia killed an estimated one hundred protesters.

Police violence against citizens was justified by a new definition of the enemy—no class socialist immigrants. The new immigrant working-class wageworkers flocking into the industrialized cities were defined by the *Chicago Tribune* as "governed by their passions; they are coarse in tastes and vicious in habits; they are ignorant and revengeful; they are readily influenced by liquor" (Schneiroy, 2008: 95). Allen Pinkerton of Pinkerton Detective Agency fame and a supplier of strikebreakers proclaimed that the strikers and protesters were communists, tramps, and misguided unionists (Salvatory, 1976). Compounding their dangerous disposition was that many of the Chicago strikers were socialists and members of the Workingmen's Party of the

United States. The *dangerous classes* now included immigrants and socialists. In the twenty-first century, immigrants and socialists would return to the popular American definition of *dangerous classes*. Illegal immigrants were threatened with deportation if they did not cooperate with the authorities in these early riots as it is alleged they are today.

1897: Lattimer Massacre of Immigrant Protesters

An 8-feet rough-cut shale boulder is located in the small coal town of Lattimer, Pennsylvania. It commemorates the killing of nineteen immigrants from southern and eastern Europe on Sunday, September 10, 1897, by local police authorities. The immigrants had migrated to rural Lattimer to work in the deep, dangerous anthracite coalmines. At the time, immigrants from these areas of Europe were considered inferior with strange customs and a threat to native-born American whites—a *dangerous class* (Shackel, 2019). On the fateful Sunday day, about 400 miners rallied to march to the mine and peacefully protest for improved working conditions. Eighty-six armed deputy sheriffs and company police opened fire on the protesters as they marched. Nineteen of the peaceful marchers died that day and five more died later in the week. The sheriff and his deputies were tried for killing one miner in February 1898. They were acquitted after the defense attorney described the dead miners as "invaders from them steppes of Hungary" who came to America to destroy peace and liberty (Shackel, 2019).

1909 Pressed Steel Car Strike

The Pressed Steel Car Company located in McKees Rocks, Pennsylvania, was the largest railroad car producer in America. The company manufactured the cars on an assembly line. The work was dangerous, with an average of one person a day being killed from moving cranes (Pitz, 2009). The company was also well known for its low pay and peonage of its workers. The workers—unskilled immigrants from southern and eastern Europe—had to live in quarters rented from the company and buy their food from a "company store" at inflated prices or be fired.

The workers went on strike on payday Saturday, July 10, 1909, after their starvation wages were cut further without explanation. The company hired 550 scabs-strike breakers— setting off a series of conflicts between the strikers and armed deputy sheriffs. The Pennsylvania State Police was called in to support the local law enforcement authorities. The conflict climaxed on August 22, 1909—Bloody Sunday—with the death of eleven to twenty-six strikers and a deputy sheriff.

1937 Memorial Day Massacre: Police Out of Control

On Memorial Day, May 30, 1937, 200 plus Chicago police officers fired multiple shots into peaceful labor demonstrators, approaching the Republic Steel Plant in South Chicago (Leab, 1967; Dennis, 2010). The marchers included women and children. Ten demonstrators were killed, and ninety were injured and several permanently disabled. Dennis (2010) describes the eyewitness account of a woman shot in the leg and a wounded ten-year-old boy being helped into a private car to be taken to the hospital (Dennis, 2010: 143). One woman claimed that she was lucky to be alive, because a cop chased her as she ran away, "shooting all the time, and he just hit my hand" (Dennis, 2010: 146). The police claimed they fired into the unruly mob because the crowd charged them while throwing bricks and sticks. However, the coroner's report revealed that 65.5 percent of those injured by gunshots were shot in the back. Existing photos and a 1937 Paramount News camera film shows uniformed Chicago PD officers chasing, shooting, and clubbing men and women as they ran from the police.

The photos and the film show multiple police officers clubbing wounded persons on the ground. Several injured persons "bled out" as they waited for help that was never summoned. One wounded person pleaded with a policeman for help. The officer's response was, "Shut up you son of a bitch; you got what was coming to you" (Dennis, 2010: 147). Thirty-five police officers were injured that day, and three were hospitalized. The police injuries were mostly cuts and bruises from falling. None had gunshots. The film created national outrage; however, none of the out-of-control police officers was ever charged for these atrocities. The police actions in Chicago are best described as a Police Riot—an example of out-of-control police officers exacting extralegal violence on a perceived *dangerous class*. There have been other examples of Police Riots.

POLICE RIOTS AGAINST PEACEFUL PROTESTERS

The extralegal violence, including examples of homicides committed by LEOs during the 1960s civil rights struggle, are too massive to summarize. One source documents 239 incidents of collective racial violence from January 1, 1963, to May 31, 1968 (Downs, 1979). It is during this period that the "escalated force" model of protest policing was in vogue. The "escalated force" force model predicts that the police will be most repressive against dangerous counter culture groups that present the most threat to political elites (Earl, Soule, and McCarthy, August 2003).

The "escalated force" model is evident in "police riots," where the police instigate, escalate, or sustain violent confrontations (Walker Report, 1968). Stark, in his seminal work on police riots, offers the following definition "'hostile outbursts' in which the major participants are police officers" (Stark, 1972: 11). During a Police Riot, the LEOs engage in unrestrained and widespread police brutality against citizens for political repression. The term was first used to describe the actions of the Chicago police during the 1968 Democratic Convention in Chicago. However, a "police riot" occurred in Selma, Alabama, three years earlier in 1965.

Bloody Sunday—Selma, Alabama, May 7, 1965

What became known as Bloody Sunday occurred during the 1960s civil rights struggle. Bloody Sunday has its genesis with police homicide and violence in the small rural town of Marion, Alabama, in Dallas County on February 18, 1965. The murder of a young black man—the precipitating event—would be unresolved for four decades until May 10, 2007, when a retired Alabama State Trooper charged with murder pleaded guilty to manslaughter and apologized for the killing (Bernstein, July 8, 2015). He received six months in jail.

On the fateful night in 1965, a twenty-six-year-old Vietnam veteran Jimmie Lee Jackson joined with a group of Negroes in a local Methodist church to protest the recent jailing of a Southern Christian Leadership Conference (SCLC) official for participating in voter registration activities. The protesters made a dangerous nighttime march to the jail one block from the church. Local police and Alabama State Troopers met the marchers, and they were brutally beaten. The club-wielding lawmen chased a group of marchers including Jackson into Mack's Café, a local black restaurant. An unidentified state trooper shot Jackson in the stomach under suspicious circumstances inside the cafe. The police custom at the time was to remove nametags and cover badge numbers when engaging in protest incidents (personal knowledge—I did the same thing at several protests in the 1960s). The trooper's identity remained hidden until 2005 when he came forward of his own volition even though he had killed another unarmed black man in May 1966 (Fleming, March 5, 2005). Jackson died several days later. No official authorities ever questioned the officer until 2007; however, Jackson was arrested and charged with assaulting a police officer while he lay dying in the hospital (Springer, 2011).

In response to Jackson's death, the SCLC planned a massive protest march on May 7, 1965, from Selma, Alabama, to Montgomery—the state capital 54 miles away. Just outside Selma at the Edmund Pettus Bridge—named after a Civil War general and a U.S. Senator—local police, sheriff's deputies, and

Alabama State Troopers met the peaceful marchers that included future U.S. Congressmen, John Lewis.

The 600 marchers were tear-gassed and brutally beaten all the way back to Selma. The whole incident was televised. The national exposure enraged many Americans and embarrassed most Alabamians and many LEOs (personal experience and interviews with working police officers). President Johnson went on TV to praise the marchers and condemn the police actions. Martin Luther King asked for civil rights activist and religious leaders to come to Alabama to support the voting rights cause. The exposed level of state violence exceeded the public's tolerance as was common for the brutal reaction of Southern law enforcement officials during the early 1960s—witness the national response to Birmingham, Alabama's Police Commissioner and the use of dogs and firehouses in 1963 against black school children. Even some Birmingham police officers refused to participate in the extra-legal violence against school children and peaceful demonstrators (personal knowledge and interviews with working officers).

Earl, Soule, and McCarthy (2003) opine that external watchdogs—national politicians, the Department of Justice, civil rights groups—and the public tend to overlook moderate repressive police actions, but the indiscriminate use of violence by Southern police officers on Bloody Sunday provoked external reactions.

Civil rights activists poured into the state and were a big part of the civil rights movement that ended the Alabama Jim Crow segregation laws. No one died on the Edmund Pettus Bridge beat-down, but white supremacists murdered two of those coming to support the movement—James Reeb, a white Boston minister, was beaten to death by white segregationists, and Viola Liuzzo was shot to death by an FBI informant as she traveled to Alabama from Michigan in a car driven by a black activist (Jeffries, June 17, 2008).

The 1968 Democratic Convention in Chicago

Significant collective events where protesters seek radical goals that threaten the political elites are most likely to receive the most severe police action—the "All Hands on Deck" approach where police use physical force, make arrests and use their weapons, including tear gas (Earl, Soule, & McCarthy, August 2003). During the four days and nights of the 1968 Chicago convention 10,000 protesters from diverse groups and ideologies—hippies, yippies, youngsters working for political candidates, professional people with dissenting political views, anarchists, revolutionaries, motorcycle gangs, black activists, and young thugs—united under one cause—Opposition to the Vietnam War. The motley group of protesters screamed obscene epithets and threw rocks, bathroom tiles, urine and feces at 23,000 Chicago police officers and National Guard troops who responded with unrestrained and indiscriminate police violence on anyone who came in contact with them.

The rioting police clubbed and hit journalists, peaceful protesters, and innocent bystanders with no consideration of age or gender. According to the Walker National Commission that examined the police riot, the victims included "persons who had broken no law, disobeyed no order, made no threat" (Walker Report, 1968). The innocent victims were peaceful protesters, onlookers, residents passing through, or living in the area. Six hundred and sixty-eight people were arrested; 425 were treated at temporary medical facilities; 200 were treated on the scene; 400 hundred were given first aid for tear gas exposure; and 110 had to go to the hospital. Unbelievably, no one died. The Chicago police did not fire into the crowd as they did at the 1937 Memorial Day Massacre.

POLICE VIOLENCE AND HOMICIDES AGAINST MEXICANS

The academic and popular discussion of U.S. LEO homicides has primarily focused on police violence against the various *dangerous classes* in the Southern states and the Northeast, particularly African Americans. Equally disturbing but primarily ignored is the Anglo-American treatment of Mexicans (Romero, 2001). Carrigan and Webb (2013) in their seminal study of Mexican lynchings refer to lynched Mexicana as the *forgotten dead.*

They use the term "Mexican" to refer to persons born in Mexico and living in the United States and those of Mexican descent born in the United States. They do not use the terms "Hispanic" or "Latino" because those terms were not in use at the time examined (Carrigan & Webb, 2013). In the western and southwestern states, racial discrimination and state violence against Mexicans has a long history (Urquito-Ruiz, 2004).

Following the end of the Mexican-American War and the 1848 Treaty of Hidalgo, Mexico lost half its geographic size with this treaty. The Mexicans already living in the conquered areas that would become Texas, Arizona, New Mexico, and California were guaranteed their property and civil rights by the treaty, but that is not what happened (Knowlton, 1970). The invading Anglos did not treat Mexican nationals who were in the seized territory as citizens. The Anglos dispossessed them of their homes and took their lands.

The Mexican hatred stirred up by the U.S.-Mexican war was deeply ingrained in the early Anglo settlers. The "Remember the Alamo" battle cry was a significant part of early Texas culture for decades and embodied in the racist and brutal policing practices of the Texas Rangers prior to August 10,1935—the establishment of the Texas Department of Public Safety. Prior to that date, Mexican nationals in the occupied lands were subjected to extra-legal violence—lynchings, murders of men and boys, and rape of the women and girls (Romero, 2001).

Mexican immigrants that came looking for work, starting with the influx of Mexican workers during the 1849 California Gold rush, were subjected to extralegal violence and murder. Mexicans were discriminated against by an established system of Juan Crow laws enforced by violent police actions up until the 1950s in Texas. Mexicans were segregated from Anglos in schools, churches, and restaurants (Martinez, 2018). They were discouraged from voting or serving on juries. Mexicans—legal and illegal immigrants—were and still are treated by some as impoverished brown-skinned criminals—the *dangerous classes*, and a threat to the "American way of life" (Gonzales, 2000).

Although the Texas Rangers, an investigative branch of the Texas Department of Public Safety, is a well-respected law enforcement agency today, this was not always true. In the early nineteenth century, the Texas Rangers were an instrument of racial oppression and terror. Some historians view the early Texas Rangers in the same light as the earlier colonial slave patrols—the first Western vigilante group to be invested with enforcement powers (Martinez, 2018). The fledgling Texas Rangers performed slave patrols objectives after Texas independence in 1836 (Prassel, 1972). Rangers brutally policed the African slaves and prevented slaves from escaping into Mexico. Rangers, at times, crossed into Mexico to bring back runaway slaves.

The Texas Ranger's Dark History—Anti-Mexican Homicides

The Texas Ranger's "dark history" reveals their murderous efforts at ethnic cleansing in the early settlement of Texas. From August 1915 to June 1920, an unknown number of Mexicans—estimates run from several hundred to several thousand—were killed by the Texas Rangers and vigilante groups during a race war between Anglos and Mexicans—the *dangerous class* (Carrigan & Webb, 2013; Onion, May 5, 2016; Martinez, 2018). A 1919 report of the Texas legislature investigation into the actions of the Texas Rangers that was sealed until 2000 has the following passage: "During the course of these events [1910 to 1919], the regular Texas Rangers along with hundreds of special rangers appointed by Texas governors killed an estimated 5,000 Hispanics along the border between 1914 and 1919" (http://legacy.lib.utexas.edu/taro/tslac/50062/tsl-50062.html). The actions of the Rangers and their collusion with vigilante groups was an ethnic cleansing effort to remove all Mexicans from Texas—Mexican American citizens and Mexican nationals (Martinez, 2018). The Texas Rangers during that period used homicide as racially motivated violence.

Knowlton (1970) gives the example of a Mexican American from Texas whose grandfather was hung by the Texas Rangers as his family watched. Anglo-American ranchers drove branded cattle on his land and accused him of stealing them. The Anglos got his grandfather's property after the hanging. Between 1848 and 1929 there were 597 documented lynchings of Mexicans in the United States—Texas (282), California (188), Arizona (59), and New Mexico (49) (Carrigan & Webb, 2003). Based on the relative size of the population, the risk of lynching was nearly as high or greater for Mexicans in the southwest as it was for blacks in the South (Carrigan & West, 2003: 414). One of the largest lynchings in U.S. history occurred in Nueces County, Texas. Forty Mexicans were randomly lynched for the murder of a white man in 1877 (Carrigan & West, 2003). The Texas Rangers were directly or indirectly involved in many of these lynching's.

In 1881, Texas Rangers crossed into Mexico to bring back a wanted Mexican national. The Rangers illegally extradited the wanted man, and once back in Texas, they turned him over to a mob that lynched him (Carrigan & Webb, 2003). Following a train robbery in Texas in 1915, Texas Rangers killed two Mexican train passengers suspected of aiding the robbers. The Rangers then took eight Mexican suspects to the banks of the Rio Grande River and executed them (Carrigan & Webb, 2003). The bodies were left on the border river as an example of Texas Ranger swift justice. The 1919 Porvenir Massacre is a tragic example of the brutal tactics of the Texas Rangers as they engaged in the removal of Mexicans from Texas.

Porvenir Massacre

Porvenir, Texas, is in a rural, rugged, isolated area of mountains, desert and the Rio Grande River just across the Texas-Mexico border and the city of Chihuahua, Mexico. In 1918, Anglo ranchers in the area complained that Mexican bandits were raiding their property. It was rumored that the Mexican residents in Porvenir were providing safe passage and support for the Marauders (Harris & Sadler, 2004; Martinez, 2018). The ranchers claimed that men from Porvenir joined the gangs on raids. At the time, only one Anglo—a schoolteacher—lived in the small community. The area was under the jurisdiction of Texas Ranger Company B at Marfa, Texas commanded by Captain J. M. Fox. Captain Fox was ordered by the commander of the Big Bend District to "clean out the nest" of bandits in Porvenir. He did that with a vengeance.

Captain Fox and Company B composed of eight rangers, four local ranchers accompanied by members of the U.S. Eighth Calvary who had been ordered to assist the Texas Rangers in searching for weapons rode into Porvenir at 2:00 a.m. The soldiers woke the residents and had them stand outside their residences. The soldiers who regularly patrolled the area were known and trusted by the residents. The soldiers assured the frightened residents that the hated and feared Texas Rangers would not harm them. Captain Fox dismissed the soldiers, and the Texas Rangers took control of the terrified residents and moved them to a nearby bluff.

According to later eyewitness testimony, the Rangers tied all the men and boys together and began shooting them (Harris & Sadler, 2004; Martinez, 2018). Soldiers heard the shots and the screaming women and rushed to the massacre scene. The soldiers found fifteen bodies, each with multiple wounds and a coup de grace headshot. One of the soldiers said the massacre scene reminded him of a slaughterhouse (Martinez, 2018: 123). He added, "A hospital corpsman who was with us went over to the bodies, but not a breath was left in a single one. The professionals had done their work well." The resulting investigation concluded that the fifteen Mexicans killed by the Rangers and the ranchers had been disarmed and were helpless prisoners when they were executed (Harris & Sadler, 2004: 354).

The Texas Governor was told that the men and boys killed were innocent farmers and not bandits. No one was ever prosecuted for the massacre, but Texas Governor Hobby disbanded Texas Ranger Company B, fired all the Rangers involved, and forced Captain Fox to resign. Within the last two years, Texas has finally acknowledged that the Porvenir Massacre and the other atrocities of the Texas Rangers occurred (Casares, February 3, 2018; Martinez, 2018).

POLICE VIOLENCE AGAINST INDIVIDUALS AND GROUPS IN EARLY AMERICAN HISTORY

Police violence and homicides against individuals and groups have a long history in the United States in addition to the multiple homicides committed against the *dangerous classes* during protests, demonstrations, and dissent outlined previously. In their history, New York police have used their official position to commit and cover up crimes from burglary to election fraud and murder (Sherman, 1978). The same could be said for most U.S. urban police departments. The best narrative of the early 1900s police violence in New York City is contained in the 1931 autobiography of NYPD Captain Cornelius W. Williams (Williams, 1931, see also Reppetto, 1978). His descriptions of police violence events are too numerous to present here. Police-perpetrated homicide was a common outcome of police-citizen interactions, regardless of race or ethnicity. The first-known U.S. LEO to be convicted and executed for a murder committed on duty was NYPD Lt. Charles Becker in 1912. Then, and now, police officers worked hand and glove with local criminal gangs, including acting as "muscle" for criminal gangs (see Haller (1976) for the working relationship between the Chicago police and criminals 1890–1925).

Seven years earlier—1905—an NYPD Patrolman had been convicted of murdering a black night watchman (Johnson, 2003: 81). The NYPD officer claimed he shot in self-defense. That did not convince the jury because the black man was shot in the back and several witnesses testified that the officer had fired several additional shots as the man lay helpless on his back. In 1926 another NYPD officer was convicted of first-degree murder and sentenced to death after murdering a shopkeeper who identified him in a line-up in a police station house as an attempted extortionist (Johnson, 2003: 117 & 118). The officer shouted, "You won't squeal against anyone again." These killer cops who commit intentional murder are not a new phenomenon in American policing and will be discussed more fully later. The 1929 Wickersham Commission—the first National Commission on Police Violence—in a volume entitled *Our Lawless Police*—documented the use of the third-degree and other forms of police violence throughout the United States. The same report found that the American police of the 1920s and 1930s engaged in "institutionalized malpractice"—violations of constitutional rights or the human dignity of civilians (Richardson, 1974).

Police violence was an accepted part of early urban policing in Chicago. For example, in Chicago, there were three justifications for police violence: First, to mete out punishment to wrongdoers, "That's my motto, scare 'em to death and knock the hell out of them, and let them go" (Haller, 1976: 318). Second, the third degree was an accepted part of investigative work. This was still in use in Chicago during the 1970s and 1980s. A Chicago police commander, Jon Burge, and his team of white detectives known as the "midnight crew" used electric shocks, waterboarding, and mock executions, accompanied by racial epithets, and attacks to the genitals to coerce false confessions from 200 predominately African American criminal suspects (Taylor, 2016). This was a part of the third reason for police violence, which was to uphold the dignity of the policeman. This is what is known as arrests for COP (Contempt of Cop) or POP(Pissing off the Police) in today's police culture. During the 1960s many police supervisors would not accept a "resisting arrest" charge unless the suspect was sent to the hospital or the morgue. The rationale was that if he was a "cop fighter," he might kill the next cop (personal experience). The "get tough on criminals" philosophy still exist in many police agencies as they conduct the War on Crime.

War on Crime and Resulting Violence

Theodore Roosevelt in 1894 was the first NYPD Police Commissioner to recognize the police as a military organization when he declared "war" against crime and corruption. He increased the officer's weaponry and gave them the license to use it against criminals (Johnson, 2003: 88). Other police CEO's have urged the police on in their "no quarter" for suspected criminals.

The American police have always had hostility toward criminals, the courts, politicians, and civilians who do not share the police view of the genesis of crime, disorder, and its control (Richardson, 1974; Walker, 1977). This ideology was the standard for the NYPD since Clubber Williams declared, "There is more law in the end of nightstick than un a decision of the Supreme Court" (Johnson, 2003: 41). Frank Rizzo, when he was the Philadelphia Police Commissioner in the 1970s, reportedly told a newsperson, "The way to treat criminals is *spacco il capa*—to bust their heads" (Skolnick & Fyfe, 1993: 139). I hear the same philosophy from working police today.

PREVIOUS INFORMATION ON
POLICE-PERPETRATED HOMICIDES

Popular Sources for Police-Perpetrated Homicides

The majority of information on homicides by LEOs, before the mid to late 1960s, is not the result of scholarly research; however, there is anecdotal evidence, some from popular sources. The 1977 publication *Killer Cops: An Encyclopedia of Lawless Lawmen* by Michael Newton is an excellent source to begin an examination of LEOs who murder in U.S. history. The fascinating book on sixty-seven American killer cops includes early nineteen-century cops and Western lawmen killer cops such as Bass Outlaw, Wild Bill Hickok, and Wyatt Earp. The popular market book was used as a reference source for research purposes, although I disagreed with many of his selections.

Stark (1972) in a footnote describes a 1968 "friendly fire" incident between three trigger happy off-duty NYPD officers on a crowded expressway unaware that they were officers that left one dead and one seriously injured. A second 1968 "friendly fire" incident by an NYPD plainclothes officer and another Housing Authority plainclothes officer left NYPD officer dead. Friendly fire police homicides still occur in the NYPD and other police departments. Although multiple police-caused deaths are rare in modern police work, the Philadelphia police did drop an incendiary bomb on a row house occupied by a militant black cult (Skolnick, May 21, 1985). The fires spread to sixty more homes and lead to eleven deaths including five children ranging from age seven to thirteen. It could happen again in the present rise of police militarization with surplus military equipment.

Early Scholarly Research on LEO-Perpetrated Homicides

Professor Gerald Robin (1963) published one of the first empirical studies of justified police homicides—intentional killings commanded or authorized by law. He reported that from 1952 to 1955, the reported rate of justifiable police homicides (JPH) was 3.2 percent of the total number of homicides in the United States. Furthermore, Robin opined that the victim-offender relationship in police justified homicides is an example of victim-precipitated homicide because the victim was killed as a consequence of his criminal actions—an interesting but biased conclusion.

Robin examined the thirty-two known police killing of criminals in Philadelphia from 1950 to 1960 according to official police records. Thirty of the cases were disposed by the medical examiner's inquest, and two officers were indicted and cleared by a jury at trial. All the deaths were the result of gunshot wounds. Twenty-five victims of the police-caused homicide victims resisted during the attempted arrest. Seven of the thirty-two victims were fleeing when shot and killed. Robin also presented JPH reported for ten U.S. urban cities from 1950 to 1960—Boston 3; Buffalo 7; Milwaukee 10; Philadelphia 32; Washington, D.C., 26; Cincinnati 23; Kansas City MO. 23; Chicago 191; and Miami 21. He reported that the national statistics show that the U.S. police were six times more likely to kill than to be killed in the line of duty. He used this statistic to opine that the dangerousness of police work may be exaggerated. The study concluded that the JPH in the sample revealed that Negro's deaths were disproportionate to whites at 7 to 1, female JPH's deaths were negligible, JPH victims were relatively young, victims were generally unskilled workers, 70 percent of the shootings occurred between 9:00 p.m. and 9:00 a.m., and two-thirds of the victims had criminal records. The author reported that six of the men killed had "strong indications of psychotic consequences" (Robin, 1963).

CONCLUSION

Complaints of police violence and LEO-perpetrated homicides are a part of American police history. The allegations are not confined to big cities or particular regions, any specific racial or ethnic group, or labeled *dangerous class*, or any type/pattern. For example, in August 1900 in Akron, Ohio, a shootout between police in a city building and civilians outside left two children killed by police gunfire (Richardson, 1974: 188). Johnson (2003) in her seminal study of NTPD police brutality complaints opined that the use of police violence progressed through several periods. In the nineteenth century, the major citizen complaint was "clubbing" where brutal police bludgeoned poor, working-class citizens, and immigrants with nightsticks and blackjacks. Severe injuries and deaths occurred during the "clubbings."

During the Prohibition era, NYPD police collusion with criminals increased police violence and the use of the third degree to elicit confessions. The victims were predominately the immigrant poor, African Americans, and other marginalized individuals and groups. Injuries and deaths occurred during these extracted false confessions. In the 1870s, the 1930s, and the 1960s mass police violence was directed at the *dangerous classes* such as Communists, labor, African American activists, strikers, and demonstrators. Johnson said that the significant police brutality complaints resulted in police brutality in the form of street justice—punishment given to criminals, wrongdoers, and disrespecters.

The historical discussion of law enforcement violence and homicides against members and groups of the *dangerous classes* is a part of American history. However, the risk to the physical security and civil rights of those labeled as members of the *dangerous classes* still exists in this country. The use of the *dangerous class* label has utility for politically charged criminal justice professionals because of its flexibility. For example, a Texas District Attorney (DA) running for reelection arrested 177 bikers at a biker/police shoot out in Waco, Texas, as members or supporters of outlaw motorcycle gangs—criminal street gang according to Texas law (Barker, 2017). Police snipers killed four of the nine persons during the shootout. All charges against those arrested have been dropped and the DA was voted out of office. The Texas criminal street gang definition—dangerous class—was used as a hammer to force plea bargains and it backfired on him. The Texas DA was not the first to do so.

However, a myopic approach centered on *dangerous classes* masks the complex nature of homicides by LEOs. The patterns/types of law enforcement homicides makes LEO-perpetrated homicide a potential risk factor for all persons living in the United States regardless of age, race, gender, ethnicity, social status, or label. However, the majority of public and academic attention belies the true nature of police-perpetrated homicides. This is slowly changing.

The August 9, 2014, shooting death of Michael Brown, an eighteen-year-old African American male, by a white police officer in Ferguson, Missouri, made a national issue of LEO homicides. The lack of reliable official data on "killings by the police enraged the public and lead to riots and demonstrations erupted nationwide" (Swaine & McCarthy, December 15, 2016). This book provides a much needed examination of the types and patterns of police homicides. It is the first step toward needed reform.

We will demystify police homicides and expose its variety and range though the development of a heuristic typology of police homicides. Then we will examine and provide examples of each type or pattern.

SOURCES

Albon, P.M. (1951). Labor competition and the New York draft riots of 1863. *Association for the study of African American Life and History.* 36(4): 375–405.

Anon. (January 20, 2017). Civil lawsuits lead to better, safer law enforcement. *Center for Justice and Democracy at New York Law School.*

Anon. (February 13, 2019). NYPD detective killed by "friendly fire" responding to robbery. *Police Magazine.*

Anon. (April 16, 2019). The latest 'No common sense' in Michigan cop's use of Taser. *Associated Press.*

Balen, B. (August 29, 2014). Police officer distracted by computer who killed cyclist not prosecuted. *Guardian Liberty Voice.*

Barker, T. (2011). *Police Ethics: Crisis in Law Enforcement.* Springfield, IL: Charles C. Thomas.

Barker, T. (2017). Massacre at Waco: Biker violence and police overreaction. *American Journal of Criminal Justice.* 42: 668–681.

Barker, T. (2020). *Aggressors in Blue: Exposing Police Sexual Misconduct.* Palgrave/McMillian.

Bernstein, A. (July 8, 2015). James Bonard Fowler dies; Alabama lawmen was convicted 45 years after killing civil rights protester. *Washington Post.*

Bittner, E. (1990). *Aspects of Police Work.* Boston: Northeastern University Press.

Blumberg, M. (1991). Police use of deadly force: Exploring some key issues. In Barker, T. & Carter, D.L. Editor: *Police Deviance*, 3rd. ed. Cincinnati, Ohio: Anderson, 201–222.

Barber, C., Azrel, D., Cohen, A., Miller, M., Thymes, D., Wang, D.E., & Hemingway, D. (May 2016). Homicides by police: Comparing counts from the national violent death reporting system, vital statistics, and supplemental homicide reports. *American Journal of Public Health.* 106(5): 922–937.

Barker, T. & Carter, D.L. (1991). *Police Deviance,* 2nd Ed. Cincinnati, Ohio: Anderson Publishing Co.

Campbell, K.M. (2014). Rising Arizona: The legacy of the Jim Crow southwest on immigration law and policy after 100 years of statehood. *Berkeley La Raza Law Journal.* 24(1).

Carrigan, W.D. & Webb, C. (2003). The lynching of persons of Mexican origin or descent in the United States, 1848 to 1928. *Journal of Social History.* 2(Winter): 411–430.

Carrigan, W.D. & Webb, C. (2013). *Forgotten Dead: Mob Violence against Mexicans in the United States, 1848–1928.* New York: Oxford University Press.

Casares, C. (February 3, 2018). Texas finally acknowledges rangers killed hundreds of latinos. *www.latina.com.*

Cooper, H.L.F. (2015). War on drugs policing and police brutality. *Substance Use and Abuse.* 50(1): 1188–1194.

Davis, A.J. (2017). *Policing the Black Man.* New York: Pantheon Books.

Downs, B.T. (September 1970). A critical reexamination of the social and political characteristics of riot cities. *Social Science Quarterly.* 51(2): 349–360.

Downs, C. (March 13, 2019). Grand jury clears deputies who fatally shot suspected car thief, 6-year-old in NE Bexar County. *San Antonio Express-News.*

Fleming, J. (March 6, 2005). The death of Jimmie Lee Jackson. *Anniston Star.*

Fogelson, R.M. (1977). *Big-City Police.* Cambridge, Massachusetts: Harvard University Press.

Frank, T. (July 30, 2015). High-speed police chases have killed thousands of innocent bystanders. *USA Today.*

Gillispie, M. (May 31, 2014). 6 Cleveland police officers charged in fatal'12 pursuit. *AP.*

Gonzales, J. (2000). *Harvest of Empire: A History of Latinos in America.* New York: Penguin Books.

Hadden, S.E. (2001). *Slave Patrols: Law and Violence in Virginia and the Carolinas.* Cambridge, MA: Harvard University Press.

Harmon, R.A. (2008). When is police violence justified? *Northwestern University Law Review.* 102(1118): 1119–1193.

Harring, S.L. (1983). *Policing a Class Society. The Experience of American Cities: 1865–1915.* New Brunswick, NJ: Rutgers University Press.

Jeffries, H.K. (June 17, 2008). Modern civil rights movement in Alabama. *Encyclopedia of Alabama.*

Johnson, M.S. (2003). *Street Justice: A History of Police Violence in New York City.* Boston, MA: Beacon Press.

Karabel, J. (December 6. 2016). Police killings surpass the worst years of lynching. Capital punishment, and a movement responds. *Huffington Post.*

Knowlton, C.S. (1970). Violence in New Mexico: A sociological perspective. *California Law Review.* 38: 1054–1065.

Madani, D. (December 7, 2018). Officer killed during Borderline shooting died from friendly fire. *NBC News.*

Martinez, M.M. (2018). *The Injustice Never Leaves You.* Cambridge, MA: Harvard University Press.

McNamara, R. (February 17, 2019). The Astor place riot of 1849. www.thoughtco.com.

Olzik, S. (1989). Labor unrest, immigration, and ethnic conflict in Urban America, 1880–1914. *American Journal of Sociology.* 94(6): 1303–1333.

Onion, R. (May 5, 2016). America's lost history of border violence. *Slate.*

Ortiz, E. & Madani, D. (January 18, 2019). Jason Van Dyke, ex-Chicago officer Sentenced to six years, 9 months for Laquan McDonald shooting. *NBC News.*

Pham, S. (April 1, 2011). Police: Teen committed suicide by cop. *ABC News.*

Prassel, F.R. (1972). *The Western Peace Officer: A Legacy of Law and Order.* Norman, OK: University of Oklahoma Press.

Rankin, K. (January 5, 2018). 2017 police shootings by the numbers. *Colorlines.*

Rawlings, P. (2002). *Policing: A Short History.* Portland, OR: William Publishing.

Reichel, P. (1988). Southern slave patrols as a transitional police type. *American Journal of Police*: 60–75.

Reid, T., Eisler, P., & Smith, G. (February 4, 2019). As death toll keeps rising, U.S. Communities start thinking Taser use. *Reuters.*

Reith, C. (1952). *The Blind Eye of History: A Study of the Origins of the Present Police Era.* Montclair, NJ: Patterson Smith.

Reppetto, T.A. *The Blue Parade.* New York: The Free Press.

Rice, R. (April 11, 2019). Man shot and killed by St. Louis police officer after a Struggle over gun, chief says. *St. Louis Post Dispatch.*

Richardson, J.F. (1974). *Urban Police in the United States*. Port Washington, NY: Kennikat Press.

Ritchie, A.J. & Mogul, J.L. (2008). In the shadows of the war on terror: Persistent police brutality and abuse of people of color in the United States. *DePaul Journal for Social Justice*. 1(2): 175–250.

Robin, G.R. (1953). Justifiable homicide by police officers. *Journal of Criminal Law and Criminology*. 34(2): 225–231.

Romero, M. (2001). State violence, and the social and legal construction of Latino criminality: From Bandido to gang member. *Denver University Law Review*. 78: 1081–1118.

Salvatore, N. (1976). Railroad workers and the Great Strike of 1877: The view from a small Midwest town. *Labor History*.

Schneiroy, R. (2008). Chicago's great upheaval of 1877: Class polarization and democratic policies. In Stowell, D. O. Editor: *The Great Strikes of 1877*. Urbana and Chicago: University of Illinois Press.

Shackel, P.A. (March 13, 2019). How a 1897 Massacre of Pennsylvania coal miners morphed from a galvanizing crisis to forgotten history. *Smithsonian. com*.

Sherman, L.W. (1978). *Scandal and Reform*. Los Angeles: University of California Press.

Sherman, L.W. (1980). Execution without trial: Police homicide and the constitution. *Vanderbilt Law Review*. 33(71): 71–100.

Silver, A. (October 7, 1965). On the demand for order in civil society. *Society for the Sociological Study for Social Problems*.

Skolnick, J.H. (May 21, 1985). Murphy's law and order in Philadelphia. *Los Angeles Times*.

Skolnick, J.H. & Fyfe, J.J. (1993). *Above the Law: Police and the Excessive Use of Force*. New York: The Free Press.

Slaughter-Johnson, E. (April 13, 2019). No accountability: How the civil justice system fails Black Americans killed. *Independent Media Institute*.

Springer, C. (2011). Jimmy Lee Jackson. *Encyclopedia of Alabama*.

Stark, R. (1972). *Police Riots: Collective Violence and Law Enforcement*. Belmont, CA: Wadsworth.

Stowell, D.O. (2008). *Editor: The Great Strikes of 1877*. Urbana and Chicago: University of Illinois Press.

Swaine, J. & McCarthy, C. (December 15, 2016). Killing by US police logged at twice the previous rate under new federal program. *The Guardian*.

Taylor, G.F. (2016). The long path to reparations for the survivors of Chicago police torture. *Northwestern Journal of Law and Social Policy*. 11(3): 50–75.

Urquito-Ruiz, R.E. (2004). Alicia Sotero Vasquez: Police brutality against an undocumented Mexican woman. *Chicana/Latina Studies*. 41(Fall): 62–84.

Verdine, R. (September 9, 2017). Detroit police stonewall investigation into Taser death of 15-year-old. *World Socialist Web Site*.

Vodrey, W.F.B. (2010). Blood in the streets: The New York city draft riots. *The Cleveland Civil War Roundtable*.

Walker Report. (1968). Summary of rights in conflict. National commission on the causes and prevention of violence. *www.chicago68.com.*

Walker, S. (1977). *A Critical History of Police Reform.* Lexington, MA: Lexington Books.

Walker, S. (1983). *The Police in America.* Lexington, MA: Lexington Books.

White, M.D., Dario, L.M., & Shjarback, J.A. (2019). Assessing dangerousness in policing: An analysis of officer deaths in the United States. 1970–2016. *Criminology & Public Policy.* 18: 11–15.

Williams, C.W. (1931). *Behind the Green Lights.* New York: Alfred A. Knopf.

Williams, H. & Murphy, P. (1990). The evolving strategy of police: A minority view. *U.S. Department of Justice. National Institute of Justice.*

Chapter 2

Law Enforcement Homicides

INTRODUCTION

As stated, LEOs as perpetrators in homicides—legal and illegal—were present and a problem in the historical unfolding of American interactions with individuals, groups, or classes of people. However, police-perpetrated homicide was not always recognized as a national social justice problem. Before the 1960s police crisis, LEO homicides received little attention and police agencies were vague or silent on how many citizen deaths were the results of police actions. That changed in the evolving modern social climate created by the tragic events following the shooting of Michael Brown in Ferguson, Missouri (Davis, 2017; Zimring, 2017; Prator, 2018). Today, law enforcement–perpetrated homicides evoke public and social media debates. Today the killing of a citizen by a LEO under questionable or disputed circumstances receives 24/7 media attention.

Sooner or later, police agencies no matter the size or the government level will experience a police-perpetrated homicide incident. The agency must be prepared to cope with the situation. Any police homicide is problematic, but controversial and contentious details require some finesse and understanding by law enforcement authorities—virtues missing in most police CEOs. The law enforcement agency must have in place plans to handle the inevitable media coverage. However, the typical law enforcement response to police-perpetrated homicides has been a public relations disaster (see Text Box 2.1).

TEXT BOX 2.1   POLICE-PERPETRATED HOMICIDES: POLICE PUBLIC RELATIONS DISASTERS

Dr. Loretta Prator is a leading spokesperson for the accountability of police agencies for homicides caused or related to U.S. police actions. She is a retired college professor and former dean of the College of Health and Human Services at Southeast Missouri State University. She was thrust into her spokesperson role by the tragic death of her thirty-five-year-old son, a police homicide victim on January 2, 2004. According to newspaper and police reports, the unarmed African American male experiencing a mental health issue was taken to the ground, handcuffed behind his back, pepper sprayed, beaten and kicked by four members of the Chattanooga, Tennessee Police Department (Zulz, February 25, 2008). The medical examiner ruled the death a homicide. No officers were charged and the police handled the family in an admitted callous manner, leading to a civil suit. In 2006, the city of Chattanooga reached a $1.5 million settlement with the family. The terms of the settlement were:

(1) Pay the plaintiff $1, 500,000, 00, (2) have an independent expert conduct an audit of Police Department's Office of Internal Affairs regarding existing and recommended policies and procedures for Internal Affairs investigators, and (3) consult with an independent expert regarding existing and recommended policies and procedures for current training on positional asphyxia and related topics. In addition the settlement will allow Loretta Prator, a college professor, to create a video explaining the loss of her son which will show to new recruits in several upcoming training academies or Ms. Prator will personally appear for a training session during the next three upcoming academies for new police officers.

Source: Anon, December 6, 2006.

Prator's (2018) recent book on the death of her son in police custody under disputed details, and the disingenuous calloused reaction of the police authorities, should be required reading for all law enforcement supervisors. The Chattanooga PD reaction to the death exacerbated the grief by the family and confused and enraged large portions of the public. The same public outrage occurred following the police homicide of Michael Brown.

MICHAEL BROWN'S DEATH

The handling, or mishandling, of Michael Brown's body by the Ferguson Missouri PD was barbaric. The heavy-handed militarized response by the authorities after the shooting enflamed the viewing public and resulted in riots and disturbances throughout the country. There were calls for the criminal prosecution of the officer from civil rights groups and social justice advocates. Suddenly, LEO homicides that have a long, sordid history in the United States became a national social justice issue with the fear-driven police homicide under scrutiny. The social reaction should have been anticipated.

Need to Identify the Types of Police-Perpetrated Homicides

The public reaction to the Brown homicide elevated U.S. police homicides to a social issue and a search for past examples of police homicides. The search for instances of police-perpetrated homicides revealed that citizen deaths at the hands of LEOs occurred under a variety of circumstances having little to do with police shootings. There was a real need for a typology or classification of police homicides. My preliminary search found multiple law enforcement homicides, including intentional murders, occurred before Michael Brown was shot to death. The police homicides found in my search of a convenience sample of police violence cases, combined with decades of researching misconduct and crime, buttressed by my personal experiences were used to develop a rough model of a typology of police-perpetrated homicides.

SELECTED EXAMPLES OF LEO-PERPETRATED HOMICIDES

Many of the following selected cases come from a "List of killings by law enforcement officers in the United States 2011, 2012, 2013, 2014 and 2016" (Wikipedia.org/wiki/List...by_law-enforcement_officers_in_the   United States). The examples in no way portray a scientific quantitative analysis of police homicides; however, they represent the variety of LEO-perpetrated homicides three years before and up to the death of Michael Brown in 2014 for the purpose of typology development. Cases two years after Brown's police homicide were also included. The examples come from open-source records and not official statistics, a recommended source for information on police shootings (Zimring, 2017). However, the open-source data describes the nature of the events presented. Therefore, it was possible to go to the original newspaper sources for additional information, a necessity for typology development. The incidents are listed by preliminary type—for example, justified shootings, accidental, suicide by cop, death from non-deadly devices, in-custody homicides, and murder.

Fatal Accidental Shootings

A twenty-one-year-old man in Merced, California, was killed by stray police bullets as officers repeatedly fired at an eighteen-year-old man who pointed a gun at them. The Merced police charged the eighteen-year-old for the murder under the felony homicide rule—2011.

A firearms instructor accidentally killed a female Georgia probation officer during a training class—2011.

A Columbus, Ohio, a man called 911 to report burglars in his home and was shot and killed by the responding officer, a seventeen-year police veteran. A gun was found near the victim, but the police did not confirm where the weapon came from or if the victim had it in his hand when he was shot (Manning, July 20, 2012).

A forty-one-year-old female hostage was killed in a Stockton, California, shootout between the police and two bank robbers—2014.

A "Cops" television crew member was accidentally shot and killed by an Omaha, Nebraska police officer. He was covering a shootout between police and armed robbers.

A retired Pennsylvania State Police Corporal pleaded guilty to five counts of recklessly endangering another person. There were five troopers, including one who died, in the room when the Corporal negligently fired a loaded weapon (Clark, May 19, 2015).

NYPD officers responding to a stabbing incident killed the assailant and accidentally killed the victim—2014.

Friendly Fire Police Homicides

A retired ATF special agent trying to arrest a pharmacy robber in December 2011 was fatally shot by an off-duty officer.

Lakewood, Colorado police officer, was killed by another officer when responding to shots fired call—2012.

A San Francisco, California detective sergeant was killed by another officer while they were making a probation check—2014.

Vehicular Police Homicides

A sixty-two-year-old man driving on a moped in the center-driving lane was struck and killed by a speeding Firerest, Washington deputy responding to a backup call. The officer making the backup call was looking for someone who fled a traffic stop—2011.

A female Avondale Estates, Georgia, police officer was driving twice the speed limit not on an emergency call when she T-boned another vehicle killing the two occupants—February 2011. The officer was indicted on two counts of vehicular homicide and reckless driving. She pleaded guilty and was sentenced to ten years with serving three in prison (Anon February 6, 2015).

A Dallas, Texas, police officer following an ambulance struck and killed a forty-three-year-old female pedestrian at 3 a.m. on January 22, 2012. The officer was exceeding the speed limit without his emergency equipment—lights and siren on. It was ruled that the deceased victim did not yield the right of way to a marked police vehicle (Heinz, January 23, 2012).

An Atlanta police officer was fired and charged with second-degree vehicular homicide after his police car traveling at high speed on an emergency call struck a BMW killing the driver (Richardson, M. July 26, 2012).

A Tucson, Arizona, officer responding to a fight call with his lights and siren on struck and killed a pedestrian crossing the street—2012.

A female pedestrian was struck and killed by a Harrisburg, Pennsylvania, police vehicle when she ran in front of the patrol car. Witnesses say she was reading a text or running to catch a bus and not paying attention—2012.

A Baltimore, Maryland, police officer on an emergency run to a shooting struck and killed a pedestrian—2012.

A Los Angeles County deputy struck and killed a bicyclist in the bike lane. The deputy was distracted by his mobile digital computer—2013.

A Minneapolis, Minnesota officer, responding to a shooting call ran a red light and struck a motorcycle killing the driver and injuring his passenger—2013.

A sixty-year-old Portsmouth, Virginia woman was struck and killed by a police vehicle, not on an emergency run—2013.

A New York State Police SUV struck a thirty-year-old Au Sable, New York woman and her small children. The woman was killed. The state trooper failed to yield the right of way—2014.

Suffolk County, New York Sheriff's deputies were responding to an emergency call when they struck and killed a pedestrian—2014.

A Franklin Township police officer driving 20 miles per hour over the speed limit without his lights and siren on struck and killed a ten-year-old boy crossing the street—2014

Justified LEO Fatal Shootings

Clear and Present Danger Police Homicides

An on-duty Santa Maria, California, police officer was fatally shot by other Santa Maria officers when he resisted arrest for illegal sexual relations with a female Police Explorer—2012.

Malden, Massachusetts, police officers were pursuing an armed bank robbery suspect when he shot three times at the officers. The suspect had car-
jacked three vehicles in his escape attempt. He was driving the third vehicle
when the officer shot and killed him—2012.

Miami, Florida, officers shot and killed a naked man while he was eating
the face off another naked man on a public causeway—2012.

A New Bedford, Massachusetts, man was fatally shot in 2012 by gang unit
detectives after he stabbed one of the detectives with a hunting knife.

Two Charleston, West Virginia, police officers pulled over a man, and an
altercation developed. The suspect took one of the officer's gun and shot both
officers. One officer died at the scene and the other a week later. The suspect
fled and was involved in a shootout with a third officer. This officer although
wounded killed the suspect—2012.

Two Philadelphia officers responded to a fight call. One of the combatants
turned to the officers with a knife and was shot to death.

A Riverside, California, man was shot to death after he rammed a police
car with a stolen car—2013.

A Santa Monica, California, man went on a killing spree that left four
dead and five wounded. He was cornered in a college library and killed in a
shootout with police. He wore body armor and a helmet and carried several
firearms—2013.

A Fort Lauderdale, Florida, police officer was indicted for manslaughter
after shooting a black man carrying an unloaded pellet gun down the street.
The man had just bought it at a pawnshop. There was conflicting testimony in
the case. The officer received an award for the shooting, which outraged the
family. The manslaughter charges were later dismissed—2013.

Fear-Driven Police Homicides

An officer fatally shot an unarmed Shreveport, Louisiana, man after
he allegedly reached for the officer's gun during a struggle with the
officer—2011.

An unarmed East Point, Georgia, man was shot and killed after making
a "threatening gesture" toward officers conducting a "knock and announce"
drug search warrant—2011.

Houston officers responded to a home burglary, and three suspects fled
when they arrived. One suspect was caught and then fatally shot when he
allegedly attempted to take an officer's gun—2012.

An unarmed man was shot to death by two U.S. Marshals pursuing him
for a probation violation. He allegedly tried to crash into their car—2012.

A man who was stopped for a speeding violation allegedly attempted to
choke the Alma, Arkansas, officer who was trying to handcuff him. The officer shot and killed him—2012.

Two members of the U.S. Marshals Fugitive Task Force shot and killed a Vancouver, Washington, man through the windshield of his car when he "escalated the situation."

Suisun City, California man was killed after pointing a pellet gun at police—2013.

Sonoma County Deputies were responding to a suspicious person call when they spotted a thirteen-year-old boy walking in a vacant lot. He was carrying what they thought was an assault rifle. The officers claimed that the boy disregarded commands to drop the weapon. One deputy fired eight rounds at the boy from 20 to 30 feet away, striking him seven times and killing him. The boy was carrying an airsoft replica of an AK-47 that fired plastic pellets. The district attorney ruled the homicide justified—2013.

Two San Diego, California, shot and killed a man while serving a drug warrant. The man was shot when he allegedly reached for his waistband after he was ordered to show his hands—2014.

Two Oak, Texas, officers shot and killed a mentally ill man who refused their orders to drop a screwdriver—2014.

Eighteen-year-old Michael Brown was fatally shot to death after assaulting a Ferguson, Missouri, police officer and reaching for his weapon. The shooting and the alleged police overreaction led to nationwide protests and demonstrations and the Black Lives Matter movement—2014.

Twelve-year-old Tamir Rice was killed. He held a replica gun. The shooting was controversial and lead to riots and demonstrations.

A Texarkana, Texas, police officer shot and killed a mentally ill man who was holding an 8-inch metal spoon.

Unjustified Shootings

In August 2011, a Eutawville, South Carolina, police chief was charged with murder in the fatal shooting of a man who complained about his daughter's traffic ticket. The white police chief was tried twice for killing the black man. Both trials ended in hung juries. A third trial was ruled out when the former chief pleaded guilty to misconduct in office and received a one year home detention sentence (CBS News, September 1, 2015).

A Del City, Oklahoma, police captain was sentenced to four years in prison for manslaughter for the fatal 2012 shooting of an eighteen-year-old man after a short police pursuit (Dinger, February 5, 2014). Evidence at trial revealed that the police captain was under the influence of hydrocodone when he shot the teenager in the back as he ran away.

A Garland, Texas, officer was charged with manslaughter after firing forty-one times at the driver of a thirty-minute pursuit with speeds up 100 miles per hour. The officer allegedly did not give the suspect time to comply before he started shooting—2012.

Two Utah detectives shot and killed twenty-one-year-old Danielle Willard in 2012 after she allegedly tried to hit them with a car as she fled a drug buy. The district attorney ruled the shooting unjustified as their stories do not match the evidence. One officer has been charged with manslaughter, and the other was fired for an unrelated offense. Civil suits are pending (Jauregul, December 6, 2017).

A former Fairfax County, Virginia, officer pleaded guilty to involuntary manslaughter in 2016 for the 2013 fatal shooting of a man during a domestic disturbance call (Jackson, April 18, 2016). The officer was initially charged with murder.

A white North Augusta, South Carolina, Public Safety Officer was indicted for the felony shooting a black man after a police chase—2014.

Two Albuquerque police officers were indicted for first-degree murder after shooting a homeless mentally disturbed man illegally camping—2014.

A Missouri Highway Patrol trooper was charged with first-degree involuntary manslaughter when a boater he arrested and handcuffed fell into the water and drowned—2014.

A white Norfolk, Virginia, police officer was indicted for voluntary manslaughter after shooting a mentally ill black man—twice in the back. Allegedly, the man threatened the officer with a small knife—2014.

Non-Lethal Devices Homicides

A Lake Arrowhead man died after being beaten and tased two dozen times by three San Bernardino County Sheriffs Deputies in August 2011.

CAUSE OF DEATH: Sudden cardiac death due to conducted electrical weapon discharge.

MANNER OF DEATH: Homicide

Office of Medical Examiner: New

The medical examiners report above set off a series of civil lawsuits.

In 2012 a hospital called the police and asked for a welfare check of a man who had been discharged the night before for a brain seizure. The man called the hospital and threatened to harm himself. The responding officer, a Vermont State Trooper, fired a Taser into the man's chest after the man made a "threatening move" toward him. The trooper was cleared of all charges (Davis, June 18, 2014).

A three-hundred-pound Fort Worth, Texas, man died after being tased multiple times—2013.

Park Forest, Illinois, police officers tased a man and shot him with five bean bag rounds. One of the rounds hit the man in the stomach and killed him. The officer was charged with felony reckless conduct—2013.

An eighteen-year-old was spray painting the outside of vacant McDonald's restaurant in Miami Beach, Florida, in 2013. When officers approached he ran off and ignored commands to stop. He charged toward an officer who shocked him with a Taser. He became unresponsive and died in the hospital.

Deputies with the Mohave County, Arizona, Sheriff's Office chased a motorcycle without a rear license. The rider became combative and was tased twice. He stopped breathing and died—2014.

A Tamaqua, Pennsylvania, man died after being tased by several officers—2014.

A Baytown, Texas, unarmed man died after being tased twice by a Chambers County Deputy. The incident was investigated by the Texas Rangers—2014.

A Kansas City, Missouri, man died after being shocked by a Taser in 2014.

Escambia, Florida County, deputies shocked a twenty-eight-year-old man until he lost consciousness. He died two weeks later—2014.

Suicide by Cop

Lakewood, Washington, officers shot and killed a woman in what appears to be an incident of "Suicide by Cop" when she pointed what turned out to be a BB gun at them and yelled "shoot me shoot me"—February 2011.

A San Antonio man called a crisis hotline saying he was contemplating suicide. The police responded and found the man walking down the street with a handgun. He fired at the police, and they shot and killed him.

A Vermont man wanted for a suspected home invasion was being chased at night on foot through a wooded area. He turned toward a Vermont State Trooper, took a shooter stance, and pointed a cell phone at the trooper. The trooper feared that the object was a gun and shot the suspect. The trooper administered first aid, called for an ambulance, and asked the man why he did what he did. The man responded, "I wanted to die" (Anon, 2012).

A man confronted Silver Springs, Florida, police officers responding to a call about a suicidal person with a gun in his hand. They shot him and found out the weapon was a replica—2012.

In what is considered an act of suicide by cop, a Martinsburg, West Virginia, woman called 911 and made a false report. She said another woman was holding her hostage at gunpoint. When the police arrived, the woman who called in the false report came out of the house with a gun in her hand and approached the officers. The officers shot and killed her (Ains & Umstead, December 28, 2012).

In what appears to be a suicide by cop incident, a Tucson, Arizona, woman called 911 and said she was going to kill herself. The responding officers found her outside her residence with a man. She took her gun out and refused to drop it. The police fatally shot her and wounded the man—2013.

A Manheim, Pennsylvania, man called 911 and announced that he would not be taken alive. When officers arrived to investigate, he pointed a Daisy Powerline air gun with a scope at them, and they fatally shot him thinking it was a real rifle—2013.

A Sunnyvale, California, man stabbed his wife to death and then called 911. When the officers arrived, he charged at them with a knife and was shot multiple times—2013.

A twenty-one-year-old female was shot and killed by responding officers after her boyfriend called and said she was suicidal—2014.

An Espanola, New Mexico, man called 911 about a suspicious and possibly armed man. He described the man with the clothes he was wearing. He presented a gun to the responding officers and was shot and killed—2014.

A Jacksonville, Florida, murder suspect was shot and killed by the Sheriff's Department SWAT team after he confronted them while holding a box stuffed in a black sock to resemble a gun.

In-Custody Homicides: Jails and Lockups

Custody officers at the Brooklyn Central Booking Jail ignored a female inmate's call for medical attention for seven hours before she died.

An Eastern Oregon Correctional Institutional Corrections officer shot and killed an inmate who would not stop beating another inmate—2014.

A Jefferson County, Alabama Jail inmate died after being shocked with a Taser by a corrections officer—2014.

An inmate was shocked three times in eight hours by officers in the New London, Connecticut Police Department Jail before his death—2014.

Murder

A Las Vegas Police Lieutenant killed his wife and five-year-old son and then set fire to the house. He called 911 and waited for the officers. When they arrived, he shot and killed himself—2013.

A female Indianapolis Metropolitan Police Officer was murdered by her ex-husband also a sergeant with the same department. He committed suicide after the murder—2014.

A Natchitoches, Louisiana, police officer kidnapped and beat another man to death in 2013 in a dispute over a woman. He was found guilty of first-degree murder in 2015 and sentenced to life in prison (Roy, October 17, 2015).

In January 2014, an on-duty Border Patrol Officer drove 160 miles to murder his wife's lover. He was convicted and sentenced to thirty years in prison after pleading guilty in 2015.

A Santa Fe, New Mexico, deputy sheriff was charged with murder for killing his partner after a drunken argument in a motel room. They were staying in the room after extraditing a prisoner—2014.

A Rocky Ford, Colorado, police officer was sentenced to sixteen years in prison after his second-degree murder conviction of an unarmed man in 2014.

A female Memphis PD officer was convicted of second-degree murder and sentenced to twenty years for killing her wife, also Memphis Police officer in 2014.

A Midland, Texas, police sergeant killed his wife and then committed suicide—2014.

A Delaware County, Pennsylvania, deputy broke into his former girlfriend's house and killed her and shot her teenage daughter—2014.

A New Jersey State Corrections killed his girlfriend and then committed suicide—2015.

A white Montgomery, Alabama, police officer was charged with murder after tasing, beating, and shooting an unarmed black man—2015. He is still waiting for trial.

TYPOLOGY OF LAW ENFORCEMENT
PERPETRATED HOMICIDES

Zimring (2017), a leading authority on police killings, confines his discussion to police shooting deaths. However, he is aware that the shooting-only distinction of police killings results in some police homicides being omitted. He cautions that including other police-caused deaths from the police use of force or misadventure may be misleading. Zimring uses the example of deaths from the use of Tasers and argues that the officer did not intend to kill when he stunned his victim. This example shows the error of not including Taser deaths. His academic opinion is disputed by legal decisions. For example, a former Michigan State Trooper was sentenced to five to ten years in prison after being convicted of involuntary manslaughter for his reckless use of a Taser (Anderson, May 13, 2019). The trooper who was riding as a passenger in the police vehicle reached out the window and stunned a fifteen-year-old boy driving an ATV, causing him to crash into a parked truck. The teenager died of his injuries. Also, in 2016, a former East Point, Georgia police officer was sentenced to life in prison for the murder of an unarmed black man who was shocked with a Taser more than a dozen times while he was in handcuffs (Hawkins, December 22, 2016). His police partner during this incident was acquitted of murder but convicted of involuntary manslaughter and reckless conduct. He was sentenced to eighteem months in prison.

The narrow approach advocated by Zimring and others does not reflect the real world of police homicides. As indicated in the selected examples, some LEO homicides are intentional, such as justified shooting, some are accidental—friendly fire deaths or driving while distracted, others are victim precipitated as in suicide by cop. Other police homicides result from careless and reckless action when performing a legal objective. Finally, some police homicides are murders for sex, to conceal a crime, to profit from crime and other personal reasons. From a criminal justice perspective, we examine the homicide type from the outcome of the act.

The incidents cited earlier document the complex nature of police homicides. There are multiple patterns or types of homicides indicated in the open-source data. Moreover, we know from official sources, open-source data, and research that LEO-caused homicides still occur.

Police-perpetrated homicides involve different patterns of police behaviors and police actors, and include accidents, friendly fire deaths, use of less-than-lethal weapons, motor vehicles, victim-precipitated deaths, and intentional murders. The book's purpose is to present a *Typology of Police-Perpetrated Homicides* based on archival information, official statistics, open-source materials, scholarly studies, and the author's personal experiences as a working police officer, police academy instructor, and police deviance researcher for over forty years (see Text Box 2.2). Prevention and intervention strategies are facilitated by the identification of types with similar characteristics.

TEXT BOX 2.2   TYPOLOGY OF LAW ENFORCEMENT–PERPETRATED HOMICIDES

- Accidental Homicides
  - Fatal Shootings
  - Friendly Fire Deaths
  - Vehicular Homicides
- Justified Shooting Homicides
  - Clear and present danger homicides and fear-driven homicides
  - Non-lethal Device Deaths—Tasers
- Suicide by Cop
- In-Custody Homicides-Jails and Lockups
- Murder

CONCLUSION

The proposed *Typology of Law Enforcement Perpetrated Homicides* is a heuristic device to move from a description of police homicide by patterns to theoretical developments and prevention. Different types suggest different causes, correlates, and consequences. One remedy does not fit all types. For example, accidental gunshot deaths appear to be a policy and training issue; pursuit deaths may involve training, policy development, and increased supervision; suicide by cop seems to require mental health awareness and de-escalation training, and numerous police homicides are the result of poor vetting. From a criminal justice perspective, the types are useful to academics, students, and practitioners. The professional law enforcement community can use this tool for research and planning, the development of policies and procedures, supported by training, and the appropriate discipline.

SOURCES

Ains, D. & Umstead, M. (December 28, 2012). Police: Woman shot, killed after pointing gun at Martinsburg officers. *Herald-Mail.*

Anderson, E. (May 13, 2019). Ex-MSP trooper Mark Bessner gets 5–15 years for the death of teen on ATV. *Detroit Free Press.*

Anon. (December 6, 2006). Prator family to receive $1.5 million settlement in death of man in struggle with police. *Chattanooga.com.*

Anon. (2012). Cambridge shooting mat have been "suicide by cop." *The Newport Daily Express.*

Anon. (February 6, 2015). Ex-officer will serve 3 years in traffic death. *CrossRoads News.*

Barker, T. & Carter, D.L. *Police Deviance,* 2nd Ed. Cincinnati, Ohio: Anderson Publishing Co.

CBS New. (September 1, 2015). White ex-police chief makes plea deal in shooting of a black man. *CBS News.*

Clark, D. (May 19, 2015). Ex-state trooper pleads guilty in accidental shooting death of David Kedra. *Montgomery News.*

Davis, A. (Ed.). (2017). *Policing the Black Man.* New York: Pantheon Books.

Davis, M. (June 18, 2014). Wrongful death suit filed in state police Taser case. *Sevendaysvt.com.*

Dinger, M. (February 5, 2014). Judge sentences former Del City police captain in 18-year-olds death. *The Oklahoman.*

Hawkins, D. (December 22, 2016). Former Ga. Cop sentenced to life in prison in Taser death of unarmed, handcuffed man. *The Washington Post.*

Heinz, F. (January 23, 2012). Pedestrian struck, killed by Dallas police. *NBC 5–Dallas-Fort Worth.*

Jackson, T. (April 18, 2016). Ex-Fairfax officer Adam Torres pleads guilty to Manslaughter in shooting death of John Geer. *The Washington Post.*

Jaregul, A. (December 6, 2017). Danielle Willard shooting: Salt Lake city police 'not justified' in women's death face criminal investigation. *HuffPost.*

Manning, A. (July 20, 2012). Police officer killed victim of break-in. *The Columbus.*

Prator, L.P. (2018). *Excessive Use of Force: One Mother's Struggle against Police Brutality and Misconduct.* Lanham, MD: Rowman, and Littlefield.

Robin, G.R. (1953). Justifiable homicide by police officers. *Journal of Criminal Law and Criminology.* 34(2): 225–231.

Roy, C. (October 17, 2015). Louisiana: Convicted cop avoids death penalty. *KSLA News.*

Richardson, M. (July 26, 2012). APD officer charged for car accident that killed Jacqueline Culp on Cascade Rd. *Cascade GA Patch.*

Sherman, L.W. (1980). Execution without Trial: Police homicide and the constitution. *Vanderbilt Law Review.* 33(71): 71–100.

Zimring, F.E. (2017). *When Police Kill.* Cambridge, MA: Harvard University Press.

Zulz, E. (February 25, 2008). Death by brutality inspires mother. *Daily Eastern News.*

Chapter 3

Accidental LEO-Perpetrated Homicides

INTRODUCTION

In order to assess the actual volume and seriousness of LEO-perpetrated homicides it is necessary to identify and make accurate estimates of the amount of each type. That is not possible at this time; however, progress is being made—witness the proposed typology and the search for reliable data. Reliable statistics on the full range of LEO homicides identified in the *Typology of Police-Perpetrated Homicides* are not currently available. That is understandable. In our fragmented law enforcement system police-perpetrated homicides occur in agencies from one sworn member to thousands of sworn members. These agencies vary in their adoption of professional standards proposed by professional associations such as the International Association of Chief's of Police. As independent actors not subject to national standards some agencies record or report these homicides; however, most do not. Nevertheless, there are attempts to provide more information and more accurate estimates.

Zimring estimates that the annual U.S. death toll from police shootings is "well over 1,000 civilians each year—three killings a day" (Zimring, 2017). His estimate is based on the existing official records and open-source data following the national attention on the spate of police shootings of unarmed black men in 2014 and 2015. This estimate is not supported by official data that measures different categories-types—of police homicides.

OFFICIAL SOURCES

Three government sources provide limited information on "on-duty" killings—police homicides—by U.S. LEOs, that is, police-perpetrated homicides. The National Center for Health Statistics of the Center for Disease Control and Prevention lists a separate category of deaths called "legal interventions." These are "deaths caused by the police or other law enforcement agents including military on duty, in the course of arresting or attempting to arrest lawbreakers, suppressing disturbances, maintaining order and other legal actions" (quoted in Barber, et al., May 2016). Legal intervention deaths come from death certificates that explicitly mention that the victim died at the hands of a police officer. This narrow definition leads to serious undercounting of police homicides. A second source, the FBI's Supplemental Homicide Reporting System is based on reports of "felons killed by the police" submitted by local police and sheriffs departments as part of the Uniform Crime Reporting system administered by the FBI. The deficiencies of the UCR are well known. In addition, homicides committed on federal property or by federal agents, non-lethal device deaths, and accidental killings are not reported. Even more troubling is that the UCR reporting system is voluntary, and many agencies do not report their homicides. The third official source is Arrest-Related Deaths (ARD). These homicides only apply to in-custody deaths. In sum, these official sources present an incomplete description of the nature and situational circumstances under which police-perpetrated homicides occur. The nature and circumstances of each homicide are necessary for an understanding of police-perpetrated homicides.

IMPROVING THE POLICE HOMICIDE DATA SOURCES

In an effort to provide more situational information on police homicides, Zimring (2017) supplemented his 1,000 annual police shooting deaths estimate with data from mass media open-source outlets. These sources assess and document LEO homicides from social media sources that sprung up since 2014. Operating under the assumption that known police killings became media events, one can reasonably assume internet listings such as Wikipedia can with caution be useful in identifying the nature and circumstances of LEO homicides (Zimring & Arsingiega, 2015). An advantage of crowdsourced data is that both sides are portrayed—police and other interested parties. Police agencies cannot be trusted as reliable sources because of their notorious impression-management techniques when reporting possibly damaging information (Barker, 2011).

   Zimring (2017) opined that the official data supplemented by crowdsourcing (open-source) data provides a better method to estimate police shooting homicides until comprehensive official statistics become available. The combination of official data and mass media sources is the only way to identify the nature and types of LEO-perpetrated homicides at this time. However, as reported earlier, Zimring (2017) cautions that the "shooting deaths only" distinction of police killings results in many police homicides being omitted. .

The *Typology of Law Enforcement–Perpetrated Homicides* indicates that some LEO-caused homicides are intentional, such as justified shooting, some are accidental—friendly fire deaths or driving while distracted, others are victim precipitated as in suicide by cop. Other police-caused homicides result from careless and reckless action when the officer is performing a legal objective. Finally, some LEO homicides are murders for sex, to conceal a crime, to profit from crime and other personal reasons.

The Utility of Crowdsourced Data

Officer-involved fatal shootings and the link to racial bias dominates the politically charged debate over police homicides (Legewie & Fagan, 2016). Unfortunately, the lack of adequate databases has led to research findings supporting racial bias in police shootings and other studies have found no racial bias in police shootings (Ruane, 2017). As James Comey, former Director of the FBI at the time is quoted as saying, "how can we address concerns about officer-involved shootings if we do not have a firm grasp on the demographics and circumstances of those incidents" (Ruane, 2017: 1131). According to Ruane, a journalist filled this gap with his innovative crowdsourcing and internet searching technique—Fatalencounters.org.

Legewie and Fagan's (2016) study used the crowdsourced database, *Fatal Encounters* in their research. Fatal Encounters goal is "to create a comprehensive national database of people who are killed through interactions with police," and it includes accidents and deadly domestic violence incidents involving police officers. Other crowdsourcing techniques are now in use, adding to what is known about police homicides.

The Counted, another open-source database compiled by the *Guardian*, collects data on "Any death arising directly from encounters with law enforcement." A third open-source database comes from the *Washington Post* that collects data on "All shooting deaths from on-duty police officers." The researchers Legewie and Fagan do not include accidental homicides or police-caused domestic violence homicides in their definition (Legewe & Fagan, 2016: 13). This approach is now the norm in police shooting homicide research and makes a significant contribution to an understanding of police shooting death homicides (see Zimring, 2017). However, as we have continually stated, LEO-perpetrated homicides encompass more than shooting deaths. We begin our discussion of types of police-perpetrated homicides with LEO-accidental homicides.

ACCIDENTAL LEO-PERPETRATED HOMICIDES

Truly accidental homicides may be excusable (O'Hara & O'Hara, 1988). Excusable homicides occur when a lawful act is done in a lawful manner and without negligence and results in death. The acts do not involve intent or reckless and negligent action on the part of the officer. For example, a police officer while responding to shots fired call accidentally slips on the wet ground and discharges his weapon and kills an innocent person standing on the sidewalk. *Caution.* The officer's negligent or reckless act may be a proximate cause of the homicide. For example, there was no reason for the officer to be running with his finger on the trigger—a violation of training and his department's policy—when the suspect was not in sight (actual case based on the author's personal experience while serving as an expert witness for the plaintiff in a civil wrongful death suit). Officers are taught that the Golden Rule of Gun Safety is "keep your finger off the trigger until you are ready to fire." In this case, the homicide was not excusable, and the officer's actions were not justified. The officer lost his job and was indicted for misdemeanor and felony charges, and was subject to civil litigation. All three outcomes or a combination of one or more can happen in similar situational circumstances. Many "accidental" homicides appear "lawful," but the situational details are questionable.

Moreover, police officers kill themselves, each other, loved ones, and civilians accidentally in two ways: first, the homicide is the result of a lawful act of violence done lawfully with no intent or expectation that harm would occur. A police cruiser is driving down the street at the speed limit and a pedestrian with his headphones on steps in front of the police car and is killed. This is an example of accidental and excusable homicide. Suppose this police cruiser was driving down the street 20 miles per hour over the speed limit without his lights or siren on. The pedestrian crosses the road in the crosswalk and does not see the speeding police cruiser and does not have time to react. In this case, the officer is driving unlawfully, but he did not intend to kill anyone. The officer's "accidental" actions could lead to criminal—involuntary manslaughter—civil, or departmental charges.

Accidental Fatal LEO Shootings

A discussion of what is or what is not an accidental homicide is clouded by heated and debated controversy. There are seldom right or wrong conclusions that satisfy the parties involved. One of the most controversial accidental police fatal shootings before the events of 2014 and 2015 occurred in the early morning hours on New Years Day 2009 when a white Bay Area Rapid Transit (BART) police officer shot and killed an unarmed black man and claimed it was an accident.

Oscar Grant Shooting 2009

Twenty-two-year-old Oscar Grant was returning home from San Francisco on a BART train when a fight broke out among the "hammered and stoned" passengers celebrating New Year. The fight was broken up, and the conductor announced that the police had been notified and would meet the train at the next stop—Fruitvalle station in Oakland. What happened at the Fruitville station is still being debated today. However, numerous witnesses and cell phone videos are clear on significant facts. Nine officers responded to the scene and were greeted by an angry and rowdy crowd. The first two officers on the scene detained Oscar Grant and his friend. His friend was handcuffed, and Grant was placed prone on the ground. Grant was told he was being arrested and BART officer Johannes Mehserie attempted to handcuff him. Mehserie had difficulty getting Grant's hands behind his back. Mehserie stood up, unholstered his semi-automatic weapon, and shot the prone Grant in the back. Why the officer shot Grant is in dispute. Several witnesses reported that Mehserie appeared stunned and said "Oh my God" several times. The officer would claim that the shooting was an accident. He meant to use his Taser to control a combative Grant and pulled his weapon in mistake. The shooting was an accident.

The video images of the incident were widely broadcast and streamlined locally, nationally, and internationally sparking several days of rioting and demonstrations and calls for the officer to be prosecuted. The news media carried dueling interpretations from police use-of-force experts. On January 12, 2009, the Alameda County District Attorney filed a murder complaint against Mehserie, and he was arrested. A change of venue was granted citing extensive media coverage and protests and riots in Alameda County. The trial was held in Los Angeles.

The defense claimed the shooting was an accident. The prosecuting attorney told the jury that Mehserie was guilty of second-degree murder. The judge offered the jury four alternatives: acquit or reach three conviction options to include second-degree murder—fifteen years to life in prison, voluntary manslaughter—three to eleven years, or involuntary manslaughter with two to four years in prison. The jury returned a guilty verdict of involuntary manslaughter, and he was sentenced to two years in prison with double-time credit for time served. Mehserie was released from prison on June 13, 2011. Several civil suits followed the conviction. BART settled with Grant's young daughter for $1.5 million and $1.3 million to Grant's murder.

Other Similar Examples

On March 3, 2013, an unnamed New Hope, Pennsylvania, veteran police officer entered the cell of an inmate being processed to aid a fellow officer in an altercation with the inmate. The second officer yelled "Taser," "Taser," and pulled his service revolver and shot the inmate in the stomach. The officers realizing the inmate had been shot and gravely wounded administered first aid and transferred the inmate to the hospital. He survived. The Buck's County District Attorney is quoted as saying the shooting "was neither justified, nor criminal, but was excused" (Rodriguez, April 12, 2019). It was excusable, he added because the shooting was the result of the mistaken belief that the officer thought he was deploying his Taser instead of his gun—an accidental shooting. The officer was allowed to retire. There are problems with this decision. There is evidence of reckless or negligent behavior by the officer. Why was the officer in a cell with a weapon, in the first place? Guns are usually not allowed inside custody settings. Even more disturbing is the mistake of drawing a gun instead of a Taser. Tasers are carried on the opposite side of the handgun and cross-drawn to prevent these kinds of errors. The shooting officer carried the Taser on the same side and in front of his weapon in violation of police department rules. This suggests reckless and negligent action by the officer, calling for criminal and civil action.

In February 2015, a leading police training blog *Blue Sheepdog.com* lamented that two months into the year there had already been two police officers from large police agencies criminally charged with negligent or reckless accidental homicides (www.bluesheepdog.com/2015/02/12). The first case involved a Pennsylvania State Police Corporal fatally shooting a fellow Trooper during a training session. The corporal was a twenty-year state police veteran and a firearms instructor. He was explaining the firearm's mechanism to a class of troopers when he pulled the trigger and shot a twenty-six-year-old trooper, killing him instantly. The corporal was indicted on five misdemeanor counts of reckless endangerment—there were five troopers in the class. The shooting was an accident but was it excusable? The corporal retired and pleaded guilty and was sentenced to three to eighteen months. The first two weeks were to be served in the county jail, followed by house arrest and four years' probation (69 news, August 28, 2015).

The second accidental homicide mentioned in the *Blue Sheepdog blog* occurred in New York City when a rookie NYPD accidentally killed a twenty-eight-year-old man waiting for an elevator in a Brooklyn public housing complex. The man and a female acquaintance tired of waiting for the elevator opened a door into the seventh-floor landing. There were no lights on in the landing. They were either burned out or knocked out. The complex was a high-crime area, and two NYPD officers were walking up the stairs in response to a disturbance call. For some unknown reason, probably fear, the rookie had his gun in his hand with his finger on the trigger. The startled rookie pulled the trigger, and the bullet ricocheted off the wall and struck the man in the chest. He died two days later. The cardinal rule of firearms safety is "keep your finger off the trigger until you are ready to fire."

The NYPD officer was convicted of second-degree manslaughter and official misconduct. He was immediately terminated from the NYPD upon conviction. At his sentencing in April 2016, the judge reduced the manslaughter and official misconduct convictions to criminally negligent homicide and sentenced the former officer to five years of probation and community service. The judge remarked, "Shooting somebody never entered his mind. This was not an intentional act. This was an act of criminal negligence" (Phippen, April 19, 2016).

A seventy-three-year-old retired librarian playing the part of a police officer in a "shoot/don't' shoot" demonstration during a Citizens Academy in Punta Gorda, Florida, was accidentally shot and killed by a police officer in August 2016 (AP, August 11, 2016). During the role-playing exercise, both the officer playing the bad guy and the citizen have guns. However, the guns are supposed to be loaded with blanks or use "simunition guns," which are real-looking weapons that fire non-lethal projectiles with reduced force. It appears that the gun fired by the officer was a personal weapon loaded with wadcutter rounds used for target practice, not blanks. The officer, contrary to all safety requirements in these role-playing demonstrations, never checked his gun. The police officer was charged with negligent manslaughter and was scheduled for trial in May 2019. The city of Punta Gorda has settled with the family for $2 million. In October 2019, the officer pleaded no contest to second-degree manslaughter (Munez, October 16, 2019). He was sentenced to ten years of probation, restitution to the family, and he agreed never to seek employment as a police officer.

Devastating Effects on Victims and Offenders

All accidental fatal police shootings are devastating for the victims and survivors. They are also troubling for the public, the police agency, and the officers involved. The deadly shootings of hostages and innocent bystanders are particularly disturbing; however, they do occur. In June 2018, the LAPD Police Chief was quoted at a news conference as saying, "It's been 13 years since an officer's gunfire has killed an innocent bystander or hostage in this department. In the last six weeks, it happened twice" (Fedschun, August 1, 2018). The first incident occurred on June 16 when a knife-wielding man held an innocent female bystander hostage. The police responded to a 911 call that a man had stabbed his ex-girlfriend. When the police confronted him, he refused to drop the knife. An officer fired several rounds from a beanbag shotgun, but the assailant deflected them with a folding chair. He then grabbed an innocent bystander and held the knife to her throat. As he began cutting the woman's throat, the officers opened fire, killing both. Two police bullets hit the innocent woman.

The second accidental LAPD police homicide of a hostage occurred on July 21, when the twenty-seven-year-old manager of a Trader Joe's market was killed by police gunfire during a hostage situation and shootout with LAPD officers (Gaydos, July 24, 2018).

ACCIDENTAL POLICE VEHICULAR HOMICIDES

There are few official sources of information on accidental vehicular homicides with non-police victims, so much of what is presented comes from open-source information. However, I was a specialized emergency vehicle operations instructor in a regional police academy covering twenty-three counties for seventeen years. In addition I have conducted research on emergency vehicle operations, and testified as an expert witness on police pursuits since 1982. Based on these experiences I have arrived at one conclusion. *The police kill and injure more citizens with the reckless and negligent operation of their vehicles than with their guns* (Barker, 1998).

A disturbing number of police officers are accidentally killed during motor vehicle operations. The "2017 FBI Law Enforcement Officers Killed & Assaulted Report" (https://ucr.fbi.gov/leoka/2017) lists 163 officers killed from 2013 to 2017 in motor vehicle crashes—20 engaging in pursuits, 49 responding to an emergency, and 9 killed responding to nonemergency. Forty pedestrian officers were struck and killed by vehicle from 2013 to 2017.

A Special Report *Police Vehicle Pursuits 2012–2013* from the Bureau of Justice Statistics (BJS) reported that in the twenty years 1996 to 2015, there were 6,000 fatal police pursuit crashes (BJS, May 2017). There were 7,000 deaths from those crashes, averaging 355 per year. Nearly two-thirds (65%) of those deaths were occupants of the pursued vehicles—4,637. A third of the deaths (29%) were innocent occupants of other cars—2,088. Four percent (277) were pedestrians hit by the pursued vehicle or the police. Eighty-eight fatalities were occupants of a police vehicle. The top five states with pursuit fatalities from 1996 to 2015 were (1) California (827), (2) Texas (762), (3) Georgia (369), (4) Florida (311), and (5) Michigan (300).

The typical pursuit begins with a traffic violation. In California, which had the most vehicle pursuit fatalities in the BJS study, the *USA Today* reports the following:

- There were 63,500 police pursuits reported from 2002 to 2014 in California:
- More than 89 percent were for vehicle-code violations, including speeding, reckless driving, and *4,898 instances of a missing plate or an expired registration.*

- *Just 5 percent were an attempt to nab someone suspected of a violent crime*, usually assault or robbery, 168 sought a known murder suspect.
- Nearly *1,000 were for safety violations that endangered a driver only*, including 850 drivers not wearing a seat belt and 23 motorcycle riders not wearing a helmet.
- In ninety instances police chased *someone for driving too slow* (Frank, July 30, 2015 italics supplied).

This information raises the question: Are these violations worth the risks involved? Police pursuit drivers must balance the known risks of the pursuit against the benefits to be gained (Barker, 1998). As I said over twenty years ago, there is a *Termination Equation* guiding all police pursuits.

Termination Equation

Justification for pursuit=Initiating Offense + The need for immediate apprehension + the known risks involved

Initiating Offense—Is the known offense a misdemeanor, felony, or equipment violation. In 2012 the Florida State Police changed their discretionary policy to only allow the pursuit of suspected felons, drunk, drivers, and reckless drivers (Frank, July 30, 2015). The number of police pursuits dropped by one half the next year.

Need for Immediate Apprehension—Does the driver represent a threat of death or injury to another person if allowed to continue? Are their alternative actions that can be taken, for example, the identity of the driver is known? The Michigan State Police Policy reads, "It is better to either delay the arrest or abandon the pursuit than to kill innocent people" (Frank, July 30, 2015).

Known Risks—roadway and traffic conditions, time of day and geographic conditions, other occupants in the vehicle, and the driver is a juvenile.

Therefore, as we see police, accidental motor vehicle homicides have several subcategories.

Pursuit Fatalities

A twenty-two-minute chase by police officers from six different agencies in downtown Cleveland on November 28, 2012, resulted in thirteen officers firing 137 shots at two unarmed homeless persons—a black male age forty-three and a black female age thirty (AP, April 11, 2015, & Wikipedia, May 24, 2019). The black male was shot twenty-four times, and the black female was shot twenty-three times. The pursuit began when a plainclothes officer observed the car in a known drug trafficking area and decided to make a well-known police "chicken crap" pretext stop for a turn signal violation.

The chase began when the car would not pull over. The vehicle passed two officers who believed they heard shots—no gun was found in the vehicle. At one point, there were sixty-two cars from six law enforcement agencies involved in the pursuit at speeds over 100 plus.

When the pursued vehicle pulled into a middle school parking lot, police officers reported they saw a gun—none was found—and started shooting. The confused officers on the scene thought they were being fired on by the occupants of the car. Thirteen officers fired 163 rounds. One officer fired forty-nine shots. This officer jumped on the hood after the others had stopped shooting and fired through the windshield. He was fired and charged with two counts of voluntary manslaughter. Five supervisors were charged with dereliction of duty, and six other officers were fired.

The incident sputtered to an inglorious ending. Five of six officers fired were reinstated by an arbitrator in 2017. In January 2019 the charges against three of the supervisors were dismissed. The trial judge acquitted the officer who was charged with voluntary manslaughter. The city settled with the families for $3 million. This case is frequently cited as an example of unequal and discriminatory treatment of police homicides against African Americans by the Black Lives Matter movement.

A bizarre pursuit related "accidental" death occurred in DeLand, Florida, in September 2013. The police attempted to pull over a vehicle occupied by a thirty-eight-year-old black man for a seat belt violation and for some unknown reason he sped off. As discovered later, the man was a known felon with numerous arrests. The suspect stopped and ran into a vegetable field. A rookie police officer drove into the vegetable garden toward the suspect. The suspect stumbled and fell in the wet grass and the rookie unable to stop ran over him. The police tried but failed to lift the car off the suspect, and he died from what the medical examiner determined to be mechanical asphyxia (Anon, September 19, 2013). The entire incident was captured on the officer's dash cam. The officer who ran over the suspect was immediately fired, but the grand jury refused to press charges. The dead man's ex-wife received a $550,000 settlement from the city of Deland.

In October 2016 a police pursuit of a stolen car that began in Kennett, Missouri, continued into Clay County Arkansas. A Clay County Deputy Sheriff joined in the pursuit. As the pursuit entered the city of Rector, Arkansas, the deputy crashed into the rear end of a vehicle not involved in the pursuit, killing the eighty-four-year-old female driver (Field, October 3, 2016). The driver of the stolen car was charged with murder.

A Newark, New Jersey, police officer was indicted and charged with aggravated manslaughter, aggravated assault, two counts of possession of a weapon for an unlawful purpose and two counts of official misconduct for shooting and killing a driver and wounding a passenger during a "bizarre" pursuit on January 28, 2019. The Essex County prosecutor is quoted as saying, "He [the officer] showed a reckless disregard for human life by shooting into a moving vehicle which had heavily tinted windows. This is the first fatal police-involved shooting to result in an indictment in Essex County in recent memory" (Norman, May 22, 2019). The details, as reported in the news article, starts with a traffic stop by a female Newark PD officer. The vehicle stopped and then sped off. The officer broadcast that she saw a gun that led to several police cars joining in the chase. The indicted officer—Officer X— was a passenger of a police car that attempted to cut the fleeing suspect. At an intersection, Officer X jumped out of the police vehicle and fired several rounds while yelling, "get out of the car." The car took off again, and Officer X jumped back in the patrol vehicle. Officer X's body camera reveals that the police driver told him to "relax." Officer X ignored the command to relax and jumped out of the car again and fired more rounds at the fleeing vehicle. Officer X jumped out a third time as the pursuit ends and fired multiple rounds into the suspect's car. As other officers approach the suspect's vehicle, Officer X's body camera footage reveals him saying, "I shot him in the head," and "I shot both of them." The driver of the pursued vehicle and the passenger were both shot in the head. The driver died, and the passenger suffered severe injuries. Officer X was suspended without pay and has not made his first court appearance.

Stop Sticks

As reported in the news, on October 19, 2012, two Baytown, Texas, teenagers had just gotten off work and were sitting at a red light at 10 p.m. when a speeding car pursued by the Baytown police entered the intersection. The police were chasing the occupants of the vehicle at speeds over 90 miles per hour for shoplifting at a nearby Academy store. The police had deployed stop sticks in the intersection—a dangerous action at a busy intersection. The pursued vehicle ran over the spike strips, lost control, and crashed into the car at the red light, killing a sixteen-year-old-boy.

US Border and Customs Pursuits

Following a high-speed pursuit that used spike strips and caused the deaths of three persons and eight others injured, the US Custom & Border Protection agency is quoted as saying, "agents may get involved in pursuits when the benefit outweighs any immediate danger created by speeding or other emergency driving techniques" (Riggins, November 29, 2018). The facts as reported speak for themselves. Border Patrol agents chased a pickup truck that had two people in the cab and nine people in the uncovered bed because they had an alert that the truck belonged to an armed and dangerous person. The Border Patrol deployed spike strips in front of the vehicle. The truck hit the spike strips at high speed, veered into an embankment and rolled over, ejecting nine or ten people from the truck. Three were killed, and eight were injured. Did any possible benefit outweigh the danger created by the pursuit and deployment of the spike strips?

Is there a pattern? The Border Patrol policy benefits versus danger calculus statement should be examined in light of previous pursuits and stop stick use. According to newspaper sources, an investigation by ProPublica and the Los Angeles Times, Border Patrol pursuits of suspected illegal immigrants resulted in 22 deaths and 250 injuries from 2014 to 2018 (Queally, Mejia, & Syrana, May 3, 2019). In those years the Border Patrol engaged in more than 500 pursuits in California, Texas, New Mexico, and Arizona—one of three of these pursuits ended in a crash. Even more troubling, the report said the Border Patrol deployed stop sticks in extremely high-speed chases, a hazardous practice. The report and the deaths in the 2018 pursuit prompted Senator Dianne Feinstein to call for an investigation. In January 2003, two women were killed, and thirteen people were injured when a pickup loaded with suspected illegal immigrants crashed and overturned after running over spike trips deployed by Border Patrol agents (Garrison & Silver, January 10, 2003). The crash occurred 25 miles east of San Diego.

POLICE "DISTRACTED" DRIVING ACCIDENTAL HOMICIDES

The information on police distracted driving homicides is limited for several reasons. There are no official statistics, and emergency vehicles—police, fire, ambulances, and EMS—are exempted by law from traffic laws when operating in emergency response and driving with due regard for the safety of others on the roadways. The last restriction—driving with due regard for the safety of others—increases the likelihood that an officer will not admit negligence or reckless driving unless there are witnesses or a visual record.

We assume that emergency vehicle operators are well-trained, qualified professionals, operating with clear guidance from their agency. Therefore, they are less likely to be affected or subject to the dangers of distracted driving. However, in most cases of police distracted driving homicides, the driver has not received any emergency vehicle training since rookie school, and the agency has no policies, procedures or rules on distracted driving such as no talking on a cell phone while driving, no typing on the in-car mobile computer while driving, or similar guidance. Inadequate training is a major contributing factor in emergency vehicle crashes (Hsiso, Chang, & Simeonov, 2018).

The performance of additional tasks during driving, especially those that draw the hands away from the steering wheel or the eyes from the road are the major factors in police vehicle crashes. The modern police patrol vehicle is a one-person car with an overwhelming amount of interactive equipment in the driver's compartment. When two-person cars where the norm, one officer drove and the other worked the radio and other equipment, in most patrol cars today, there is no room for another person. Numerous simulator studies have shown that drivers are significantly slower in responding when operating interactive equipment (Hsiso, Chang, & Simeonov, 2018). A simulator study of eighty experienced police patrol officers in the Pacific Northwest came to the same conclusion (James, 2015). The in-vehicle equipment—radios, onboard computers, radar equipment, cell phones—serve as distractors when in use.

Examples

On Sunday, December 8, 2013, at 1:05 p.m., Milton Olin Jr., a prominent lawyer and COO of the music streaming site Napster, was riding his bicycle in a marked bicycle lane in Calabasas, California. A Los Angeles County Deputy Sheriff was driving in the same direction as the victim. According to published reports, the deputy who was not on an emergency call "was distracted by using his cellular telephone or viewing and using the Mobile Digital Computer in his radio car at the time" swayed into the bike lane striking and killing Mr. Olin. In other words, the deputy was texting when he collided with the victim (Pamer & Wynter, July 16, 2014). California state law prohibits texting or making calls while driving. However, the law does not apply to emergency services personnel operating an authorized vehicle in the course and scope of their duties. Therefore the deputy was not charged with any state crimes. The district attorney, according to published reports, said the texts to his wife before the collision did not contribute to the deputy's inattention (Edwards, August 29, 2014). However, the subpoenaed Verizon phone records showed that the deputy had made more than 100 recorded calls before the collision, including five before he crashed into the cycle rider (Pamer & Wynter, July 16, 2014). No charges were ever filed against the distracted deputy sheriff. However, a lawsuit was settled in 2018 by the Los Angeles County Board of Supervisors for $11.5 million to avoid a jury trial (Silva, May 31, 2018). The outcome for the next "distracted" driving homicide would be quite different.

Three years later a California Highway Patrol officer was involved in a "distracted" driving homicide. On June 7, 2016, a twenty-year CHP veteran was the cause of a four-car collision at a construction site. The motor vehicle chain-reaction collision resulted in the death of a fifteen-year-old boy. The teenager was a passenger in the back seat of a car the CHP officer rear-ended while he looked at his computer screen (Oide & Locke, June 9, 2016; KCRA staff, June 9, 2016). According to the newspaper accounts, the trooper was approaching a construction site when he looked down at his computer screen. The CHP's officer was unaware that the construction had slowed the cars in front of him. When he looked up, it was too late, and he rear-ended the vehicle in from, killing the teenager in the back and injuring three teenagers in the car. In 2018, the ex-officer pleaded guilty to a misdemeanor count of vehicular manslaughter and was placed on three years probation and ordered to serve 160 hours of community service (Bylk, May 30, 2018).

A sixty-one-year old Spanish teacher was struck and killed by a marked NYPD van at 4:30 p.m. on July 6, 2013, in the Williamsburg neighborhood of Brooklyn. The police reported that the man had the crossing signal in his favor, and the NYPD van was not answering a call (Robbins, July 7, 2013). The police van made a left turn and struck the man in the crosswalk. The incident had the appearance of a tragic traffic accident until witnesses reported that the female officer was talking on her cell phone during the crash—talking on a cell phone while driving is illegal in New York. Internal Affairs investigators asked for her cell phone, and she refused to give it to them (Weiss, July 8, 2013). The cell phone records were subpoenaed, but no information is available as to the resolution of this incident. According to published sources, the NYPD has declined to comment. A lawsuit was filed.

BLUE-ON-BLUE ACCIDENTAL HOMICIDES

Blue-on-Blue homicides aka *Friendly Fire Police Homicides*, are rare, but as with all preventable deaths their rare occurrence offers no solace to the widow or widower, children, family, and friends of the deceased. Although empirical research on this issue is virtually nonexistent, there is one 2010 New York state study, numerous anecdotal accounts, and police training narratives. According to one source, the National Law Enforcement Memorial in Washington, D.C., lists 180 cases of blue-on-blue homicides since 1893 (Anon, June 26, 2000). Thirty-two of those cases involved accidental discharges of a weapon. Twenty-four officers were killed in cross-fire situations between criminals and police. Fourteen officers were killed in training exercises, and twenty-eight were killed because of mistaken identity, the remaining cases did not have information for classification.

We can venture some basic conclusions from what we know. The majority of the police officers killed by other police officers on- or off-duty were shot because of mistaken identity. Most police officers shot were not in uniform, and had a gun in their hand. Many of those shot refused commands to drop their weapon and made reflexive quick turns toward the officer/s who shot them with the gun in their hand. I have worked plainclothes, and I have trained police officers in shoot/don't shoot simulations. Police officers are trained to shoot whenever someone points a gun at them and refuses commands to drop it. That is not going to change in the near future. Officers have to make a quick decision—less than a second—when confronted with a person with a gun in their hand (Anon, June 26, 2000). The wrong decision to shoot or not to shoot can cost them their lives.

The current training reinforces reflex action to the presence of a weapon. However, the training of officers in responding to off-duty incidents and while working in plainclothes can be improved to prevent many of these tragic accidental shootings (Scoville, June 20, 2012; Markel, September 17, 2013; Blake, January 5, 2018). Once again, we see that there is no one solution to all accidental police-caused homicides.

Examples

Lakewood, Colorado Police Department was established in 1969, and the first officer killed in the line of duty was slain by another officer—Blue-on-Blue homicide (Mitchell, Nicholson, & Gurman, November 8, 2012; Farberov, November 11, 2012). On September 9, 2012, at about 1.45 a.m., a police officer was dispatched to a possible prowler call and reported shots fired in the area. Several police officers responded, including SWAT officers. The house where the shots were fired was located, and the officers formed a perimeter around the house. Officer James Davies, a six-and-a-half-year veteran officer in uniform, was one of those officers on the perimeter in the back of a neighbor's house. Ten feet away from officer Davies in another backyard with a fence separating the two Lakewood officers was a Lakewood SWAT officer. The SWAT officer spotted Davies and did not recognize the man with a gun as a police officer. The SWAT officer claims that he ordered the man with the gun to drop it and he did not obey the command. He shot officer Davies in the head, killing him. Officer Davies's widow has sued the Lakewood Police Department.

The first California BART (Bay Area Rapid Transit) officer killed in the forty-two-year history of the department was killed by a fellow BART police officer in January 2014 (Debolt, Nelson, & Thomas, January 21, 2014). Forty-two-year-old Detective Sergeant Tom Smith Jr., a twenty-year veteran, was leading a group of eight officers—four BART and four officers from the Dublin PD and Alameda County Sheriffs Department when he was fatally shot. They were searching for a robbery suspect. The suspect had already been arrested, and the officers were searching the apartment room by room. The officers entered a room with their guns in their hands, and the officer who fired the shot said he mistook the sergeant for an armed criminal. The wife of the slain officer, also a BART officer, filed a civil suit against BART alleging that police officials denied numerous training requests submitted by her husband and denied the use of SWAT officers for potentially high-risk searches (Johnson, June 1, 2015). The widow also alleged that her husband urged her to sue BART if he was killed during these raids. The suit was settled for $3.1 million (Staff, December 9, 2016).

The shooting of a black undercover police officer from Prince George County, Maryland, by a white police officer was deliberate but without malice, according to the chief of police (Staff, March 17, 2016). The slain officer was responding in street clothes to a gun battle between three black men who launched a planned and unprovoked attack on a police station. The undercover officer responded to the call, and was shot by an officer on the scene who mistook him for one of the shooters. The grand jury did not indict the fellow officer.

Confusion and disorder is the best way to describe the scene that unfolded in the Borderline Bar & Grill in Ventura County, California, on a Friday night in December 2018 (Staff, December 7, 2018). The mass shooting between a gunman and police officers resulted in the friendly fire death of a sheriff's deputy. The deputy was shot five times by the suspect; however, the fatal six shot to his heart was fired by a California Highway Patrol officer.

Two detectives responded to broadcast calls of a store robbery. They were close on another call, so they responded (Moore, Celona, & Marino, February 12, 2019, Staff, February 13, 2019). As they entered the business, the suspect pointed a firearm replica at them, and the detectives started shooting at him and backing out of the store to seek cover. Unformed officers in patrol cars were arriving on the scene as the detectives backed out of the store. The uniform officers mistaking the detectives opened fire. Newspaper reports say the police fired forty rounds. One detective was killed, and the other was shot in the leg.

CONCLUSION

The lack of reliable data on police homicides is, and always will be, an obstacle to overcome in our fragmented system of criminal justice. However, police homicide data collection is improving with the use of several data sets supplemented with open-source information. Open-source data includes information on a number of variables on the victims and the police officers involved, and the situational setting under which the homicide occurred. This sort of information is necessary to make clear that there are several "types" of police homicides—*Typology of Police-Perpetrated Homicides*. The variety of Accidental Police Homicides dimensions ensures that there is no one "Silver Bullet" fox for this type of police homicides. This finding will hold true for all the police homicide types we examine.

SOURCES

69 news. (August 28, 2015). Firearms instructor sentenced for state trooper's death. *69 News.*

Anon. (June 26, 2000). Officers killed by friendly fire. *Policeone.com.*

AP. (January 26, 2015). Six Cleveland officers sacked after 137 shots killed two unarmed black people. *The Guardian.*

AP. (August 11, 2016). Florida officer who killed a woman during a demonstration has checkered past. *The Guardian.*

Barker, T. (1998). *Emergency Vehicle Operations: Emergency Calls and Pursuit Driving.* Springfield, ILL: Charles C. Thomas.

Barker, T. (2011). *Police Ethics: Crisis in Law Enforcement.* Springfield, ILL: Charles C. Thomas.

BJS. (May 2017). Police vehicle pursuits, 2012–2013. *Bureau of Justice Statistics.* Office of Justice Programs.

Blake, D. (January 5, 2018). 8 ways to prevent blue-on-blue shootings. *Policeone.com.*

Bylk, A. (May 30, 2018). Ex-Willows CHP officer granted probation in crash that killed teen. *Chico Enterprise-Record.*

Debolt, D., Nelson, K., & Thomas, J. (January 21, 2014). BART police sergeant shot and killed by a fellow officer during search in Dublin. *Mercury News.*

Edwards, J. (August 29, 2014). Police Officer will not be charged for killing Napster Exec while texting and driving—because it's apparently OK for police to do it. *Business Insider.*

Farberov, S. (November 11, 2012). James Davies: Tragedy as a veteran police officer and father of two shot to death by fellow cop. *Daily Mail.*

Fedschdun, T. (August 2, 2018). LAPD releases video of fatal police shooting of Female hostage held at knifepoint. *Fox News.*

Field, H. (October 3, 2016). Arkansas deputy hits, kills motorist during chase. *Arkansas Democrat.*

Frank, T. (July 30, 2015). High-speed police chases have killed thousands of innocent bystanders. *USA Today.*

Garrison, J. & Silver, B. (January 10, 2003). Border pursuit crash kills 2, hurts 13. *LA Times.*

Gaydos, R. (July 24, 2018). Trader's Joe's employee, who died in hostage situation, killed by LAPD gunfire, chief says. *Fox News.*

James, S. (2015). Distracted driving impairs police patrol officer driving performance. *Policing: An International Journal of Police Strategies and Management.* 38(3): 505–516.

Johnson, A. (June 1, 2015). Widow of slain bart officer files suit against agency. *Pleasanton Patch.*

KCRA staff. (June 9, 2016). CHP identifies officer involved in crash that killed Willows teen. *KCRA.*

Lam, K. (June 22, 2018). Washington police officer killed after being struck by patrol vehicle during pursuit, officials say. *Fox News.*

Legewie, J. & Fagan, J. (May 2016). Group threat, police officer diversity and the deadly use of police force. *Columbia Law School.* Paper Number 14-512.

Markel, P. (September 17, 2013). Blue on blue shootings. www.officer.com.

Mitchell, K., Nicholson, K., & Gurman, S. (November 8, 2012). Lakewood officer fatally shot by another officer. *Denver Post.*

McMahon, G.H. (September 1, 2012). Bulletin alert: Deployment of spike strips. *FBI Law Enforcement Bulletin.*

Moore, T., Celona, L., & Marino, J. (February 12, 2019). 'Absolutely tragic': NYPD detective killed by friendly fire responding to robbery. *New York Post.*

Munez, C.R. (October 16, 2019). Former Punta Gorda officer who shot and killed librarian won't go to jail. Herald-Tribune.

O'Hara, C.E. & O'Hara, G.L. (1988). *Fundamentals of Criminal Investigation.* 5th ed. Springfield, IL: Charles C. Thomas.

Oide, T. & Locke, C. (June 9, 2014). Distracted officer slams CHP cruiser into car on I-5, killing teen. *The Sacramento Bee.*

Pamer, M. & Wynter, K. (July 16, 2014). Lawsuit filed in death of cyclist Milton Olin, struck by deputy who was texting before collision. *KTLA.*

Phippen, J.W. (April 19, 2016). Sentencing for Peter Liang. *The Atlantic.*

Queally, J., Mejia, B., & Surana, R. (May 3, 2019). Feinstein calls on Border Patrol to review pursuit tactics after L.A Times-ProPublica investigation. *Los Angeles Times.*

Robbins, C. (July 7, 2013). Police van strikes & kills Williamsburg man crossing the street. *Gothamist.*

Ruane, J.M. (2017). Re[searching] the truth about our criminal justice system: Some challenges. *Sociological Forum.* 12(81).

Scoville, D. (June 20, 2012). Blue-on-blue shootings. *Police Magazine.*

Silva, M. (May 31, 2018). $11.5 million awarded to the family of Ex-Napster executive Milt Olin. *Digital Music News.*

Staff. (December 9, 2016). Family of CA transit officer gets $3.1 million wrongful death settlement. *Police Magazine.*

Staff. (March 17, 2016). Maryland undercover officer killed by "friendly fire" was mistaking for attacker. *Police Magazine.*

Staff. (December 7, 2018). Sergeant killed in California mass Shooting was struck by "friendly fire." *Police Magazine.*

Staff. (February 13, 2019). NYPD detective killed by "friendly fire" responding to robbery. *Police Magazine.*

Weiss, M. (July 8, 2013). Brooklyn teacher fatally hit by cop using cell phone behind wheel: Sources. *DNAinfo.*

Wikipedia. (May 24, 2019). Shooting of Timothy Russell and Malissa Williams. *Wikipedia.*

Xiong, C. (August 23, 2013). 101-year-old St. Paul woman dies after being struck by police squad. *Star Tribune.*

Zimring, F.E. & Arsingiega, B. (2015). Trends in killings of and by Police: A preliminary analysis. *Ohio State Journal of Criminal Law.* 13(1): 110–125.

Zimring, F.E. (2017). *When Police Kill.* Cambridge, MA: Harvard University Press.

Chapter 4

Justified Police Shooting Homicides

INTRODUCTION

Justified police homicides (JPH) occur during police proactive and reactive *legal interventions*—arrests, investigatory stops, and other seizures—as defined by the Fourth Amendment. The principal official government source for information on JPH is the Supplemental Homicide Reporting (SHR) system compiled by the FBI's Uniform Crime Reporting section (Zimering, 2017). However, we have no way of accurately knowing how many police justified homicides are missing in these official reports. The reporting is voluntary, and many police agencies do not report their police homicides. Furthermore, there is no internal audit judging the accuracy of the submitted information.

As stated, police perpetuated homicides as a social issue did not generate sustained national attention until 2014, and the riots and national protests fueled by the Black Lives Matter movement. The national interest ignited a call for accurate statistics and police accountability (Zimring, 2017). The increased attention resulted in an increase of officers charged and tried for unjustified criminal homicides. In 2005, there was one case reported in the media of an officer charged with criminal homicide for shooting a citizen (Zimirng, 2017). That figure rose in 2014 to seven reported and seven charged. Eighteen officers were charged with criminal homicide in 2015. My research supports this escalating police criminal homicide prosecution trend and increased interest. However, a 2001 Bureau of Justice report was prescient in its findings and foreshadowed the developing storm over JPH

2001 BUREAU OF JUSTICE REPORT

A Bureau of Justice publication reported that the killing of a felon by police was considered justified when it prevented deaths or serious bodily injury to the officer or another person (Brown & Langan, March 2001). The report published by the Department of Justice's Bureau of Statistics reported on two types of police homicides: (1) justifiable homicides of felons by the police and (2) the murder of police officers by felons. The "felon" designation was used "because at the time of the homicide, they [the deceased] were involved [or were thought to be involved] in a violent felony" (Brown & Langan, 2017: 4). The authors pointed out that the data was not accurate because of the known underreporting by police agencies. For example, they reported that from 1988 to 1998, Florida did not report any justifiable police homicides, an unlikely event. Nevertheless, during the period examined (1976–98), 8,578 police justified homicides were reported. There was a yearly average of 373 JPH from 1976 to 1998.

Although an eleven-year-old was killed in 1981 and a twelve-year-old was killed in 1992 (no additional information supplied on these two death), the average age of felons killed was thirty-one. Thirty-five percent of those killed were black in 1998. During that same year, blacks represented 12 percent of the population of age thirteen or older and 40 percent of the persons killed by police. The victims by gender and race were 55 percent white males, 41 percent black males, 1 percent white females, and 1 percent black females. The remaining 1 percent was males from a variety of racial groups. The homicides were predominately intraracial, as are all homicides. Officers of the same race killed sixty-five percent of the persons killed: white officer killed white felon—53.1 percent; black officer killed black felons—11.8 percent. One-third of the justifiable homicides were interracial. The report provided thirty-five examples of justifiable homicides from Atlanta, Baltimore, Cleveland, Houston, New York City, Oklahoma City, Los Angeles, and Philadelphia.

FEAR-DRIVEN POLICE PERPETRATED HOMICIDES

A review of the study's examples reveals thirty incidents that are easily recognized as threats to the officer's safety—a deadly weapon was produced and pointed at the officer(s) or the felon fired shots. One hundred and twenty justifiable homicides from 1987 to 1998 were felons who had murdered a police officer. Five cases were judgment calls by the officer on the scene as to the threat. The term *fear-driven homicide* is used in the proposed *Typology of Police-Perpetrated Homicides* as a factor to describe these judgment-based incidents. That is, the officer based on the totality of the circumstances fears that the perpetrator represents a clear and present danger to him/her or others (see chapter 2).

Fear is not a pejorative term in *fear-driven homicides*; it means that the officer's reaction was judged reasonable under the circumstances—the officer feared for his or her life. From a criminal justice perspective in the case of *fear-driven homicides*, someone(s) must decide later if the officer's actions were reasonable under the circumstances. That someone takes a variety of forms—a shooting team from the department or from another police agency, a coroner or medical examiner, a prosecutor, a judge or jury. Court decisions and prior court rulings guide these outside agencies or examiner's actions. The U.S. Supreme Court has weighed in on this issue and defined what is and what is not a justified legal shooting homicide.

Supreme Court on Police-Justified Homicides

The Warren Supreme Court recognized that the self-regulation of the U.S. police by the police was not adequate to regulate the behavior of police actors in our fragmented system of criminal justice (Harmon, 2012). The court recognized that state and federal courts were also not up to the task of regulating police behavior. Therefore, the Warren Supreme Court embarked on a systematic endeavor to have that regulation performed by the courts through adherence to constitutional law. The efficacy of the application of constitutional law applied by the courts on police misconduct is beyond this inquiry. Furthermore, we do not examine how civil service law, police unions, collective bargaining contracts, Police Officer Bill of Rights, and how employee discrimination law effects police departments as they pursue reform efforts (Harmon, 2012). These areas need attention and scientifically sound research; however, the first step to prevention and regulation of police homicides from a criminal justice perspective is to identify the patterns/types of police-caused homicides. Our focus is the development of a taxonomy of police-caused shooting homicides. Therefore, we examine the movement of the U.S. Supreme Court into the police use of deadly force and how the court defined the definition of justified and unjustified police use of deadly force.

Background of the Issue

Historically, coercion—the use of violence—is a core function of policing (Harmon, 2008). Moreover, numerous U.S. police officers at all levels of government have been sued and criminally prosecuted for the use of excessive—not justified—use of force. Harmon (2008) reports that thousands (2,300) of federal civil court cases—a violation of constitutional rights under the Fourth Amendment—and hundreds of local, state, and federal officers have resulted in conviction for excessive use of force.

Legal/Justified Use of Deadly Force

Every community in history has used physical force, including deadly force, as a means to secure the effective observance of laws and achieve justice (Reith, 1952). Deadly force has always been allowed if there is credible evidence to believe that the suspect/s presents a threat of serious physical injury to the officer/s or the public. However, there are long-standing limitations on the discretionary decisions to use deadly force. The typical restrictions include (1) deadly force may not be used if the offense is a misdemeanor crime, not a felony; (2) police officers can only use deadly force, in the performance of professional duties and not to advance their own personal reasons or the personal reasons of others; and, (3) police officers may not use deadly force maliciously, frivolously, negligently, or recklessly (Bittner, 1990).

Following the common law history of use of force, a police officer may be *justified* in using force, including deadly force, to affect an arrest for any crime or protect themselves from any attack that could cause death or serious bodily injury. However, that force may not be used as punishment.

The U.S. Supreme Court addressed the excessive police use of force three times—*Tennessee v. Garner* (1985), *Graham v. Connor* (1989), and *Scott v. Harris* (2007). The first two cases have a direct bearing on police shooting homicides. The third case involves the use of deadly force in a pursuit incident. The current interest in police shootings has been directed at police-citizen street encounters—arrests, investigatory, and other "seizures." For that reason, we examine the first two Supreme Court decisions on the police use of deadly force. The Supreme Court in *Tennessee v. Garner* and *Graham v. Connor* grounded all police excessive force claims in the Fourth Amendment's right to be free from unreasonable seizures (Thompson, October 30, 2015). However, we proceed with caution when addressing the U.S. Supreme Court decisions because these decisions provide legal situational circumstances that determine if a police shooting homicide is justified or not justified. These legal distinctions are not necessarily the arguments that take place in the public arena.

PUBLIC ARENA DISCUSSIONS

The interested public and special interest groups often reject the legal view, and proceed in "common-sense" examinations based on emotion not law. For that reason, riots, disturbances, and other protest actions will not cease when the homicide is declared legally justifiable, and no police officer is charged.

Police shooting homicides, especially of minority group members will always be controversial. The general public makes their decisions on such question as the following: Were their alternative actions? Was the threat real and imminent? Did the officer overestimate the threat? Alternatively, was the police response too extreme? Was the police reaction a result of explicit or implicit bias? These questions arise because LEO homicides are real tragedies for families, relatives, and friends. The family and friends of the deceased want someone held accountable for their loss, and, regrettably, the media and special interest groups "whip up" these emotions. Police agencies have traditionally reacted in such a manner to support this emotional outpouring with defensive missteps. The failure of the criminal justice professionals to recognize the views of the survivors and interested public causes major police-community relations problems.

The problems arising from unnecessary and unreasonable police shooting homicides were recognized by the U.S. Supreme Court and dealt with in the dismantling of the ancient fleeing felon rule.

THE FLEEING FELON DOCTRINE

> "[It] is not better that all felony suspects die than that they escape. Where the suspect poses no immediate threat to the officer and no threat to others, the harm resulting from failing to apprehend him does not justify the use of deadly force to do so." *Tennessee V. Garner.* 471 U.S. 1, 11 (1985).

As communities and modern societies evolved, they attempted to remove unnecessary and wanton deadly violence from the use of force in the administration of justice (Bittner, 1990). For example, the outdated common law use of deadly force to apprehend any "fleeing felon" is no longer applicable in modern societies such as the United States.

The "fleeing felony doctrine" as a legal use of deadly force developed in eleventh-century England, and was transported to the Colonial states. The English common law fleeing felon doctrine was necessary in early societies where (1) there were no weapons available that could kill at a distance—no guns and rifles; (2) felonies were punishable by death; and (3) there was little, if any communication among law enforcement agencies in different communities—felons who escaped were lost forever (Sherman, 1980).

Tennessee v. Garner (1985)

ACTS

Edward Garner was an unarmed fifteen-year-old black male in Memphis, Tennessee, who was shot and killed by a Memphis police officer in October 1973 (Harmon, 2008 & https://legaldictionary.net/tennessee-v-garner). A Memphis police officer was responding to a house burglary call when he spotted the young Garner in the yard of the house. He was ordered to stand still. Instead, Garner ran to a chain-link fence and started to climb the fence. The officer testified that Garner was likely not armed. However, the police officer shot Garner in the back of the head to prevent his escape. Garner died shortly after that. The Tennessee statute and police policy allowed the use of deadly force to stop a fleeing felon. Garner's family sued alleging that Garner's constitutional rights were violated. The district court found no constitutional violations, but the Sixth Circuit Court of Appeals reversed this decision. The case went to the U.S. Supreme Court.

The U.S. Supreme Court

The U.S. Supreme Court, in deciding this case, relied on a variety of sources to render their decision (Stoughton, 2014). The court reviewed the policies of the FBI and the NYPD that "forbade the use of firearms except when necessary to prevent death or serious bodily injury." The court examined the written policies of forty-four police departments that had the same restrictions. The court reviewed a study of large cities conducted by the Boston Police Department of Planning and Research Division. The BPD study concluded that a "majority" of the U.S. cities surveyed had adopted restrictive deadly force policies that cut back the use of deadly force against fleeing felons. The court also reviewed the findings and official position of the International Association of Chiefs of Police and the Commission on Accreditation for Law Enforcement. Both of these professional associations recommended a restrictive deadly force policy as the policing industry's best practice.

Finding

Stopping a suspect with deadly force is a Fourth Amendment seizure. The government's use of deadly force is not *justified* when a fleeing suspect is not armed. Deadly force cannot be used against a fleeing felon unless the suspect poses a threat to the officer or others. The court went on to say,

> If the suspect threatens the officer with a weapon or there is probable cause to
> believe that he has committed a crime involving the infliction or threatened with

serious physical harm, deadly force may be used if necessary to prevent escape, and if, where feasible, some warning has been given. (Thompson, October 30, 2015: 3)

The U.S. Supreme Court on *Fear-Driven Homicides*

The next U.S Supreme Court decision introduced *fear-driven police homicides* into the police deadly force controversy.

Graham v. Connor (1989)

ACTS

Police officers pulled over Graham a suspected shoplifter. He acted erratically because he had Type 1 diabetes and was experiencing the onset of an insulin reaction. The officers handcuffed Graham and slammed him on the hood of the car, and ignored his attempts to explain his behavior. Graham sustained serious injuries from his rough treatment. Once the officers learned that Graham was innocent, they released him. Graham sued the officers under 42 U.S. C 1983, claiming that the officers violated his civil rights and used excessive force during the stop (Thompson, October 30, 2015; Anon, March 20, 2017).

Decision

Although *Graham v. Connor* is not a deadly force case, it has implications for whether a police shooting homicide is justified or unjustified. The Supreme Court held that "*all* claims that law enforcement officers have used excessive force—deadly or not—in the course of an arrest, investigatory stop, or other 'seizure' of a free citizen [legal intervention] should be analyzed under the Fourth Amendment and its 'reasonableness' application clause" (Thompson, October 30, 2015: 2). What is reasonable depends on the circumstances of each case, including the severity of the crime alleged, whether or not the suspect poses an immediate risk to the officers or others, and whether the suspect is actively resisting arrest or attempting to flee. Chief Justice Rehnquist said the "reasonableness" is determined by, first, examining the facts from the perspective of a reasonable officer on the scene not the 20/20 vision of hindsight; second, the judgment must take into account that police officers make split-second decisions about the use of force in tense, uncertain and rapidly developing circumstances; and third, the reasonableness inquiry must be objective in light of the circumstances without regard to any underlying intent or motivations (Thompson, October 30, 2015, see Text Box 4.1).

TEXT BOX 4.1   ASSESSING THE USE OF EXCESSIVE FORCE

Based upon Supreme Court case law, the following rules apply to an assessment of excessive use of force:

- All claims of excessive force occurring in the course of an arrest, investigatory stop, or other seizure [legal interventions] are reviewed under the Fourth Amendment prohibition against unreasonable seizures.
- An officer's use of force must be "objectively reasonable" under the totality of the circumstances.
- Reasonableness is determined by balancing the interests of the individual and the government. *Reasonableness is evaluated from the perspective of a reasonable officer in the field."

Source: Thompson, October 30, 2015: 5.

Below is the actual "Reasonable Force" instructions given to the jury that acquitted a St. Anthony (Text Box 4.2), Minnesota police officer charged with the fatal shooting of Philandro Castille. The shooting was captured on video by his girlfriend and shown nationally and led to protests and demonstrations, and it is still cited by special interest groups as proof of police bias.

TEXT BOX 4.2   REASONABLENESS STANDARD

As to each of the counts, the "reasonableness" of a particular use of force must be judged from the perspective of an officer acting reasonably at the moment he is on the scene, rather than with the 20/20 vision of hindsight. The reasonableness inquiry extends only to those facts known to the officer at the precise moment the officer acted with force. The determination of reasonableness must embody allowance for the fact that police officers are often forced to make split-second judgments about the amount of force that is necessary in a particular situation under circumstances that are tense, uncertain, and rapidly evolving.

Source: Kaste, June 30, 2017.

JUSTIFIED HOMICIDES

In order to examine examples of whether or not a police shooting homicide is justified or not justified, we examine the officer's actions after the fact, based on the actions of the agency, the prosecutor, or in some cases, the trial judge or jury. We make two distinctions within the justified category—*clear and present danger homicides* and *fear-driven homicides*. The first category—*clear and present danger homicides*—generally do not elicit any controversy. An examination of the known facts demonstrates that the officer/s killed the suspect because he/she was subjected to a direct threat. The classic example is that the suspect was shooting or attacking the officer with a deadly weapon. The majority of all police homicides are in this category (Zimring, 2017). The second category—*fear-driven homicide*—requires that the officer is judged with 20/20 hindsight—the critical element of the "reasonableness" standard of the *Graham* decision. The classic example of this category is an officer who reasonably believes the suspect is pointing a gun at the officer or is going to do so. However, it is later determined that the object was harmless or the purported assailant is unarmed. *Fear-driven homicides* are the most controversial, often resulting in civil suits and or criminal charges.

From a criminal justice perspective, we are most interested in the process involved in determining whether or not the police homicide is judged justified or not justified and who determines that distinction. Before we present a recent actual justifiable police homicide and the criminal justice determination process, we examine a selected sample of recent police shooting homicide information.

Recent Police Shooting Homicides

Following the aftermath of the fatal shooting of Michael Brown in 2014, the *Washington Post* began compiling a database on every U.S. police line of duty shooting homicide reported in local news reports, law enforcement websites, and social media (Tate, Jenkins, Rich, Muyskens, Elliott, Mellnick, & Williams, May 7, 2016). The project began on January 1, 2015, and is continuing. The data consists of what is known about the gender, race, age, whether the person killed was armed, type of weapon, or if the deceased was experiencing a mental illness issue. At this time, it is one of the "best" sources for information on fatal police shootings. The database reports twice as many police shootings as the official statistics. Unfortunately, we do not know the outcome of each incident; therefore, we do not know if the shooting was ruled justified or not from this data source (Table 4.1). However, the authors in their summary mention several incidents where police officers were charged with murder.

There is no information on the disposition of these fatal shooting incidents; however, it is reasonable to assume certain outcomes. There was a total of 4,359 reported fatal shootings with 3,295 incidents reporting that the person shot was armed with a deadly weapon—gun or knife. These shootings

Table 4.1   Washington Post Fatal Police Shootings by Year 2015 to 2019

Total persons shot dead by police	2015	2016	2017	2018	2019
	994	962	986	992	425
Gender					
Male	952	922	939	739	398
Female	42	40	45	52	25
Unknown	0	0	2	1	2
Race					
White	497	465	459	452	85
Black	258	234	223	229	56
Hispanic	172	160	179	164	44
Other	38	42	44	40	9
Unknown	29	61	81	107	231
Age					
Under 18	18	16	16	15	6
18–29	331	295	295	284	120
30–44	355	392	392	378	146
45+	279	234	234	251	104
Unknown	11	25	25	64	49
Weapon					
Deadly Weapon	830				
Gun		520	577	551	231
Knife		172	156	183	75
Vehicle	0	1	0	38	31
Toy Weapon	43	44	26	33	9
Other		117	132	105	21
Unarmed	94	51	69	47	16
Unknown	27	57	26	35	42
Signs of Mental Illness					
Yes	257	242	237	213	70
No or Unknown	737	720	749	64	355
Threat Level					
Attack in Progress	732				
Other	218				
Undetermined	44				

represent 76 percent of the total shootings and fit our category of justified *clear and present danger police homicides*—the most numerous police shooting homicides according to all studies and police use of force experts. Seven percent (159) of the fatal police shootings involved unarmed persons, or persons "armed" with a toy weapon. We can assume that the person shot is in the category of a *fear-driven homicide*, where the officer made a reasonable decision to shoot based on the fear that his or her life was in danger. That assumption may be in error, but we do not have any information to challenge it at this time.

Fear-Driven Police Homicides

We provide an in-depth analysis of a *fear-driven homicide* to demonstrate from a criminal justice perspective how the justified or non-justified decision is made. First, newspaper accounts of a police homicide are presented, and then we examine the official report, to observe the discrepancies between the two accounts.

Newspaper Account

In August 2017, a manager of a sandwich shop in Jacksonville, Florida, called the Sheriff's office and reported that an intoxicated man was in the shop, and they were afraid he was going to drive off and endanger other motorists. The manager called back and said the man had a gun and was sitting in his truck in the parking lot (Callaway, August 25, 2017). The responding officer parked his car and walked up to the truck. According to published reports, the officer walked up to the driver's window and engaged the man in conversation. As they were talking, the man allegedly reached for his waistband. According to the newspaper account, the officer said he saw the man reaching for a gun in his waistband and fired thirteen shots killing the forty-four-year-old man. Three witnesses claimed to have seen the man reaching for the gun. The man, who could legally carry a gun, had a 9-millimeter handgun with one round in the chamber and 11 rounds in its magazine. The State Attorney General investigated the shooting and released its report on December 10, 2018.

Official Report

The Daniel Byler Death Investigation—State Attorney General—Fourth Judicial Circuit of Florida Duval County—December 10, 2018.

ACTS

The officer-involved shooting took place on August 25, 2017, at approximately 12:20 p.m. Officer X shot and killed Man Y in the parking lot of a sandwich shop in Jacksonville, Florida. At the time, Man Y was intoxicated and refused to obey commands from Officer X. The encounter evolved from a call from the shop's owner that Man Y, who was a frequent customer, was intoxicated, acting strangely, and having trouble standing. The shop's owner feared that Man Y would drive off and become involved in an accident. A customer told the shop owner that Man Y had a holstered gun on his right hip. The owner called and alerted the Sheriff's Office that the intoxicated man was armed.

Officer X arrived on the scene and was told that the intoxicated man was in the parking lot. The officer approached the man with his gun held low against his body and gave several commands to "show his hands" to Man Y. The man ignored the commands and reached for his right hip. At this time, the officer shot and killed Man Y. The State's Attorney's Office concluded that "Officer X shot and killed Man Y while Man Y was highly intoxicated, refusing to comply with Officer X's commands, and reaching for his gun. Officer X, therefore justifiably shot and killed Man Y.

The autopsy results revealed the following substances in Man Y's system: alcohol (.014), methadone (treatment for opioid addiction), Buprenorphine (controlled substance for treating opioid addiction), and topiramate (an anti-convulsant with depression effect). Although Man Y had a concealed weapons permit, he was in violation of federal offense by being a drug addict in possession of a firearm.

How Was the Justified Shooting Decision Determined?

The State's Attorneys in Florida employ sworn LEOs who have limited investigative duties. Their primary function is to investigate criminal offenses for prosecution in court. However, an Officer Involved Shooting (OIS) Team within the State's Attorney's Office composed of experienced prosecutors and investigators responds to, and reviews every officer-involved death in their circuit. This is their report. According to the report, "Once a report like this is issued, the investigative agency has reviewed the matter, an experienced prosecutor and investigator have reviewed the matter, and the full team of experienced prosecutors and investigators have reviewed the matter, and the elected State Attorney has reviewed the matter" (State Attorney's Office, December 10, 2018: 5).

Potential Outcomes

The report is a summary of the legal framework for their decision and the findings that led to that decision. There are three potential outcomes of their independent review:

- The police shooting death was justified under Florida law.
- There is no reasonable probability of conviction.
- The OIS Team cannot affirmatively say the shooting was justified or not justified. However, the likely result of a criminal trial would be an acquittal.
- The police shooting was not justified, and it can be proved not justified beyond a reasonable doubt.

POLICE CRIMINAL HOMICIDES

Any police homicide that is not excusable or justified is a *criminal homicide*—manslaughter or murder. We provide numerous examples of unjustified police homicides throughout the chapters on types of police perpetrated homicides. However, three recent interracial—white officer, black victim—Texas police perpetrated homicides are definitive examples of police shooting deaths that were declared unjustified and resulted in the police officer charged with murder. The first incident occurred in the Balch Springs Community—a suburban community of Dallas, Texas, in April 2017. A fifteen-year-old unarmed black male and several other black teenagers were leaving a suburban house party when a Balch Springs Officer fired into the car, killing the fifteen-year-old. The officer and his partner were responding to a loud noise complaint (Manna, August 29, 2018). The officer claimed that the car the teenagers were in was backing up in an attempt to strike him, and he fired because he feared for his life. Both officers were wearing body camera. The chief watched the cameras the next day and fired the shooter. The camera video showed the car was driving away not backing up when the officer shot into it. The officer was convicted of murder and sentenced to fifteen years in prison.

This case is noteworthy for two reasons. A spokesman for the Dallas Police Association—the officer was a member—condemned his actions and only equivocated on whether the police homicide was manslaughter or murder (AP, August 31, 2018). The second noteworthy element is the value of the body camera in the determination of a not justified designation and the prosecution of criminal police homicide (McCullough, August 28, 2018). The officer's body camera was used in the termination and charge of murder, and was also shown to the jury to debunk his fear-driven defense.

The second case occurred on September 6, 2018, at about 09.59 p.m., when a four-year white female veteran of the Dallas, Texas, Police Department, Amber R. Guyger, entered the wrong apartment in her apartment complex and fatally shot the black resident, Botham Sherm Jean, of that apartment. Officer Guyger had just finished a thirteen and a half-hour shift and was in full police uniform. At first the DPD handled the shooting as an officer-involved shooting, but the decision was made to bring in the Texas Department of Public Safety and the Texas Rangers for possible criminal violations. Guyger was placed on administrative leave. On September 7, 2019, Texas Ranger, David L. Armstrong filed an Affidavit for Arrest Warrant for the offense of manslaughter second degree (see Text Box 4.3).

TEXT BOX 4.3   ARREST AFFIDAVIT
FOR AMBER R. GUYGER

The facts of the case are as follow:

Complainant Jean is the resident of apartment #1478. Guyger, who is a Dallas Police Officer, lives in the same apartment complex, directly beneath the Complainant in apartment #1378. Apartment #1378 and apartment #1478 and their respective interior floor plans are in most ways identical or extremely similar to the exterior surroundings, structure, and description of each other. Complainant Jean was home alone when Guyger, who had ended her shift, but was still in her Dallas Police uniform, arrived at the apartment complex, parked her vehicle on the fourth floor of the parking garage, which should correspond to the floor the resident lives on. Guyger entered the building and walked down the fourth floor hallway to what she thought was her apartment. She inserted a unique door key, with an electric chip into the door key hole. The door, which was slightly ajar prior to Guyger's arrival, fully opened under the force of the key exertion. Upon the door being opened, Guygar observed that the apartment interior was nearly completely dark. Additionally, the door being opened alerted Complainant Jean to Guyger's presence. Believing she had encountered a burglar, which was as a large silhouette, across the room in her apartment; Guyger drew her firearm, gave verbal commands that were ignored by Complainant Jean. As a result, Guyger fired her handgun two times striking the Complainant one time in the torso. Guyger then entered the apartment, immediately called 911, requesting Police and EMS, and provided first aid [discounted by later court testimony] to Complainant Jean. Due to the interior darkness of the apartment, Guyger turned on the interior lights while on the phone with 911. Upon being asked where she was located by emergency dispatchers, returned to the front door to observe the address and discovered she was at the wrong apartment (#1478). Guyger called 911 from her cell phone requesting an ambulance and police to the offense location. Complainant Jean was transported to Baylor Hospital where he died as a result of his injury. Guyger remained at the scene and informed the responding officers and the 911 operator that she thought she was at her apartment when she shot the Complainant. Guyger believed she was in her apartment and confronted by a burglar when she fired her handgun, striking and killing him.

Source: Warrant of Arrest, September 9, 2018. The State of Texas.

On September 8, Guyger reported to the Kaufman County Jail and was charged with manslaughter. She posted $200,000 bail and was released. On September 24, Amber Guyger was fired from the DPD. The family filed a civil lawsuit against Guyger and the city of Dallas. The lawsuit alleges that the police chief, City Council and the city manager failed to implement and enforce DPD measures "that respected Jean's constitutional rights" (Cardona & Steele, October 2, 2019).

The shooting and social media attention raised the issue of racial bias where white police officer kill unarmed black man. During this heightened social media call for justice a Texas grand jury upped the charge from manslaughter to murder raising the possible penalty from twenty years to life in prison (Cardona & Steele, October 2, 2019). Guyger turned herself into the Mesquite County Jail and was booked for murder. She posted a $200,000 bond and was released. On September 5, 2019, one year from the death of Botham Jean, Amber Guyger trial began with the selection of the jury.

The trial lasted seven days and the jury deliberated for five hours over two days before finding Guyger guilty of murder. The jury sentenced Guyger to ten years in prison. She will be eligible for parole after five years. Once again a police body camera was used in the trial. A responding officer's camera was shown to the jury (Anon, September 24, 2019).

Less than two weeks after Amber Guygar was convicted of murder, thirty miles away in Fort Worth, a third police homicide ignited a national debate. On Saturday October 12, 2019, at approximately 2:25 a.m., a white Fort Worth, Texas police officer that had been on the job for eighteen months shot an armed black woman in her home. Two Fort Worth police officers responded to an "open structure call." The call came in on the department's nonemergency line and reported that the caller had seen that his neighbor's lights were on and doors were open (Allyn, October 13, 2019). At this time, the "facts" are confusing. However, it appears that one of the officers was walking down the side of the house, when he noticed a person standing near a window with a gun in their hand. He claims to have perceived a threat and ordered that person to show their hands. Two seconds later he fired one shot, killing a twenty-eight-year-old black woman. Why he shot and why was the police homicide justified is being investigated (Balko, October 16, 2019). The officer resigned before he was fired and is charged with murder.

CONCLUSION

The examined Florida case encapsulates the current thinking of the courts on *fear-driven police shooting homicides*—the most controversial category. In arriving at the decision of justified homicide, the law does not require that the danger be real. The law requires that the danger appeared so to the officer. For example, Florida law does not allow a police officer to retreat or desist because the person resists or threatens to resist. It is well settled in law that LEOs operate by compulsion not consent. The totality of the circumstances revealed that Officer X reasonably feared for his life and the lives of his fellow citizens who called for his help. Officer X only shot Man Y after he ignored his commands and reached for the firearm on his hip.

The latest Texas incidents of *fear-driven police shootings* that were judged to be criminal homicides are important for our discussion of police homicides. In particular, the use of body cameras and dash cams—a key factor in the 2014 Laquan McDonald police homicide in Chicago—as evidence in these cases demonstrates their viability in police perpetrated homicide incidents. Convicting police officers of criminal homicides is hard to do; however, a conviction is much easier when it is shown that they are lying (Curriden, May, 1996). Video evidence can show this. Body cameras are a part of the technological supervisory assists for policework, just as DNA analysis is a technological assist for crime investigation. We will examine DNA as a technological assist later in selected murder investigations.

SOURCES

Allyn, B. (October 13, 2019). Fort worth officer kills women in her bedroom in response to "open structure call." *NPR*.

Anon. (March 10, 2017). Graham V. Connor. https://legaldictionary_net/graham-v-connor.

Anon. (September 24, 2019). Bodycam footage played in court shows moments after cop fatally shot her neighbor. *CBS News*.

AP. (August 31, 2018). Dallas police group applauds "bad cop" Roy Oliver held responsible for Jordon Edwards death. *Associated Press*.

Balko, R. (October 16, 2019). Radley Balko: Civilians are dying in politicians' 'war on cops'. *The Washington Post*.

Bittner, E. (1990). *Aspects of Police Work*. Boston: Northeastern University Press.

Brown, J.M. (March 2001). Policing and homicide, 1976–1998: Justifiable homicide by police, police officers murdered by police. *Bureau of Justice Statistics. U.S. Department of Justice*.

Cardona, C. & Steele, T. (October 2, 2019). Timeline: How the case has unfolded since Dallas officer Amber Guyger killed Botham Jean. *Dallas Morning News*.

Curriden, M. (May 1996). When good cops go bad. *ABA Journal*.

Harmon, R.A. (2008). When is police violence justified? *Northwestern University Law Review*.

Harmon, R.A. (2012). The problem of policing. *Michigan Law Review*. 110(30): 781–817.

Kaste, M. (June 30, 2017). Cop shooting death cases raise question: When is fear reasonable? *NPR*.

Manna, N. (August 29, 2018). Ex-Balch springs police officer Roy Oliver guilty of murdering teenager Jordon Edwards. *Fort Worth Star-Telegram*.

McCullough, J. (August 28, 2018). Police officers are almost never convicted of murder. Body camera may have made the difference in this Texas case. *The Texas Tribune*.

Reith, C. (1952). *The Blind Eye of History: A Study of the Origins of the Present Police Era.* Montclair, NJ: Patterson Smith.

Sherman, L.W. (1980). Execution without trial: Police homicide and the constitution. *Vanderbilt Law Review.* 33(71): 71–100.

State Attorney's Office. (December 10, 2018). *The Daniel Blyer Death Investigation.* Fourth Judicial Circuit of Florida Duval County.

Stoughton, S.W. (May 2014). Policing facts. *The Tulane Law Review.* 66(3): 847–898.

Thompson, R.M. (October 30, 2015). Police use of force: Rules, remedies, and reform. *Congressional Research Service.*

Zimring, F.E. (2017). *When Police Kill.* Cambridge, Massachusetts: Harvard University.

Chapter 5

Non-lethal Use of Force?

Taser-Related Homicides

INTRODUCTION

Tasers are designed to deliver a high voltage, low current electrical charge designed to disrupt the central nervous system and cause uncontrolled muscle contractions in order to allow for the temporary incapacitation of the suspect (Amnesty International, 2008). In theory, the use of a non-lethal or less than lethal weapon such as the Taser prevents or lessens the use of deadly force by LEOs; for that reason they were introduced in street-level and custody settings. However, an unknown number of persons' have died or been seriously injured by the use and misuse of this weapon. Amnesty International (AI) was the first worldwide organization to call attention to the deaths and serious injuries associated with the police use of electrical shock weapons—conducted energy devices (CEDs) such as Tasers. However, the actual number of LEO homicides related to the use of "less than lethal" devices such as Tasers is hampered by the lack of independent research and reliable statistics. No government agency collects data on Taser-related deaths.

There is a critical need for medical research on Taser effects on vulnerable groups such as those under the influence of drugs and alcohol, suffering from mental illnesses, or other health issues. These special populations of vulnerable persons are typically encountered in the field during legal interventions or in custodial settings after an arrest. However, the majority of physiological research has been conducted with animals, not humans, because of ethical concerns (Amnesty International, 2008). Animal research is relied on because researchers must ensure the safety of voluntary human research volunteers. However, researchers know Taser use is often dangerous. The limited research confirms that the use and misuse of the Taser have been the direct or proximate/contributing cause of multiple deaths and serious injuries in the United States and other countries.

A full discussion of all the issues surrounding the use and misuse of the Taser is beyond the scope of our inquiry. Our discussion focuses on Taser-related deaths as a type of *Police-Perpetrated Homicides.*

ALTERNATIVES TO DEADLY FORCE

Less than lethal weapons were introduced into police work to reduce the use of deadly force, and they have done so when appropriately used (Alpert, Smith, Kaminski, Fridell, MacDonald, & Kubu, May 2011). Tasers, as with all non-lethal force weapons and techniques, were supposed to be used in situations that would rise to the necessity of deadly force if not brought under control. Tasers and other CED's were supposedly designed to incapacitate potentially dangerous suspects with an electrical shock temporarily. They were an alternative to deadly force—to reduce officer-involved shootings. Instead, Tasers are used as a routine force tool to force compliance to officer demands, including common verbal commands. They are routinely used in jails and other custody settings on intoxicated and mentally disturbed persons to force compliance. The use of Tasers on persons who are handcuffed or have been placed in other mechanical restraints is for no other purpose than in inflicting pain or punishment (Amnesty International, March 27, 2006). AI reports a twelve-year-old-boy in Florida tased by a School Resource Officer while he was handcuffed and restrained by other officers (AI, March 27, 2006: 26). They also recount the use of a Taser on a fourteen-year-old boy by the Chicago PD. The boy was living in a residential treatment center and had become violent, threatening staff and breaking windows. When the police arrived, the boy had calmed down and was sitting on a couch. According to the police, the boy assumed "an aggressive stance." They tased him and handcuffed him on the floor. The minor went into cardiac arrest and remained in critical condition for three days.

TASER MISUSE

What is the cost in terms of death and serious injury when Tasers are misused? In 2008, AI reported that 334 people had died in the United States since June 2001 after being shocked by a Taser administered by a LEO (Amnesty International, 2008). Twenty-five similar deaths were reported in Canada during that period. In fifty deaths in the United States, Tasers were reported to be the cause or the contributing factor. A recent (2017) Reuter's Investigation found 1,005 Taser-related deaths. The autopsy reports of those deaths found that the Taser was the cause or contributing factor in 153 of the deaths. Not unexpectedly, the manufacturer discounts these reports and says only twenty-four deaths were associated with the use of a Taser—eighteen from neck or head injuries from falls after being shocked and six from fires caused by the electrical shock (Eisler, Szep, Reid, & Smith, August 22, 2017: 4). The manufacturer does keep statistics on Taser-related deaths, but according to Reuters, they will not share this data.

The known criminal, negligent, and reckless Taser misuse combined with the number of police caused homicides and serious injuries following Taser shocks raises serious concerns about their use (Stinson, Reyns, & Liederbach, 2012; Eisler, Szep, Reid, & Smith, August 22, 2017). Tasers have been used on school children, pregnant women, the mentally ill, elderly persons with dementia, and persons suffering from medical conditions such as epileptic and diabetic seizures. AI cites the case of a medical doctor who crashed his car during an epileptic seizure and died after multiple Taser shocks when he failed to comply with the officers' commands (Amnesty International, 2008). He was dazed and confused. The leading critic on the misuse of Tasers is AI.

Amnesty International and the Use of Tasers

AI, the worldwide voluntary movement "who are campaigning for a world where human rights are enjoyed by all" is a leading critic of the use or misuse of the TASER, an acronym for Tom A. Swift Electric Rifle (See Text Box 5.1), especially in combination with supposedly other non-lethal weapons such as batons and pepper spray (Amnesty International March 27, 2006). The non-profit group is critical of its use by the police in the United States , Canada, the United Kingdom, Australia, France, and South Korea. For the most part, our discussion centers on the use in the United States.

TEXT BOX 5.1   TASERS

Tasers are powerful electrical weapons used by law enforcement agencies in, and among other countries, the USA, are designed to incapacitate by conducting 50,000 volts of electricity into a suspect. The pistol-shaped weapons use compressed nitrogen gas to fire sharp darts up to 27 (7m) [35 feet now]. The darts can penetrate up to two inches (5 cm) of clothing. Electricity is then conducted down wires connecting the darts and the Taser gun. The electrical pulses induce skeletal muscle spasms immobilizing and incapacitating a suspect and causing them to fall to the ground. They may also be used in "drive stun" mode, as a close up stun weapon. The "drive stun" is specifically designed or pain compliance [with less or no neuromuscular incapacitation].

Source: Amnesty International, March 27, 2006.

AMNESTY INTERNATIONAL'S INVOLVEMENT

The AI's first report issued in 2004 documented more than seventy persons in the United States and Canada who had died after being shocked by a Taser (AI, March 27, 2006). AI noted the lack of guidelines in the United States for the application of this pain-causing electro-shock weapon that left no visible signs and called on "all US police departments and authorities to suspend their deployment of Tasers pending a rigorous, independent inquiry into their use and effect" (AI, March 27, 2006: 1). This call was ignored, and the AI issued another report in 2006.

Amnesty International 2006 Report

The 2006 AI report stated that from 2001 to 2006, one hundred and fifty persons in the United States had died from being shocked—direct or contributing factor. Most of those who died were under the influence of drugs and had received multiple and prolonged shocks—forty received more than three shocks, and one was shocked nineteen times. Most of those who died were unarmed males who did not appear to represent a threat of death or serious injury to anyone. The report also stated that the reported Taser deaths had been continually rising—2001, 3 deaths reported, 13 in 2002, 17 in 2003, 48 in 2004, and 61 Taser-related deaths in 2005. The AI concluded the following:

- Most of those who died in custody were unarmed and were not posing a serious threat to police officers, members of the public, or themselves,
- Those who died were generally subjected to repeated or prolonged shocks.
- Use of the Taser was often accompanied by the use of restraints and chemical incapacitate sprays.
- Many of those who died had underlying health problems, such as heart conditions or mental illness, or were under the influence of drugs.
- Most of those who died went into cardiac or respiratory arrest at the scene (AI, March 27, 2006: 3–4).

The 2006 Amnesty report listed thirteen Taser-related deaths from October 2004 to 2006. Three of the cases were ruled homicides by the coroner, and the other ten cases listed the Taser as a contributing factor in the deaths. The youngest shocked victim was seventeen, and the oldest was sixty-two. Nine of the victims were tased multiple times—2 times (3), 3 times (2), 4 times (2), 6 times (1), 3 to 7 times (1), and one was shocked 20 + times. Four of those who died were subject to Tasers and pepper-sprayed. Two were shocked while in custody, and two victims were shocked while they were handcuffed. One deceased victim in custody was shocked six times, and one of the shock cycles lasted 2 minutes and 49 seconds—an example of unreasonable force.

One of the homicides ruled justified by a grand jury inquest was the death of a forty-seven-year-old man in Las Vegas on June 2005. The police were called to a hotel because the man was creating a disturbance. He struggled with the officers and was tased. He was handcuffed and then shocked again. He was placed on a gurney for transportation to the hospital. He was given a third shock from a Taser while on the gurney. He stopped breathing and was declared dead at the hospital. The police homicide was ruled justified even though police policy forbade shocking handcuffed persons and multiple shocks from a Taser (AI, March 27, 2017: 4).

In September 2005, a twenty-one-year-old man who had been taking LSD and smoking marijuana was ejected from a Nashville, Tennessee, nightclub for acting erratically. The responding Metropolitan Nashville Police Department officers found him stripped naked at the scene. He struggled with the officers and was shocked nineteen times. He had difficulty breathing, and the police sent him to the hospital. He died two days later. The family filed suit, and the jury found that the force used was not excessive.

AI reported eighty-five Taser-related deaths in the United States between November 2004 and February 2006. The cause of death was one of the variables listed for each incident. Twenty-six incidents had no information on the cause of death (31%). Homicide or Taser contributing factor was listed for twelve causes of death (20% of the fifty-nine with the cause listed).

AI's 2006 report stated that Tasers were being used as "routine force" tools by U.S. police agencies whenever anyone failed to comply with an officer's commands whether or not they were a danger to the officers or anyone else. Tasers were unnecessarily used in jails and other custody settings. AI was concerned with the use of Tasers on vulnerable groups such as children, the disabled, pregnant women, and the mentally ill. Electrically shocking, these groups should only be done as a last resort before the use of deadly force. They called for more research, improved training, and rigorous investigations of all complaints.

The report found that the lack of independent studies is a serious problem. A UK study found that the majority of the studies on the physiological effect of Taser use have used healthy volunteers being exposed to short to five-second or shorter Taser shocks (Peel, July 2017). However, in the field, Tasers are used on persons who are under the influence of alcohol or drugs, often both; experiencing a mental health issue; or have been running, struggling, or fighting. These suspects experienced expended and repeated shocks and be retrained for long periods and in a prone position. Research on these variables will not be easy and probably not possible on live subjects.

2008 Amnesty International Report

This report is an update to the previous AI reports-2004 & 2006. The AI reviewed ninety autopsy reports, media reports, lawsuits, and reports of official investigations. Their key findings are summarized below:

- Most of those who died were agitated, disturbed, and under the influence of drugs, and a significant proportion had heart disease.
- Many were subjected to multiple or prolonged shocks, often for more than the standard five-second cycle, despite warnings for several years of the potential health risks of such deployment.
- In most cases, the deceased is reported to have gone into cardio-respiratory arrest at the scene, shortly after being shocked. Some died at the scene, and others were pronounced dead later in hospital after failing to regain consciousness. The proximity of Taser shocks to the deceased cardiac arrest in many cases raise concern that the shocks may have triggered or contributed to the fatal collapse.
- In some cases the deceased had no drugs in their system or underlying health problems and collapsed shortly after being shocked, raising further concern about the role of the Taser.
- In a significant proportion of cases (43% of autopsy reports) the deceased was shocked in the chest. Some cardiac experts have suggested that CED strikes to the chest may carry a high risk of disturbing the heart rhythm.
- In many cases additional forms of restraint were applied, including methods known to impair breathing such as hog-tying, chokeholds, and pepper spray.

Source: Amnesty International, 2008.

Those Who Died

The 2008 AI reported that 334 people had died in the United States since June 2001. Ninety-seven percent were males. The ages ranged from seventeen to sixty-three. Most of the deceased died after being shocked by sheriffs or municipal police officers. Thirty died in jails and will be discussed later. California (55) and Texas (52) reported the most deaths. The Las Vegas Metropolitan PD was the agency with the most deaths (6). Race was only reported for 200 cases (60%). Ninety of the deceased were black (45%); 74 (37%) were white; and 33 (17%) were Hispanic. Two of the deceased were Native American, and one was Haitian.

Only ten of the deceased were reported to have a weapon of any kind—four had handguns. Thirty-seven of the autopsy reports listed a Taser as the cause or contributing factor in the death. Eighteen cases listed the Taser along with other factors such as heart disease or physiological stress as the cause. In all, fifty of the ninety-eight autopsies reported that there was a link between the Taser shocks and death.

2012 CRIMINAL MISUSE OF TASERS REPORT

Stinson and his colleagues (2012), as part of a more extensive study of police crime, examined the criminal use of Tasers. Through a content analysis of newspaper articles in a sixty-five-month period—January 2005 to May 2010—they identified twenty-four non-federal U.S. LEOs who were arrested for criminal misuse of Tasers. The majority (96%) of the LEOs arrested were males between the ages of thirty-two and forty-seven (84%). Most were non-supervisory rank (83%)—officer, trooper or deputy. Seventy-nine percent had three or more years of experience. They were not rookies. Three-quarters of the Taser incidents occurred while the LEO was on duty. Municipal police agencies employed seventy-five percent of the LEO. Sheriff's offices employed almost 17 percent of the officers. Fifty-four percent of the arrested LEOs came from the Southern region of the United States. The remaining arrested officers came from the Midwestern region (21%) and Western Region (21%). Only one case was reported in the Northeastern region. Several states had multiple officers arrested—Florida had five reported cases, Michigan three, Texas three, Colorado two, and Louisiana two.

Almost 84 percent (n = 20) of the LEOs arrested were charged with assault-related cases. An equal number of officers were arrested for misdemeanor charges—harassment, simple assault, and felonies—aggravated assault, non-negligent manslaughter, and one aggravated sexual assault where a police officer held a Taser to his victim's leg as he raped her. Forty-nine officers lost their jobs or resigned as a result of the arrests. The case disposition was available for eighteen cases. Eight cases resulted in criminal convictions. Four officers were acquitted at trial, and five cases were dropped. One case was dropped when the charged officer committed suicide.

There were other disturbing findings. None of the Taser shocks occurred due to a threat to the officer or anyone else. The criminal uses of Tasers in these twenty-four cases were most likely to occur when the suspect was already handcuffed. Or not charged with a crime. Tasers were used against spouses, friends, other relatives, and even police officers. One officer tased thirty-four students attending a career fair. Frequently officers engaged in "grab-ass" tased each other. A male officer tased his female partner while she was driving the police vehicle. They were having a soft drink dispute. A police officer used his Taser on another police officer after he walked in on him having sex with his wife. The researchers concluded that "the TASER was more likely to be deployed against girlfriends, cheating spouses or troublesome citizens—perhaps those who needed to be taught a lesson—rather than resistant criminal suspects" (Sinson, Reyns, & Liederbach, 2012: 14).

AI has continually reported that Tasers are subject to abuse and misuse because they are easy to carry, easy to use, and they inflict pain at the touch of a button. Also, the Taser does not leave any evidence of its use in direct stun use. When pepper spray was first introduced into police work, many officers thought it was funny to spray one another or a suspect to teach them a lesson (personal experience). The study's conclusion supports the call for more research on the criminal use of Tasers.

2017 REUTER'S INVESTIGATION

In 2017, a Reuter's investigative team published the results of what they claim is a "first of its kind" of deaths and litigation that followed the use of Tasers (Eisler, Szep, Reid, and Smith, August 22, 2017; Morisey, October 3, 2017). The data came from a review of court documents, public records, and news accounts. The review covered all reported Taser deaths since the first in 1983 through July 31, 2017. They found 1,005 deaths where Tasers were the cause, contributing factor, or part of the mosaic of force used. In 153 of the deaths , the Taser was cited as the cause or contributing factor in the death (p. 17). Wrongful death suits were filed in 442 of the incidents against the officers or the agency that employed them.

Autopsy Findings

The Reuter's team was able to obtain official cause-of-death ruling for 712 cases—70 percent of the total. Tasers were listed as the cause or contributing factor in 278 cases. Another 348 cases listed Tasers as part of the contributing factors. The team was able to obtain cause-of-death information from other sources—court records or state investigation reports.

Civil Litigation

_There were 442 civil lawsuits where Tasers were mentioned in the court filing. In 120 of the suits, a Taser was the only weapon mentioned in the force used. In 332 of the cases, Tasers were a part of the array of police use of force. There were 366 cases concluded at the time the data was gathered. The results were 220 settlements, and 12 judgments—193 had a total of $172 million paid by cities and their insurers. Some of the settlements had nondisclosure agreements.

A Note on Taser Use in England and Wales

In 2017, A British Police Custody Nurse published an informative article on Taser use in England and Wales. It has implications for US use even though the UK standards are universal, and that is not the case in the fragmented police system with 18,000+ law enforcement agencies. In the UK, all CED's, including Tasers, are classified as prohibited weapons under Section 5 of the Firearms Act of 1968. The law prohibits possession or sale by non-specially trained and authorized police officers. The Taser is not classified as a firearm in the United States; therefore, civilian purchase and possession are permitted. The police custody nurse wrote the article because "nurses working in pre-hospital, emergency departments (ED) or police custody settings" are likely to encounter persons who have been tased by the police (Peel, April 19, 2017). In the United States, custody personnel accept tased prisoners and use and misuse the shock weapon as a control device.

Tasers were introduced in the UK in 2003, and in 2016 they were presented or used by the police in England and Wales 11,294 times. The actual use number was 1,910 incidents—17 percent. This is evidence of the tightly regulated Taser use by police officers in England and Wales. Peel reports that there have been seventeen Taser-related deaths in the UK since 2003. Two of those deaths listed the Taser as the cause of death. One of the possible reasons for the low number of deaths is the safety feature of the Taser model used in the UK. The safety feature limits the Taser discharge to the "safe" five seconds (see Text Box 5.2).

TEXT BOX 5.2   U.S. TASER DEATHS
FROM PROLONGED USE

Many deaths in the United States are attributed to long discharges, sometimes up to two minutes. In June 2019, a U.S. federal jury awarded the family of a Taser-related death $4 million (Petreqin & Casert, June 21, 2019). The forty-one-year-old man was tased six times and handcuffed after he struggled with officers over an outstanding arrest warrant. He stopped breathing and died. A twenty-two-year-old mentally ill man was shocked fifteen times after the police tased him eighteen times—each shock was 30 to 45 seconds in duration (Barton, June 19, 2019). He was reported to be running up and down the hall of his apartment building naked. The police broke down the door or his apartment and tased him as he showered. The family received a $2.5 million settlement. In 2014, a mentally ill Hollywood, California man, was shocked 10 times by two rookie police officers (Byran, December 20, 2018). The nude man was shocked four times while he was handcuffed and lying on the ground with his legs shackled, and at least one discharged lasted nine seconds. The family received a $750,000 settlement.

Another factor contributing to the low Taser death rate in the U.K. is the attention given to training and calling attention to the possible adverse effects linked to Taser use. According to the College of Policing—UK national police training and research—the typical effects of a Taser shock are:

- Persons who have been tased may:
- Be unable to control their posture and may be at risk of injury from accidental falls.
- Experience leg rigidity that can mimic "kicking out" to the prone position.
- Convulse, curl up in a ball, spasm, or stiffen.
- Experience intense pain.
- Call out or make involuntary noise.
- Be unable to respond to a verbal command.
- Experience confusion of disorientation.
- Feel exhausted.
- Freeze" on the spot.

These effects are included in the training of Taser qualified British police officers. The author says it is "essential" for Custody Nurses to seek medical attention. Under the following circumstances (Text Box 5.3)

TEXT BOX 5.3   TRANSFER TO EMERGENCY DEPARTMENT

- People with significant co-morbidities, such as heart disease, neurological disorders, or a history of neurosurgery.
- People with a pacemaker, internal cardiac defibrillator, vergus nerve stimulator, or an electric implanted device for device interrogation.

- Individuals who take anticoagulants, because of the increased risk of bleeding, or statins, because of the increased risk of rhabdomyolysis [skeletal muscle breakdown].
- Pregnant women. They should also be referred for the potential effects of a Taser on a fetus, and the link between Taser use and miscarriage.
- Individuals who are intoxicated with drugs or alcohol, as they may have a condition that mimics intoxication.
- People with abnormal ECG.
- People whose heart rate does not settle to what is considered normal within 30 minutes of Taser discharge.

Source: Peel, July 2017:26.

The circumstances for referral listed above should be posted in all U.S. custody settings. In the field where police officers use the Taser, there is little possibility that the officer could identify the conditions; however, every Taser user should be aware of the conditions that could lead to a medical emergency. U.S. police officers have tased pregnant women with disastrous results. The most famous case—cited on all anti-Taser websites—occurred in 2001 in Chula Vista, California. Cindi Grippi was six months pregnant when she was tased for not obeying the command of a cop. He told her not to come into her house, and she did. She fell on her stomach and delivered a stillborn baby several days later (Whitehead, April 7, 2008). She settled a lawsuit against the city of Chula Vista for $675, 000.

Police Policy on Taser Use

Police policy on Taser use on the vulnerable groups described above varies throughout the United States. A Department of Justice survey of more than 500 state and county agencies found that 31 percent forbid CED used against pregnant women (Kaminski, Alpert, & Fridell, May 2011). Almost 26 percent forbid its use against moving vehicles. We already cited a Michigan State Trooper who shocked a teenager on an ATV out the window of a police vehicle. The teenager crashed and was killed, and the trooper was tried and convicted of criminal homicide. Twenty-three percent of the agencies will not allow officers to shock a handcuffed person, yet the incidents reported by AI and the Reuter's investigatory document the frequent use of Tasers against handcuffed prisoners. Twenty-three percent of the agencies forbid shocking persons in elevated areas. There are incidents where shocked persons have fallen to their deaths. Ten percent of the 500 agencies would not allow shocking the elderly, although who was determined to be elderly varied. Given that Tasers can and do cause death to these vulnerable groups combined with the lack of unbiased research on the physiological effects of Tasers, a skeptical approach to their use is warranted. This skepticism is reinforced by recent newspaper accounts of Taser-related deaths that resulted in U.S. LEOs being charged with a crime.

RECENT TASER-RELATED CRIMINAL LEO CHARGES

The author performed an illustrative, not exhaustive search of the U.S. Department of Justice website and found press releases of the following law enforcement Taser-related criminal charges.

LEOs

Bridgeport, Connecticut—Two Bridgeport PD officers pleaded guilty to violating the civil rights of a man at the end of a police pursuit. The man was repeatedly tased even though he was incapacitated after the first shock. One of the officers kicked the victim several times (DOJ. U.S. Attorney's Office. District of Connecticut, June 10, 2014). The officers were sentenced to three months imprisonment and six months of supervised release.

Oglala Sioux Tribe Police Officer—The female tribal police officer was indicted for excessive force and deprivation of civil rights. She allegedly repeatedly used her Taser against a man in her custody without justification (DOJ, U.S. Attorney's Office, District of South Dakota, August 27, 2014).

Marion, South Carolina—Two Marion PD officers pleaded guilty to using excessive force when tasing a woman with mental disabilities. One officer tased the woman, and she fell to the ground and injured her head. The officer continued tasing the woman repeatedly while she was on the ground. The second officer came on the scene and tased the woman who was now sitting on the curb handcuffed. Both officers admitted in court that there was no legitimate law enforcement purpose for repeatedly the victim, as she did not pose a threat to the two officers (DOJ. U.S. Attorney's Office. District of South Carolina, October 28, 2014).

Homer, Louisiana—A Homer PD officer was indicted for tasing three victims and then lying to the FBI. He allegedly deployed his Taser on three different victims at different times, causing physical injuries and violating their civil rights (DOJ. U.S. Attorney's Office. Western District of Louisiana. December 18, 2014).

Millvale, Pennsylvania—A small-town Pennsylvania police officer was convicted in federal court for violating the civil rights of a man she arrested for public drunkenness in September 2012 (Department of Justice, March 13, 2015). She shocked the man at least three times with her Taser while laughing and calling him a "retard" (Mandak, March 13, 2015). The man was hand-cuffed and sitting on the floor in the squad room when she shocked him. A 52-second cellphone video of the incident was taken by another officer and leaked to the press. She was sentenced to three years probation—first three years to be home confinement followed by nine months of in-home confine-ment (could leave to go to work or other approved areas with a GPS device). She was also required to perform two hundred hours of community service. The community service required her to outreach to LEOs on the use and con-sequence of using excessive force.

Independence, Missouri—An Independence PD officer was sentenced to four years in prisons for violating the constitutional rights of a minor he arrested. The minor was tased in the chest four times for 20 seconds each time. The minor went into cardiac arrest and became nonresponsive. The officer handcuffed the minor and then picked him up and dropped him face-first into the pavement. Luckily, the minor survived (DOJ. Office of Public Affairs, June 1, 2016).

Lake Charles, Louisiana—A Lake Charles PD officer was indicted for using excessive force on an arrestee. He is accused of the unjustified use of Taser that resulted in bodily harm (DOJ. U.S. Attorney's Office. Western District of Louisiana, April 10, 2019).

In-custody Taser-Related Criminal Violations

Carroll County, Tennessee—A female Lieutenant with the Carroll County, Tennessee Sheriff's office, pleaded guilty to using a Taser on a restrained pretrial detainee. The inmate was secured in a restraint chair and posed no threat to her or any other officer (DOJ. Office of Public Affairs, November 18, 2015).

Mamou, Louisiana—The Police Chief of the Mamou police department was sentenced to a year and a day for using a Taser on a non-combative prisoner. He admitted in court that he knew his actions were unlawful (DOJ. Office of Public Affairs, January 14, 2016).

Tate County, Mississippi—A Lieutenant with the Tate County Sheriff's Office was sentenced to two years in prison for unlawfully tasing a pretrial detainee. The shocked victim fell backward and hit his head on the concrete floor, cracking his skull. The victim had to have brain surgery (DOJ. U.S. Attorney's Office. Northern District of Mississippi, March 24, 2016).

Dekalb County, Georgia—A sergeant with the Dekalb County Jail pleaded guilty to unlawfully tasing a female prisoner. The prisoner asked to see a supervisor about the abrupt cancellation of her family visitation. The sergeant, rather than explaining the cancellation, tased her until she defecated on herself. The inmate suffered permanent taser burns to her chest. The sergeant admitted that he knew what he was doing was wrong (DOJ. Office of Public Affairs, November 22, 2017).

Cheatham County, Tennessee—A corporal and a sergeant with the Chatham County Jail were indicted for the same unlawful Taser incident. The corporal unlawfully tased an eighteen-year-old inmate four times for a total of fifty seconds while he was incapacitated in a restraint chair. The sergeant was indicted for filing false accounts of the incident (DOJ. U.S. Attorney's Office. Middle District of Tennessee, June 26, 2018). The sergeant later pleaded guilty.

Fulton County, Kentucky—A deputy jailer was convicted of assaulting an inmate after repeatedly shocked him with a Taser after the inmate cursed at him. The inmate cursed the jailer from inside his cell, and the jailer opened the cell door and entered and began shocking the prisoner (DOJ. Office of Public Affairs, May 1, 2019).

TASER-RELATED CRIMINAL POLICE–
PERPETRATED HOMICIDE CHARGES

Winnfield, Louisiana—In 2008, a police officer from the small town—5,800 people—was fired from his police position, indicted and charged with manslaughter over a Taser-related homicide. Allegedly, the white police officer used a Taser in the stun-mode eight times while the black victim was on the ground and refusing to get up. The twenty-one-year-old victim was tased again when he refused to get out of the police car. It was also alleged that the officer failed to get medical treatment when it was needed. The officer went on trial in October 2010 and was found not guilty by a jury of ten whites and two blacks (AP. August 13, 2008, and Foster, November 12, 2010).

East Point, Georgia—Two black East Point Georgia PD officers—Sgt. Marcus Eberhart and Cpl. Howard Weems—were convicted of criminal homicide for the Taser-related death of a black 281 pound twenty-four-year-old handcuffed man they had just arrested (Hawkins, December 2, 2016, Cook, December 21, Cook, December 21, 2016, and Rankin, June 20, 2019). The often confusing newspaper accounts describe the incident as the result of a domestic violence call. The victim ran when the first officer arrived at the scene. The officer chased him into a nearby wooded area, and when the obese victim tripped and fell, the officer handcuffed him. The officer called for help and noticing the suspect's breathing problems called for an ambulance.

According to court testimony, Sgt. Eberhart, on his way to the scene, heard the call for an ambulance and canceled the ambulance. Eberhart, when he arrived at the scene, told the suspect to get up and walk out of the woods to the police vehicle. The suspect said he was too tired to walk and to let him rest. Sgt, Eberhart told the corporal that if the suspect would not get up to tase him. The victim was tased in the "stun gun mode" at least fourteen times and died at the scene. Sgt. Marcus Eberhart was convicted of murder at trial and was sentenced to life in prison. Cpl. Weems was acquitted of murder but convicted of two felonies—involuntary manslaughter and violating his oath of office— and a misdemeanor, reckless conduct. He was sentenced to eighteen months in prison and three and a half years of supervised probation after he finished his prison term. The family received a $1 million settlement from the city.

Michigan State Trooper—A Michigan State Trooper was sentenced to 5 to 15 years after he was convicted of involuntary manslaughter for the 2017 Taser-related death of a Detroit teenager. The trooper, who has a law degree, had a history of deploying his Taser without justification, and using the CED to punish suspects, used the Taser in a bizarre manner (Anderson, May 14, 2019). The trooper was a passenger in a police vehicle that was pursuing a fifteen-year-old on an ATV. The teenager slowed down, and the trooper reached out the car window and shocked the young boy who crashed into a parked car and died. The trooper claimed that he thought the teenager was reaching for a gun in his waistband. No gun was found at the scene, and the trooper did not make this claim until sometime later.

CONCLUSION

The Taser properly used by trained and certified LEOs is a valuable less than lethal alternative to deadly force. However, it is criminally misused. Tasers are preferable to killing an individual and are necessary to use for officer safety and minimizing the risk of injury to others, including suspects. However, more research is needed to examine the effects of its use, and police agencies must increase the training and administrative controls on the use of Tasers.

SOURCES

Amnesty International. (2008). '*Less Than Lethal?*' *The Use of Stun Weapons in US Law Enforcement*. United Kingdom: Amnesty International.

Anderson, E. (May 4, 2019). Ex-trooper sentenced in death of a teenager on ATV. *The Detroit Free Press*.

AP. (August 13, 2008). Ex-Louisiana cop was accused of repeatedly shocking a hand-cuffed man. *Associated Press*.

Barton, G. (June 19, 2019). West Milwaukee to pay $2.5 million settlement. *The Post-Cresent.*

Byran, S. (December 20, 2018). Police shot him with a stun gun10 time. Now his family is getting $750, 000. *TCA Regional News.*

Cook, R. (December 21, 2016). Former East Point cop sentenced to life in prison in Taser. *Actkon New.*

Department of Justice. (March 13, 2015). Former Millvale Police Officer Sentenced for Tasering Handcuffed Man. U.S. Attorney's Office. Western District of Pennsylvania.

Eisler, P., Szep, J., Reid, J., & Smith, G. (August 22, 2017). Shock tactics: The toll. *Reuters Investigations.*

Foster, M. (November 12, 2010). Jurors find ex-officer not guilty in Taser case. *The Final Call.*

Hawkins, D. (December 22, 2016). Former Ga. Cop sentenced to life in prison in Taser death of unarmed, handcuffed man. *The Washington Post.*

Kaminski, R.J., Alpert, A., & Fridell, L. (May, 2011). Police use of force, Tasers and other less-lethal weapons. *Department of Justice.*

Mandak, J. (March 13, 2015). Judge wants ex-officer in stun case to be a cautionary tale. *Associated Press.*

Morisey, M. (October 2, 2017). How they did it: Reuters' database of Taser deaths. *Global Investigative Journalist Network.*

Peel, M. (July 22, 2017). Assessment of people who have been Tasered. *Evidence and Practice.* 25(4): 22–29.

Petrequin, S. & Casert, R. (June 21, 2019). $4Million awarded over death of a man in Rohnert Park police custody. *New York Times.*

Rankin, E. (June 20, 2019). Ex-Fulton cop appeals murder conviction in man's Taser death. *The Atlanta Journal.*

Stinson, P.M., Reyns, B.W., & Liederbach, J.L. (2012). Police crime and less-than-Lethal coercive force: A description of the criminal misuse of TASERS. *International Journal of Police Science and Management.* 14(1): 1–19.

Whitehead, J.W. (April 7, 2008). Police state tactics: Tasering pregnant women and the elderly. *The Rutherford Institute.*

Chapter 6

Suicide by Cop

INTRODUCTION

A depressed, intoxicated suspect who has just stabbed his wife slowly advances on a police officer called to the scene. He has a knife in his hand. The officer tells him several times to stop and drop the knife. The man continues his advance while telling the officer to shoot him. The officer keeps backing up and calling for backup. The man suddenly lunges at the officer and is shot four times and dies—*Suicide by Cop.*

Suicides by Cop (SBC) are "incidents in which individuals, bent on self-destruction, engage in life-threatening and criminal behavior in order to force police to kill them" (Geberth, July 1993: 105). SBC is a type of police-perpetrated homicides where the victim essentially "forces" the LEO to be an unwilling instrument in his or her death (Miller, 2006). The tragic situation creates two victims—the suicide victim and the officer/s. There is an emotional toll on officers who feel that they are manipulated into assisting a person to commit suicide (Homant, Kennedy, & Hupp, 2000). This toll is especially tragic when the perceived risk was inaccurate—the weapon was not loaded or real.

However, there is a real danger to SBC incidents; both parties are armed or perceived to be. Furthermore, SBC is a more dangerous and lethal form of suicide because the subject often threatens the lives of others, including the officer, to provoke the use of deadly force. Homant et al.'s (2000) study of 123 SBC incidents found that the subject killed one or more persons in eight incidents, eight other people were seriously wounded, and fifty-three police or bystanders were directly threatened by lethal force. The police killed eighty-nine persons—72 percent of the 123 incidents. A 2009 study of officer-involved shootings (OIS) from March 2006 to January 2007 from ninety North American police departments in the United States and Canada identified 256 SBC incidents. In these incidents, two police officers were killed and forty injured (Mohandie, Meloy, & Collins, 2009). Nine bystanders or non-law enforcement persons were killed, and thirty injured. The police killed 131 (51%) of the suicidal persons, 101 were injured, and 17 committed suicide on their own.

CONTROVERSIAL CONCEPT

"Suicide by Cop" is, by definition, a controversial concept. "Suicide" is the intentional killing of oneself, whereas "homicide" is the killing of another person. In this case, we have a person killing themselves by using another person as a lethal weapon. Further complicating this police-caused homicide phenomenon is once again the lack of reliable statistics, and the lack of agreement about SBC among the U.S. medical examiners and coroners (ME/C) on the death certification (Neitzel & Gill, 2011). Some ME/C's classify the deaths as justifiable homicides, and others certify them as suicides, making it virtually impossible to get an accurate official count of "suicides by cop" (Patton & Fremouw, 2016).

Despite the lack of official statistics, SBC is recognized as a problem for law enforcement agencies. According to a study of OIS in Los Angeles County from 1987 to 1997, 25 percent of the OIS's were SBC (cited in Neitzel & Gill, 2011: 1657). The researchers in the Los Angeles County survey based their conclusion on specific criteria: evidence of the individual's suicidal intent, evidence that the individual specifically wanted police officers to shoot them, evidence that the individual possessed a lethal weapon or what appeared to be a lethal weapon, and evidence that the individual intentionally escalated the encounter and provoked the officers to shoot. Neitzel and Gill, 2011 (Gill is an MD with the Office of Medical Examiner and Department of Forensic Science, New York University School of Medicine) examined all gunshot deaths from police officers in New York City between January 1, 1996, and October 1, 2006. They identified five cases that they defined as SBC. One of those five cases is presented in Text Box 6.1.

TEXT BOX 6.1   CASE NO. 2

A forty-three-year-old man with a history of anxiety and depression (recently lost his job and was on medications) had beaten his mother, slashed his wrists and torso, and was then menacing the police with a gun and a knife. After numerous orders to drop the gun and knife, he was shot by the police. Multiple witnesses expressed the opinion that he "definitely wanted to die" and even told the police to "aim higher." Postmortem toxicology analysis detected no ethanol or drugs of abuse.

SBC TYPOLOGY

Homant and Kennedy (2000) developed a SBC typology from a database of 143 incidents from the professional literature and newspaper databases. The incidents were divided into three categories—*Direct Confrontation, Disturbed Intervention*, and *Criminal Intervention.* The three categories were then divided into different types.

Direct Confrontation (DC)

Forty-four of the incidents—30.8 percent—were placed in this category. The subjects planned to attack LEOs and be killed by the police officer. The category is divided into four types.

DC Type 1

Kamikaze Attack—The subject uses deadly force to suddenly attack a police officer, a group of police officers, or a police station. Four incidents of this type were found in the SBC database. The authors give the May 14, 1998, attack by a depressed man on a Detroit police precinct as an example of this type.

The man called his brother-in-law and asked him to take care of his son if anything happened to him. He sounded depressed. Then, he dribbles a basketball into the main entrance of a Detroit police precinct and announces that he is going to "kill everyone." He says, "Everybody down, Detroit ain't shit." At first, four officers behind the desk do not take him seriously. When he bounces the basketball toward them and pulls out two guns, they order him to drop the weapons. He points a weapon at an officer and says, "Now what are you going to?" several times as he backs up. He started firing and riddled the station with bullets as he crouches behind a vending machine with a pistol and a sawed-off rifle, saying, "I'm invincible." Bullets hit the front desk and a back wall, but the four officers and the three civilians in the room were unhurt. The four officers fired back, as the assailant crouches behind two vending machines reloading. Four other officers leave the rear of the building, circle around, and fire through the front window. They shoot some fifty to seventy-five times at the assailant, hitting him six times. He was taken to the hospital and later died. The assailant's behavior surprised everyone who knew him, although he was described as "having mood swings" and being depressed over the breakup with his son's mother (page 345; see Text Box 6.2).

TEXT BOX 6.2   RECENT KAMIKAZE SBC ATTACK

A recent example of a DC Type 1—Kamikaze Attack occurred on July 2018 in Fredericks, Virginia. A police officer answered a domestic disturbance call between a man and his brother. When the officer knocked on the door, the twenty-five-year-old male suspect came barreling out of the door, swinging a box cutter (Epps, July 12, 2019). The officer received severe cuts on his face and neck. The officer backed up shooting at the subject but missed hitting him. The subject was later apprehended and asked the officer to shoot him. He said his original intent was to get killed. The man received a twenty-year sentence for attempted capital murder.

DC Type 2

Controlled Attack—Six incidents fit in this type where the suspect confronts the officers rather than attack them. The suspect may or may not be armed. The suspect approaches and presents a weapon or threatens that they have a weapon and demands that the officer kill him, or they will engage in a deadly confrontation. Remember, a real or perceived danger is required for a police homicide to be justified (Homant, Kennedy, & Hupp, 2000).

Example: A thirty-two-year-old security officer in Shelby, North Carolina, parked his car in the middle of the street on January 6, 1997. He approached a nearby police station on foot and started yelling. He has two handguns. Thirty police officers surround him. He says, "Do your job, it gonna end today." A sheriff, an experienced negotiator, talked to him for 45 minutes. The subject started to withdraw from the conversation, then fired a shot, hitting himself in the leg (apparently on purpose). Then the subject raised the gun toward the sheriff. A police marksmen fired, hitting and killing the subject. Relatives described him as paranoid (page 345).

DC Type 3

Manipulated Confrontation—This was the Direct Confrontation type with the most incidents—22. The suspect orchestrates a confrontation with the police. A variety of ruses are used. Some suspects call to report a crime or to tell the police they are suicidal. Some drive erratically to provoke a traffic stop or a pursuit. Then the suspect confronts the officer with real or perceived deadly force. The example provided was a woman who called the police and said she was at a mall and was going to kill the first person she sees. Three officers respond, and a standoff began. She has a gun and points it at the officers who retreat. A supervisor orders the officers to shoot her. She was hit seven times and said, "Thank you, God. Thank you, God," as she dies. Later, a note was found addressed to the unknown police officer she expects to kill her. In the note, she apologizes and says she is "too chicken" to kill herself.

DC Type 4

Dangerous Confrontation—This type is similar to DC Type 3, but is a more dangerous confrontation. The suspect commits a serious crime and is more interested in the deadly encounter than getting away. The confrontation may involve hostages and the desire for the subject to take them or the officer with him. There were eleven cases in this type.

The example provided demonstrated the lethal consequences of SBC. A twenty-two-year-old man with a history of arrests was wanted for parole violations. He was also depressed over a domestic dispute. He proceeded to a bank with a shotgun. On the way, he shot and seriously injured a passing jogger. He stole a car and drove to the bank. Entering the bank, he ordered everyone to lie down and say the Lord's Prayer. He joins them in the praying, mixing in some obscenities. He killed two bank employees and injured another. He never tried for any money. He watched out the windows until the police arrived. He exited the bank, grabbing a man using the ATM as a hostage. Police surrounded him. Holding the hostage by the neck, he fired several rounds at the police. Then, he pushed his hostage down and killed him. Police opened fire and killed him (page 346).

Disturbed Intervention (DI)

Eighty-two percent of the SBC incidents were in this category. The subject was acting in an irrational, emotionally disturbed manner. The subject may be overtly suicidal or seize on the arrival of the police as an opportunity to become suicidal. There are three types in this category: suicide intervention disturbed domestic, and disturbed person.

DI Type 1

Suicide Intervention—The police intervene in what is a bona fide suicide attempt; however, the subject may be hesitant and ambivalent. Twenty-nine of the examined incidents fit in this type.

A mother is concerned about her twenty-three-year-old son. He shouted profanities at her and threatened suicide. She called the police twice complaining about his behavior that included her hearing shots fired, and him breaking a window when she locked him out. After an officer arrives, the young man returns and asks to come in. The officer goes outside to talk to him. The man points a gun at his head and tells the officer that he wants to say goodbye to his mother. Gun drawn, the officer orders him to put the gun down. He points the gun at the officer. The officer fires twice, and the man falls to the ground with wounds to his hand and stomach. The suicidal man raised the gun and shot himself in the head (page 347).

DI Type 2

Disturbed Domestic—A domestic dispute results in the police being called, and the subject reacts with hopeless, suicidal resistance. Twenty-four of the SBC incidents were included in this type.

A seventeen-year-old teenager with learning disabilities jumped in front of traffic after his girlfriend attempted to break up with him. He was hospitalized for several days. He made up with his girlfriend, but after several weeks she again ended the relationship. Armed with a pellet gun, designed as a replica of a .357 revolver, he entered the supermarket where she worked. The police are called. He runs from the police. They see he has a gun and yell for all in the store to get down. The police chase him up and down the aisles. At the checkout counter, the subject points the "gun" at a man and his nine-year-old daughter. Police shoot and kill him (page 347).

DI Type 3

Disturbed Person—The police are confronted with a person who is drunk, drug-influenced, mentally ill, or otherwise disturbed. Drug and alcohol intoxication is a bad sign because this increases the instability and impulsivity of the subject (Miller, 2006). The person is observed acting strangely or in a dangerous manner. The disturbed person reacts to police intervention in a manner that demonstrates death over submission. Twenty-nine incidents were classified as this type.

A twenty-three year-old-man gets in an argument at a bar. He leaves but returns with a shotgun and fires two shotgun blasts at the bar's back door. Police confront him at a nearby gas station. At first, he lies down on the ground in response to a police command. Then, as more police arrive, he gets back up. He ignores police commands, dares them to shoot him, and then walks toward the shotgun he had dropped. Nine officers have him surrounded. He hesitates, then picks up the shotgun and points it at the officers. The police shoot and kill him (pages 247 & 348).

Criminal Intervention (CI)

The incidents in this category begin with a common or ordinary crime that is interrupted by police intervention. The perpetrator expected to get away but was stopped by the police. However, the subject prefers death over capture. There were nine incidents in the two types of this category.

CI Type 1

Major Crime—The SBC subjects in this type are unwilling to go to jail or prison. Most often, they are on parole or probation and have served time. Nine cases were in this category.

A twenty-nine-year-old man on parole is caught burglarizing a home by the homeowner. The homeowner pursues the fleeing burglar in a car chase while talking to the police on his cell phone. The police join the chase. During the chase, the burglar throws out a rifle and a shotgun. Forty-five minutes later, the burglar abandons his car and runs between some houses. Police find him holding a pistol to his head and threating suicide. The officers talk to him for two hours. Finally, he turns and points the gun at the police, and they shoot and kill him (page 248).

In 2009, a Summerville, South Carolina man was shot and killed by a Summerville PD officer following a traffic stop (Jacobs, October 5, 2009). The coroner ruled the death a "SBC." The twenty-five-year-old man was a two-time ex-con and wanted for credit card fraud and probation violation. Also, the man had a gun in his possession. He would be fast-tracked to prison. A friend said the man often said he would rather be dead than go back to prison. After he was stopped, the man exited with the gun in his hand and ignored several commands to put the gun down. He raised the gun, and the officers shot him multiple times. He died in the hospital.

CI Type 2

Minor Crime—A person commits a minor crime such as a simple assault or traffic infraction and resists the police intervention as a matter of principle. The subject does not appear to be a psychologically disturbed person but becomes "unglued" by the police intervention. Eight incidents fit in this type.

Female SBC

Although the "typical" SBC victim in previous studies is a white male with a mean age of thirty-five, a recent California possible SBC, demonstrates that there are exceptions to statistical profiles. A seventeen-year-old girl sped by a marked Fullerton, California police vehicle. The officer gave pursuit, and the driver slammed into the police vehicle and then made a U-turn facing the wrong way on an Anaheim freeway (Stimson, July 13, 2019). The officer called for backup. The teenager exited her vehicle, and the officer's body camera shows her pointing a pistol at the officer. The officer shot her in the chest. The officer and a citizen tried to help her, but she died. The weapon she pointed at the officer turned out to be a replica of a Beretta and Recent 92 FS handgun. Some 90 minutes after the incident, the girl's father called the police, not knowing of the shooting, and said that she had taken the family's rental car and may want to harm herself.

RECENT STUDIES AND RECENT EVENTS

Studies

Mohandi and Meloy (2010) used the Homant and Kennedy SBC typology to analyze fifty-five SBC cases. Fourteen of the cases were Criminal Intervention Minor Crime incidents. An equal number—fourteen—were placed in the Criminal Intervention Major type. Fourteen cases fit into the Criminal Intervention Domestic Violence type with seven in the Disturbed Intervention type. Finally, six were Direct Confrontation incidents.

The demographic characteristics of the fifty-five SBC subjects fit the typical subject profile from other studies. The subject's mean age was thirty-six, with a range of eighteen to sixty-nine. The seventeen-year-old California girl cited earlier is an outlier. Ninety-four percent of the SBC subjects were male, 5 percent were female, and 1 percent was a known transgender person. Thirty-one percent were Hispanic; 31 percent were Caucasian; 18 percent were African American; and the rest were Asian Pacific Islander, Native American, or unknown.

The subjects' status at the time of the incident reveals interesting findings that suggest the need for additional research. However, it should be pointed out that the following subject characteristics are generally not known or knowable to the officer at the time of the incident. Fifty-one percent of the subjects were unemployed, and 25 percent were homeless. Sixty-eight percent—N=57—had recently experienced behavioral changes, and 63 percent—N=53—had recent relationship problems. Fifty-eight percent had known histories of violence, and 49 percent had been to jail or prison before. Thirty percent were having criminal justice problems, and 20 percent were on parole or probation.

Prior to or during the SBC incident 89 percent of the subjects communicated suicidal intent to the officer—"I am going to kill myself," "I wish I

Table 6.1   SBC Risk Factors and Stressors (N=68)

Prior suicidal ideation	45 (62%)
Substance use at the time of the incident	45 (62%)
Previous arrests	45 (62%)
History of depression	45 (62%)
Symptoms of mental illness—stressor	41 (60.3%)
Diagnosed mental illness	29 (42.6%)
Facing jail time	26 (38.2%)
Relationship problems—stressor	24 (35.3%)
History of domestic problems	23 (33.8%)
Criminal activity—stressor	21 (30.9%)
Psychiatric medication currently prescribed	20 (29.4%)
Previous suicide attempt	16 (23.5%)
Previous psychiatric hospitalization	11 (16.2%)

Adapted from Dewey et al. (2013): 453.

were dead," or something similar. This is a common finding in SBC studies (Dewey, Allwood, Faava, Arias, Pinzzotto, & Schlesinger, 2013). Fifty-six percent of the subjects were intoxicated or under the influence of drugs at the time.

Dewey and her colleagues (2013) examined eighty-five closed state and local cases of possible SBC cases that took place between 1979 and 2005, across fifty-five law enforcement jurisdictions in twenty-six states. The average age of the subjects was 35.9, with 62 males and 6 females. The majority of the subjects were Caucasian (64.7%) followed by Hispanics (17.6%) and then African Americans (14.7%). The majority of the sample had prior suicidal ideations, previous arrests, or a history of depression. The sample was classified into risk factors and stressors related to SBC (see Table 6.1)

Events

In July 2017 a Valdosta, Georgia, man who had expressed the wish to be killed by the police called 911 to report a vehicle break-in (Miller & Reeter, July 8, 2016). The responding officer was immediately shot when he arrived at the man's apartment. The wounded officer called for assistance, saying he had been shot. The man was shot multiple times but survived. The officer also survived. The assailant told Georgia Bureau of Investigation agents that he had nothing against the police; however, he wanted them to kill him. In 2017, the man pleaded guilty to attempted murder and possessing a firearm during the commission of a felony.

On June 8, 2018, the Suffolk County, New York, alerted the New Jersey State Police (NJSP) to be on the lookout for a GMC Sierra whose driver had shot and wounded a fifteen-year-old boy in Middle Sound, New York. The New York authorities said the driver was armed with a rifle, was suicidal, and might attempt to commit suicide by cop (New Jersey Department of Law and Public Safety, July 2, 2019). The suspect vehicle was spotted turning into a rural road leading into a National Recreational Area. Four NJSP troopers and a National Park Ranger converged on the road. Three of the troopers parked their cars and began a search of the area on foot. A fourth trooper saw the pickup truck on the road and gave chase. The truck pulled into a cutoff where the other NJSP vehicles were parked just as the three troopers came out of the woods. The troopers ordered the man to drop his weapon and show his hands. He ignored their commands, and they heard the weapon being racked. Then he shot at the troopers. The fourth trooper shot four times into the pickup with his rifle. The autopsy found five gunshot wounds—four from the trooper and a self-inflicted chest shot.

On March 17, 2019, at 6 a.m. University City, Missouri man with numerous health problems was shot by police officers in a SBC incident (Bell, March 19, 2019). At 1 a.m. that morning, paramedics had taken the sixty-one-year-old man to a VA hospital. He was released and returned home. He was acting strangely and threatening suicide, so his wife called the police. Two officers arrived and persuaded the women to leave the house. They stood on the porch and yelled for the man to come out and talk about it. The man came out with a shotgun in his hands. The officers backed up as the man put the shotgun in his mouth. The distraught man took the shotgun out of his mouth and told the police, "You are going to have to kill me." He pointed the shotgun at the officers and was shot three times. He died several days later.

CONCLUSION

SBC is another example of police-perpetrated homicides that must be recognized and addressed by the professional and academic communities. Keeping in mind that what we know about this type of police-caused homicides comes from retrospective analysis, SBC is a major social issue for the law enforcement community.

The link between SBC and mental illness is well known, and every experienced police officer can provide horror stories of dealing with the mentally ill, and that is not going to change in the near future. The National Alliance on Mental Illness (2017) reports that over 2 million jail bookings every year involve mentally ill persons. Fourteen of the thirty-eight people shot by LAPD officers in 2015 had documented signs of mental illness (Mather & Queally, May 1, 2016). These events are real nightmares and police-community relations disasters in most cases, especially when the person killed was mentally ill and or unarmed. The general public does not understand why the police are trained to shoot center mass multiple times when shooting at an armed—real or perceived—person, even if that person may be suspected of being mentally ill (Malmin, 2017). They ask why didn't the officer shoot to wound?

Most police officers or combat veterans who have been in a shooting incident consider this last suggestion ridiculous and coming from those who have never been in similar settings. Furthermore, it is contrary to police training and hard to do when an armed person is rapidly approaching. Also, shooting to wound or disable is still the use of deadly force. The fear and adrenaline experienced by the officer at the time are overwhelming (Miller, 2006). The officer who is forced to kill the person is traumatized by the event.

There is a need for the law enforcement community to review training procedures and protocols in this area. Suggested solutions have included more training, including de-escalation training, the introduction of less than lethal weapons, and the creation of Crisis Intervention Teams. The LAPD requires all officers to carry Tasers and keep beanbag shotguns in the front of the car and not in the trunk (Mather & Quelly, May 1, 2016). Some 3,000 U.S. police agencies provide crisis intervention training (Mincer & Johnson, 2015). However, there are over 18,000 U.S. police agencies and no national law enforcement standards. Moreover, as we see from the types of police homicides discussed, there is no one solution that fits all types.

SOURCES

Bell, K. (March 19, 2019). Man shot by University City police officer was distraught over recent stroke, wanted "suicide by cop." *St. Louis Dispatch.*

Dewey, L., Allwood, M., Fava, J., Arias, E., Pinizzotto, A., & Schlesinger, L. (2013). Suicide by cop: Clinical risks and subtypes. *Archives of Suicide Research.* 17: 448–461.

Epps, K. (July 12, 2019). Man gets 20 years for slashing Fredericksburg officer with a box cutter. *TCA Regional News.*

Geberth, V.J. (1993). Suicide by cop: Inviting death from the hands of a police officer. *Law and Order.* July: 105–108.

Homant, R.J. & Kennedy, D.B. (2000). Suicide by police: A proposed typology of law enforcement assisted suicide. *Policing: An International Journal of Police Strategies & Management.* 21(3): 339–356.

Homant, R.J., Kennedy, D.B., & Hupp, R.T. (2000). The real and perceived danger in police officer assisted suicide. *Journal of Criminal Justice.* 28: 43–52.

Jacobs, H. (October 5, 2009). Suspect shot by officer dead: Coroner calls it suicide by cop. *Live5News.*

Malmin, M.B. (2017). Suicide by cop—A psychology of institutional betrayal. *Psychology.* 8: 903–928.

Mather, R. & Queally, J. (May 1, 2016). More than a third of people shot by L.A. police last year were mentally ill, LAPD report finds. *LA Times.*

Miller, L. (2006). Suicide by cop: Causes, reactions, and practical intervention strategies. *International Journal of Emergency Mental Health.* 8(9): 185–174.

Miller, D. & Keeter, K.P. (July 8, 2016). Police: Valdosta shooter wanted suicide by cop. *WALB News.*

Mincer, J. & Johnson, E.M. (December 20, 2015). U.S. police get little training to handle crises with mentally ill. *Reuters.*

Mohandi, K. & Meloy, J.R. (2010). Hostage and barricade incidents within an officer involved shooting sample: Suicide by cop, intervention efficacy and descriptive characteristics. *Journal of Police Crisis Interventions.* 10: 101–115.

Neitzel, A.R. & Gill, J.R. (November 2011). Death certification of "suicide by cop." *Journal of Forensic Sciences.* 56(6): 78–85.

New Jersey Department of Law & Public Safety. (July 2, 2019). Investigation determined that Todd died of self-inflicted gunshot wound. *Office of Attorney General.*

Patton, C.L. & Fremouw, W.J. (2016). Examining "suicide by cop": A critical review of the literature. *Aggression and Violent Behavior.* 27: 107–120.

Stimson. (July 13, 2019). Teen who died had pointed fake gun at police, officer's bodycam footage suggests. *Fox News.*

Chapter 7

In-Custody Police-Perpetrated Homicides

Jails and Lockups

INTRODUCTION

The Bureau of Justice Statistics (BJS) defines jails as "as a locally operated correctional facility that confines persons before or after adjudications for 72 hours, excluding temporary lockups" (Noonan, December 2014: 21). Jails are controlled environments that should be safe, but are not. Jails should provide medical care for those with health problems, but some do not. About 1,000 jail inmates die every year in the United States (Reilly & Liebelson, December 16, 2016). Some of these deaths are law enforcement officer (LEO)-perpetrated homicides. In-custody deaths, including LEO-caused homicides, are not randomly distributed throughout the United States. Some jails are notorious for the violence that occurs between the staff and the inmates. These jails are overrepresented in the inmate death count. As is common in all types of police-perpetrated homicides, a minority of officers and agencies are the problem. Why? We address this question in this chapter.

JAIL INMATE DEATHS

Although 14,787 jail inmate deaths were reported from 2000 to 2014, the majority of the approximately 2,800 U.S. jails have no in-custody deaths in any given year (Noonan, December 2016 & Reilly & Liebelson, December 15, 2016). In 2014, 80 percent of all jails reported no inmate deaths (Noonan, December 2016). A Texas jail—Brazos County Sheriff's Jail—reported in 2016 that there had not been an inmate death in eight years (Reilly & Liebelson, December 16, 2016). From 2000 to 2014, 82 percent of the U.S. jails reported no deaths. However, 2 percent (327) of the reported deaths were homicides. This last finding is disturbing because the overwhelming majority (70%) of the jail inmates are pretrial inmates not convicted of any crime.

According to one study, those jails reporting at least one death were small jails—399 in 2014—with an average inmate population of 363 inmates (Noonan, December 2016). Jails with an average of 1,683 inmates were most likely to report inmate deaths of two or more—182 in 2014. Suicide accounted for 31 percent of all inmate in-custody deaths between 2000 and 2014 (Noonan, December 2016). In-custody homicides defined as "homicides committed by other inmates, incidental to the staff use of force, and resulting from assaults sustained prior to incarceration" are rare (Noonan, December 2016).

DEATH IN CUSTODY REPORTING ACT (P.L. 106-297)

There are statistics about the number of police assaulted by citizens and every other category of crime. It's insane that no one keeps the number of people killed or injured in police custody or by the police. (Donald Wilkies, Law Professor, University of Georgia quoted in Curriden, May 1996: 63)

Official historical information on in-custody deaths is nonexistent. Before 2000, there was no national standardized accounting of inmate deaths in U.S. jails and prisons (Zeng, Noonan, Carson, Binswanger, Blatchford, Smiley-McDonald, and Ellis, April 2016 & Noonan, December 2016). In 2000, the Death in Custody Reporting Act (P.L. 106-297) was passed. The DOJ's BJS began collecting data from jail and state departments of corrections on inmate in-custody deaths. The respondents are asked to report "causes of death" identifiers, as stated by a medical examiner or pathologist and provide the inmate characteristics such as name, date of birth, date of death, race, and sex. An average of 2,850 jails reported the information per year since 2000. The act also directed the BJS to begin the recording of arrest-related deaths (ARD). These ARD are essential to the study of in-custody deaths because, in some instances, a person injured in the arrest process may die from those injuries while in jail.

ARREST-RELATED DEATHS

Since 2003 the BJS has conducted a census of deaths that occur during the process of arrest or during an attempt to make an arrest—ARD program, see Text Box 7.1.

The ARDs reported include justified and unjustified police homicides, suicides, deaths due to natural causes, deaths resulting from accidents, and undetermined or unknown manners of death. From 2003 to 2009, 61 percent of all ARDs were homicides by LEOs—low of 54.7 percent in 2005 to a high of 68.2 percent in 2009 (Wihbey and Kille, July 2, 2016). A later study found that 268 (63.2%) police homicides and 50 accidental deaths (11.8%) occurred from June–August 2015 (Banks, Planty, Couzens, Lee, Brooks, Scott, and Whyde, July 2019).

TEXT BOX 7.1   ARREST-RELATED DEATHS: ARD

All deaths attributed to any use of force by law enforcement personnel acting in an official capacity. Any death that occurs while the decedent's freedom to leave is restricted by a state or local law enforcement agency prior to, during, or following an arrest which includes:

- while detained for questioning
- during the process of questioning
- while in the custody of, or shortly after restraint by law enforcement (even if the decedent was not formally under arrest).
- during transport to or from law enforcement or medical facility.

Any death that occurs while confined in lockups or booking centers.

Modified from: Banks, Ruddie, Kennedy, and
Planty, December 2016.

Death of Freddie Gray (2015)

The death of twenty-five-year-old Freddie Gray on April 12, 2015, is a text-book example of an ARD and what we have defined as a police-perpetrated homicide. The death was ruled a homicide by a competent medical official and determined to be unjustified by the state's attorney.

Freddie Gray's police-perpetrated homicide was the unintended consequence of change in police strategies dealing with street-level drug sales that occurred three weeks before the fatal encounter. At that time, the Baltimore Police Department (BPD) began a more aggressive, reactive strategies. These aggressive strategies often result in ARDs and police-perpetrated homicides. Proactive, aggressive police strategies against street drug dealing include stop and frisk encounters, foot patrols, zero-tolerance policing, undercover buy and busts operations, and bike patrols. Amadou Diallo's police-caused homicide on February 4, 1999, by NYPD anti-crime plainclothes officers, and

Eric Garner's chokehold death on July 17, 2014, resulted from aggressive zero-tolerance police aggressive crime control strategies. The same aggressive crime control tactics led to Freddie Gray's death.

Policy Change

The Baltimore City State's attorney, who would later charge, indict, and prosecute six BPD officers—3 white and 3 black—ordered a change in police department proactive policing strategies against street drug dealing. Street drug dealing was common in the crime-ridden area, where the police homicide of Freddie Gray took place (Rector, June 9, 2015). The BPD, as a result of the prosecutor's order, used aggressive bike patrols, and increased stop and frisk tactics against street drug dealing. As reported in the social media and court documents, the tragic saga began when Gray spotted the officers on their bikes and ran. After a short foot chase, he was apprehended, and the officers found an illegal knife in his possession. Gray was arrested and placed in a police van for transportation to the police station. The handcuffed—behind his back—Gray was put in the van without a seatbelt restraint, a violation of a BPD policy passed six days earlier. After several stops, the van arrived at the police station. Gray was motionless and in medical distress. He was taken to the hospital and died a week later. He had injuries to his vertebrae, a crushed voice box, and 80 percent of his spine was severed at the neck. The injuries suggested that Gray received a form of police brutality known as a "rough ride" where a police van is driven erratically to injure an unruly suspect.

According to newspaper accounts, the autopsy report stated that Gray suffered a single "high-energy" injury to his neck and spine when the police van suddenly decelerated (Fenton, June 24, 2015). The state medical examiner's office concluded that Gray's death was a homicide because the officers failed to follow safety procedures through acts of omission—not putting on a seatbelt and ignoring evidence of injury. The medical examiner opined that Gray might have gotten to his feet and was thrown into a van wall during an abrupt change in direction (Fenton, June 24, 2015). The police actions of handcuffing Gray behind his back with his ankles shackled, and not restrained by a seatbelt contributed to the homicide.

The six officers involved were all suspended with pay, and the Baltimore State's Attorney charged all six with felonies. The van driver was charged with second-degree depraved-heart murder—indifference to human life (Blinder & Perez-Pena, May 1, 2015). The lieutenant in charge was charged with manslaughter, assault, misconduct in office, and false imprisonment. Two officers, one a sergeant, were charged with manslaughter, assault, and misconduct in office. The remaining two officers were charged with assault, misconduct in office, and false imprisonment.

The officers' trials began in December 2015. The first officer's trial was declared a mistrial when the jury was unable to reach a verdict. The second officer charged with two counts of second-degree assault, misconduct in office, and false imprisonment was found not guilty of all charges after a bench trial in May 2016.

A third officer, the van driver, was acquitted of all charges in June 2016. The charges against the remaining police officers were dropped. In September 2017, the U.S. Department of Justice announced that no federal charges would be prosecuted against the six officers. The city of Baltimore reached a $6.5 million settlement with the Gray family. Gray's death was technically an arrest-related police homicide; he was in-custody but not yet placed in jail. However, his death is an example of how arrest-related injuries often become in-custody death in transportation to the jail. Our focus in this chapter will now move to actual in-custody jail police-perpetrated homicides.

IN-CUSTODY JAIL POLICE-PERPETRATED HOMICIDES

According to the U.S. Department of Justice Statistics (BJS), the eleven major causes of jail deaths are heart disease, AIDS-related complications, cancer, liver disease, respiratory disease, other illness, suicide, homicide, drug and alcohol intoxication, accident and other (Zeng, Noonin, Carson, Binswanger, Blatchford, Smiley-McDonald, and Ellis, April 2016). The Deaths in Custody Reporting Program lists the same eleven categories and reports that 279 of the 15,693 in-custody deaths from 2007 to 2010 were homicides (Zeng et al., April 2016). The Noonan report lists 327 homicides—homicides committed by inmates, staff, and the result of assaults before incarceration—from 2000 to 2014 (Noonan, December 2014—Table 1 page 5).

The information on in-custody homicides should be viewed with caution. Jail and prison authorities provide the data: a source of possible error. The use of force deaths may be attributed to another cause to protect the agency. For example, the inmates may have been tased before their deaths from the listed heart disease, thereby masking a homicide (Reilly and Liberson, December 15, 2016). Nevertheless, however flawed, this may be the most reliable official information available at this time on in-custody police-perpetrated homicides. Because of the U.S. fragmented criminal justice system, jail deaths vary by state and jurisdiction.

Jails with Multiple Deaths

The *Huffington Post* tracked jail deaths from July 13, 2015, to July 13, 2016, and found 800 jail deaths. The report focused on those jails that had three or

Table 7.1   Top-Ten Jails with Over Three In-Custody Deaths (July 13, 2015–July 13, 2016)

Jail	Number of Deaths	Average Daily Population
Richmond City Jail (Richmond, Virginia)	7	1,079
Hampton Roads Regional Jail (Portsmouth, Virginia)	6	1,150
St. Louis County Justice Center	6	1,199
Floyd County Jail (Rome, Georgia)	6	630
Imperial County Jail (El Centro, California)	4	436
Pinal County Jail (Florence, Arizona)	4	600–650
Charles County Detention Center (La Plata, Maryland)	3	300
Delaware County Jail (Delaware, Ohio)	3	240
Roanoke City Jail (Roanoke, Virginia)	3	560
Warren County Regional Jail (Bowling Green, Kentucky)	3	508

Modified from Reilly & Liebelson, December 15, 2016.

more deaths during the period and compared those deaths to the jail's average daily population reported in 2013 or later. They found forty-two jail facilities during that year that fit the criteria of three or more inmate deaths. From that group, they found fifteen jails that had death rates double the average rate of 135 in-custody deaths per 100,000 inmates (see Table 7.1).

Selected States with In-Custody Deaths

Texas—Although no Texas jail is mentioned in the *Huffington Post* study, 1,111 inmates died in Texas county or city jails between 2005 and 2015 (Silver, July 27, 2015). Fifty-four percent died of natural causes, and 27 percent died of suicide, and 9 percent died from alcohol or drug intoxication. There is no statistic given for homicides in the Texas data. However, a 2015 death at the Dallas County Texas jail was ruled a homicide, and a civil suit has been filed (McCarthy, August 31, 2015).

According to newspaper sources and the lawyer's website, it is alleged that the victim was forced to the ground onto his stomach, and a jail video shows two deputies putting their knees on the victim's back and neck (Anon, August 2, 2017). It is alleged that CPR was not administered for seven minutes, even though the victim was clearly in distress. The victim was transferred to the hospital where he was pronounced dead.

Oklahoma—The state has had jail problems for years, several sheriffs have been removed from office for sexual misconduct and sentenced to prison (Barker, 2019). Custer County Oklahoma Sheriff Mike Burgess allegedly ran a sex-slave operation from his jail and was a member of a drug court team. He is serving a seventy-nine-year prison sentence. Sheriff Burgess had been in office for twelve years when he was arrested in 2008 for thirty felony counts that alleged fourteen counts of second-degree rape and seven counts of forcible oral sodomy. He was accused of running a sex-slave operation at the county jail. He was also accused of repeatedly sexually harassing a female deputy during her three-year employment at the Custer County Sheriff's Department. The sexual harassment allegations included unwanted touching, putting his hand inside her uniform pants and touching her bare buttocks, groping her legs, touching her breasts outside her clothing, and continually making sexually suggestive statements.

Latimer County, Oklahoma Sheriff Melvin Holly, was arrested on October 2005 and accused of having sex with four inmates, having sexual contact with four others, and inappropriately touching three employees and the teen-age daughter of an employee. Holly's trial lasted five days, and thirty-two witnesses testified, including the defendant himself. Holly was convicted of fourteen criminal counts, including eight counts of misdemeanor deprivation of civil rights under color of law, five counts of felony deprivation of civil rights involving aggravated sexual abuse, and one count of tampering with a witness, threatening to kill an inmate if she told anyone. His appeal for a new trial was rejected, and the disgraced former lawman was sentenced to twenty-five years in federal prison.

There have been allegations of guard violence against inmates in Oklahoma jails including in-custody LEO-perpetrated homicides. In 2015, a jail supervisor for the Oklahoma County Jail was charged with second-degree murder in the death of an inmate from massive bleeding after being subdued by guards (Clay, January 25, 2015). He was acquitted at trial in 2015 (Schwab, September 4, 2015). In 2017, a former McClain County Jail Administrator pleaded guilty to violating an inmate's civil rights by depriving him of medical care, resulting in his death—law enforcement perpetrated homicide. The victim was an insulin-dependent diabetic deprived of insulin. The former jail administrator was sentenced to fifty-one months in prison and a $10,000 fine (DOJ. August 9, 2017).

California—Three San Jose, California, jails guards were found guilty of second-degree murder of a mentally ill inmate in 2015 (Anon, June 1, 2017). The victim was beaten to death. He had lacerations to his liver and spleen, which was severed in two.

NOTORIOUS AMERICAN JAILS

Hells Island—Rikers Island in New York City

A retired black female Correction's Officer (CO) who spent years working in Rikers Island wrote that a culture of violence against inmates and their colleagues existed among a minority of corrections officers on Hells Island (Miller, 2016). She divided the deviant CO's into a variety of broad categories: (1) loose cannon COs—these officers became extremely violent at work; (2) nasty ass officers who were too lazy to keep the housing areas they worked in clean; (3) abusive drug dealing officers who smuggled in drugs and actively engaged in drug dealing, some even got "stoned" at work; (4) CO sexual predators involved in sexual misconduct with inmates and staff members (see also Tucker June 24, 2018, and Barker, 2019). A 2014 report from the U.S. Attorney's Office for the Southern District of New York found that a "deep-seated culture of violence" was perpetrated by guards and inmates (Clark & Kleinman, August 4, 2014). There is also empirical support for the categories of guard misconduct Miller outlined. There is a link between guard misconduct/crime and LEO homicides.

Guard Misconduct at the Nation's Most Notorious Jail—Rikers Island

Rape at Rosies's—The all-female facility on Rikers Island is Rose M. Singer Center, which is known as "Rosie's." An expose in *New York Magazine* is the latest of a long list of reports on sexual misconduct by Rikers custodial staff (Tucker June 24, 2018). According to the article, a twenty-two-year-old black female arrested on prostitution charges entered into what she perceived to be a consensual sexual relationship with a CO that ended in forcible rape and physical violence. The magazine article concluded that at any given time, about 50 of the 800 women in "Rosie's" are sexually assaulted by the guards (Tucker, June 24, 2018: 6). In 2016 there were 109 CO sexual misconduct allegations. In 2017 there were 198 allegations.

August 2019—Riker Guard Smuggles Drugs—A twenty-four-year-old male CO admitted that he smuggled a package of marijuana into the New York City jail. He coated the package of marijuana with nail polish to mask its odor (AP, August 10, 2019).

February 2016—Female Guard Exchanges Drug for Sex with Inmate—A drug-sniffing drug alerted on a female smuggling drugs into Rikers Island. She was swapping the drugs for sex with an inmate. She was charged with rape in the third degree, sexual misconduct, official misconduct, promoting prison misconduct, and criminal possession of marijuana in the fourth degree. This was the second drug-sniffing dog bust in the same week. The earlier drug bust involved a guard with marijuana in his socks. The female guard claimed that she was in love with the prisoner; however, he and his mother were charged in 2009 with paying a female CO with smuggling tobacco, alcohol, and marijuana into Rikers Island (Rose, February 9, 2016).

May 2016—Corrupt Drug and Weapons Smuggling Crew—A criminal organization composed of COs, a jail cook, and inmates smuggled drug and weapons into Rikers Island. Allegedly, the ringleader, a thirty-one-year-old three-year veteran guard, received $10,000 to smuggle drugs and seventeen blades wrapped in duct tape into the jail from September 12 to November 24, 2015 (Kochman, May 19, 2016). When he was arrested, he had seven shanks hidden in his pants. He delivered the contraband to inmates who sold it to other prisoners.

In-Custody Jail Homicides—Rikers Island

December 2014—In-Custody Jail Homicide—A Rikers Island captain—the shift supervising guard—was convicted and sentenced to five years in federal prison for a 2012 inmate homicide (Valiquette, March 24, 2014; AP, December 17, 2014). The former captain was convicted of violating the civil rights of a burglary suspect who had bipolar disorder. The mentally ill pretrial detainee swallowed a "soap ball," a toxic disinfectant detergent used to clean cells. A CO informed the captain what had happened and said the inmate was suffering and needed medical attention. The captain said, "Don't bother me until there is a body." He ordered other guards not to call for help. The man was left unattended and died the next day. The medical examiner ruled the death a homicide.

December 2016—In-Custody Jail Homicide—A Rikers Island CO was convicted of violating the civil rights of a seriously ill inmate who died. The inmate was repeatedly kicked in the head while other officers pinned the inmate face down on the floor. At the time of the homicide in 2012, the inmate was a pretrial detainee in the infirmary unit suffering from diabetes, heart disease, and end-stage renal disease (Weiser, September 13, 2017, and Weiser, December 15, 2016). The repeated kicks caused the death of the inmate, and the convicted guard repeatedly lied to cover up the homicide. However, another officer who participated in holding down the inmate cooperated and testified against the convicted guard, even though there was a supposed culture of violence and a code of silence among correctional officers and staff. The reality of the Code of Silence among LEOs and criminals is that it always breaks down when a prison sentence is a realistic option (Barker, 2011). That is why agencies should have a zero-tolerance approach to criminal police homicides. It should be agency policy "that the first rat gets the best deal." The former guard was sentenced to thirty years in prison. The sentencing judge remarked, "This was a particularly vicious and callous attack, and that's what makes it such a serious offense" (Weiser, September 13, 2017). New York City settled with the inmate's family for $2.75 million.

Two years earlier, the city paid $2 million to settle a case of an eighteen-year-old inmate who was beaten to death by inmates enlisted by corrections officers to help control the jail unit he was in (Weiser, July 21, 2014).

LARGEST MENTAL HEALTH FACILITY IN THE
UNITED STATES—CHICAGO'S COOK COUNTY JAIL

In Chicago, police officers have three choices when they encounter a mentally ill person. They can take them home, to a shelter, or to the Cook County Jail (CCJ) (Ford, June 8, 2015). The CCJ is the largest single-site jail in the United States. According to a 2008 Department of Justice report, CCJ has a daily population of 9,800 of male and female inmates (DOJ, July 11, 2008). A third of that annual inmate population suffers from some form of mental illness, leading one author to conclude that CCJ is America's Largest Mental Health Hospital (Ford, June 8, 2015). The 2008 DOJ report found that "CCJ fails to address the specific needs of inmates with mental illnesses, including: (1) failure to timely and appropriately evaluate inmates for treatment; (2) inadequate assessment and treatment; (3) inadequate psychotherapeutic medication administration; and (4) inadequate suicide prevention" (DOJ, July 2008: 59). The report also found that the inmates were regularly subjected to excessive and inappropriate use of force by CCJ corrections staff. There appears to be a link between the inmates' mental issues and the officers' use of excessive force.

The report stated that retaliatory force was used against mentally ill inmates with impulse control problems. For example, a mentally ill inmate exposed himself to a female officer. He was taken to a room without surveillance cameras, and a group of officers kicked and beat him while he was restrained. Serious guard misconduct is a persistent problem in the CCJ.

Guard Misconduct in the CCJ

Inmate Beating—On January 17, 2014, a twenty-year veteran sheriff's deputy was captured on a jail surveillance camera repeatedly punching an inmate in the head for no reason. This was a dumb move on the deputy's part because there were 2,500 fixed cameras in the jail, and he wore a body camera. His assault of the inmate was captured on two of the cameras. The officer was formally charged with a felony—official misconduct—and a misdemeanor battery in 2016 after being charged with two additional acts of official misconduct—one was the allegation he spit on an inmate. He resigned at that time. The former officer pleaded guilty in 2019 to a reduced charge of battery and was sentenced to eighteen months probation and agreed to never seek another law enforcement position (Grimm, July 12, 2019).

Guard Sexual Misconduct—A forty-seven-year-old female guard resigned after admitting that she had a sexual relationship with a twenty-seven-year-old male prisoner (Parker, February 12, 2015). She had been a guard at the jail for twelve years. She was charged with custodial sexual misconduct: a charge that carries a five years sentence.

Inmate Beating—In 2013, two six-year veteran guards were charged with felony counts of obstructing justice, mob action, official misconduct, and perjury (Anon, February 22, 2013). The guards were mad at an eighteen-year-old inmate. They opened his cell and directed two larger inmates to enter and "Go in there and f----him up." They did.

CORRECTIONAL OFFICER VIOLENCE AND ABUSE OF POWER

What follows are additional selected, not exhaustive Department of Justice Press Releases on detention/custody officers who have been indicted, convicted, or pleaded guilty for using excessive force and violating the civil rights of inmates in jails or lockups from 2013 to 2019. They are a convenience sample selected from a larger sample of crimes committed by U.S. LEOs 2013. A deputy with the Murray County Sheriff's Office in Sulphur, Oklahoma, pleaded guilty to using unreasonable force and violating the civil rights of an inmate. The deputy assaulted a handcuffed inmate who was not a threat to him at the time. The deputy tackled the inmate and positioned himself over the inmate and banged the inmate's head against the floor. The inmate sustained a mild concussion, pain, and swelling to his head. The inmate was beaten because he verbally offended the deputy (U.S. Department of Justice. FBI Oklahoma City Division. Office of Public Affairs Press Release January 11, 2013).

The jail superintendent and assistant jail superintendent of the Muskogee County Jail in Oklahoma City, Oklahoma, were indicted on multiple counts of civil rights violations between August 2009 and May 2011. The indictment alleges that defendants did unjustifiably strike, assault, harm, and punish inmates who were restrained, compliant, and represented no threat. Jailers would "meet and greet" incoming inmates from neighboring counties by throwing and slamming handcuffed prisoners upon the ground. They threatened to fire any jail employees who encouraged the inmates to file complaints (U.S. Department of Justice. FBI Oklahoma City Division. Office of Public Affairs Press Release February 13, 2013).

Two separate indictments named nine COs at the Roxbury Correctional Institution (RCI) in Hagerstown, Maryland. The indictments alleged that the defendants on two occasions assaulted the same inmate and engaged in a cover-up to conceal the truth. Six of the custodial officers have pleaded guilty (U.S. Department of Justice. Baltimore Division. Office of Public Affairs Press Release February 27, 2013; and May 24, 2013).

CONCLUSION

The violence, including the use/misuse of deadly force against inmates by LEOs acting as detention/custody officers, is a national disgrace calling for more information and empirical study. We can only scratch the surface in this work and suggest that a more thorough research project will uncover additional unreported in-custody law enforcement perpetrated homicides. The lack of research is due to the lack of reliable official information and the "secret" setting of the acts. However, as reported above, in-custody homicides, although rare, have a historical tradition is certain American jails.

SOURCES

Anon. (February 22, 2013). Bond set for cook county jail guards charged in inmate beating. *DNInfo*.

Anon. (June 1, 2017). 3 Calif. Jail guards found guilty in death of mentally ill inmate. *CBS*.

Anon. (August 2, 2017). A lawsuit is filed against the Dallas County Sheriff's Office in the death of Joseph Hutcheson. http://police-misconduct-lawyer-texas.com. A.P. (August 10, 2019) Former Rikers Island guard admits smuggling drugs. *Associated Press*.

A.P. (December 17, 2014). Correction Officer, Terrence Pendergrass, convicted in Riker's Island Inmate 2012 Death. *Associated Press*.

Banks, D., Ruddie, P., Kennedy, E., & Planty, M.G. (December 2016). Arrest-related deaths redesign study, 2-15-16: Preliminary findings. *DOJ. Office of Justice Programs. Bureau of Justice Statistics*.

Banks, D., Planty, M.G., Couzens, L., Lee, P., Brooks, C., Scott, E., & Whyde, A. (July 2019). Arrest-related deaths program pilot study of redesigned survey methodology. *DOJ. Office of Justice Programs. Bureau of Justice Statistics*.

Barker, T. (2011). *Police Ethics: Crisis in Law Enforcement*. Springfield, ILL: Charles C. Thomas.

Barker, T. (2020). *Aggressors in Blue: Exposing Police Sexual Misconduct*. Palgrave McMillian.

Blinder, A. & Perez-Pena, R. (May 1, 2015). 6 Baltimore police officers charged in Freddie gray death. *The New York Times*.

Clark, M. & Kleinman, R. (August 4, 2014). DOJ finds "deep-seated culture of violence" at Rikers Island. *MSNBC*.

Clay, N. (January 25, 2016). Oklahoma County inmate's jail death case will go to trial. *The Oklahoman*.

Curriden, M. (May 1996). When good cops go bad. *ABA Journal*.

DOJ. (July 11, 2008). *Cook County Jail*. U.S. Department of Justice—Civil Rights Division.

DOJ. (August 9, 2017). *Former Jail Administrator Sentenced for Depriving Inmate of Medical Care*. Department of Justice. Office of Public Relations.

Fenton, J. (June 24, 2015). Autopsy of Freddie Gray shows "high-energy" impact. *The Baltimore Sun.*

Ford, M. (June 8, 2015). America's largest mental hospital is a jail. *The Atlantic.*

Grimm, A. (July 12, 2019). Jail guard pleads guilty of beating inmate. *Chicago Sun-Times.*

Kochman, B. (May 19, 2016). Rikers correction officers, jail cook, inmates busted for smuggling contraband into jail. *New York Daily News.*

McCarthy, C. (August 31, 2015). Texas jail death caused in part by sheriff's deputies, authorities say. *The Guardian.*

Miller, R.K. (2016). *Inside the Dark Underbelly of Rikers Island.*

Noonan, M. (December 2016). Mortality in Jails, 2000–2014—Statistical tables. *DOJ. Office of Justice Programs. Bureau of Justice Statistics.*

Parker, A. (February 12, 2015). Cook county jail guard had sexual relationship with prisoner: Sheriff. *Chicago Tribune.*

Reilly, R.J. & Liebelson, D. (December 15, 2016). We wanted to find troubled jails, so we counted the bodies. *HuffPost.*

Rose, S. (February 9, 2016). Rikers island guard charged with raping drug dealer inmate. *Sandrarose.com.*

Schwab, K. (September 4, 2015). Oklahoma County jurors acquite [sic] ex-jailer in inmate's death. *Tulsa World.*

Tucker, J.H. (June 24, 2018). Rape at Rosie's: When the bad guys are the guards. *New York Magazine.*

Valiquette, J. (March 24, 2014). Corrections officer arrested on federal civil rights charges in Rikers inmate "soap ball" death: Prosecutors. *NBC New York.*

Weiser, B. (July 21, 2014). New York city to pay $2.75 million to settle suit in death of Rikers island inmate. *New York Times.*

Weiser, B. (September 13, 2017). Ex-Rikers guard is sentenced to 30 years in the fatal beating of inmate. *The New York Times.*

Weiser, B. (December 15, 2016). Ex-Rikers island Guard is found guilty in inmate's death. *The New York Times.*

Zing, Z., Noonan, M., Carson, A., Binswanger, I., Blatchford, P., Smiley-McDonald, H., & Ellis, C. (April 2016). Assessing inmate cause of death: Deaths in custody reporting program and national death index. *BJS-Technical Report-249568.*

Chapter 8

Killer Cops

Overview

INTRODUCTION

In a free society, few things are as frightening as a badge-packing criminal with the authority and power of the state behind them. This is especially true when the badge packer is bent on murder—a Killer Cop. Killer Cops are stone-cold killers and in a class all by themselves. They don't kill because they "fear for their lives" or because of an accident, confusion, or poor judgment. They murder by intent and premeditation not to accomplish a perceived legal objective that turns deadly. The difference between them and other murderers is that they carry badges and use their official position to facilitate and conceal their heinous acts.

The print and non-print, social media coverage of cops who kill focuses on minority citizens killed as a result of real or perceived racial animus. Cops who kill under questionable circumstances elicit sensationalized media and TV coverage, leading to political outcries, false narratives, TV coverage, demonstrations, and social movements such as Black Lives Matter and Blue Lives Matter. Unfortunately, Killer Cops, a violent subset of the more extensive typology of LEO-perpetrated homicides, is a dark secret discussed primarily by popular fiction and nonfiction writers. Few in law enforcement today or the past openly admit that Killer Cops exist. However, most police veterans, especially in urban areas, know they exist. When one is discovered, the usual management technique is evoked: circle the wagons and insist that they are Rotten Apples in a noble profession. Admittedly, Killer Cops who murder by intent are an aberration in American law enforcement; but they are more common than the law enforcement community, or academic scholars will admit. Killer Cops appear in all law enforcement agencies at all levels of government—local, state, county, federal, and special district.

My first personal contact with Killer Cops occurred in 1964 while stationed at the Naval Air Station in Meridian, Mississippi, as a member of the Shore Patrol. I was a member of the search party for the three slain civil rights workers. I came face to face with Killer Cops who were murderers and Klan members. Since then, my personal on-the-job experiences, interviews with working and former police officers, and research projects have revealed other Killer Cops. My research has documented that Killer Cops are not a recent phenomenon in American policing.

HISTORICAL PHENOMENON

The first National Commission on American Law Enforcement in 1931 was titled *Our Lawless Police* (Hopkins, 1931). The Commission had plenty of historical documentation to support the sensational title. The first-known U.S. Killer Cop to be convicted and executed was NYPD Lt. Charles Becker in 1912 (Root, 1961; Cohen, 2006). Police officers and other law enforcement engaged in systematic murders of Osage Indians in Oklahoma in the 1920s to gain control of their lands and finances (Grann, 2017). Since then, other Killer Cops of both sexes joined this historical tradition. A Phenix City, Alabama chief deputy assassinated an incoming State Attorney General in 1954 (Barnes, 1998). In the 1970s, a Florida Sexual Serial Killer Cop hung and butchered young girls and women (Barker, 2019). Four Texas Killer Cops have been tried and convicted of murder since 1975 (Barker, 2019). A Washington, D.C., female Killer Cop was convicted of conspiracy to murder as part of a drug gang in 1993. Two NYPD detectives were convicted of murder in support of the Mafia in the 1990s (Lehr & O'Neal, 2001). Two FBI agents were convicted of murders for the Boston Whitey Bulger gang (Smith, 2006). In 1995 Antoinette Frank, a black female New Orleans Police Department officer walked into a Vietnamese restaurant with an eighteen-year-old gang-banger and murdered three people—an off-duty New Orleans cop working as security and two employees (Hustmyre, 2004). She sits on death row along with another New Orleans Police Department officer, awaiting execution.

CATEGORIES OF KILLER COPS

The empirical research and personal observations lead to the conclusion that Killer Cops fit into three distinct categories: (1) Sexually Motivated Killer Cops; (2) Domestic Violence Relationship Killer Cops; and (3) Rogue Killer Cops with ties to criminal organizations, and those who commit outlandish murders—Bad to the Bone Killer Cops. We will examine each of these categories.

SOURCES

Barker, T. (2019). *Aggressors in Blue: Exposing Police Sexual Abuse.* Palgrave.

Barnes, M.A. (1998). *The Tragedy and the Triumph of Phenix City, Alabama.* Macon, Georgia: Mercer University Press.

Cohen, S. (2006). *The Execution of Officer Becker: The Murder of a Gambler, the Trial of a Cop, and the Birth of Organized Crime.* New York: Carroll & Graff.

Grann, D. (2017). *Killer of the Flower Moon.* New York: Doubleday.

Hopkins, E.J. (1931). *Our Lawless Police: A Study of the Unlawful Enforcement of the Law.* New York: DA CAPO Press.

Hustmyre, C. (2004). *Killer with a Badge.* New York: Berkley Publishing.

Lehr, D. & O' Neill, G. (2001). *Black Mass: The True Story of the Unholy Alliance between the FBI and the Irish Mob.* New York: Perennial.

Root, J. (1961). *The Life and Bad Times of Charles Becker.* London: Seeker & Warburg.

Smith, G.B. (2006). *Mob Cops: The Shocking Rise and Fall of New York's 'Mafia Cops.'* New York: Berkley Books.

Chapter 9

Sexually Motivated Killer Cops

Police-Perpetrated Sexual Murders

INTRODUCTION

Police-perpetrated sexual murders are criminal homicides and involve nonconsensual sexual activity before, during, or after the commission of a crime. In spite of the sensationalized media attention they receive, they are extremely rare (Barker, 2019). On occasion, police-perpetrated sexual murders are a hybrid offense between sexual assault and murder. In these incidents, the police perpetrator did not intend to kill his victim (Stefanska, Higgs, Carter, & Beech, 2017). However, sexual assaults are violent crimes, and death is always a possibility. The empirical evidence shows that there are two categories in this type of police-caused homicides: LEO serial murderers and LEO rape plus murders. LEO serial sexual murderers intend to kill their victims. LEO serial sexual murderers, as all serial murderers, are driven by personality disorders. Sexual serial murderers are psychopaths or sociopaths, who show no remorse, lack empathy, and see others as objects for their sexual pleasure. Torture is their "turn on." An unknown number of these disturbed individuals are, or have been, LEOs. Their presence in law enforcement agencies is disturbing and appears to be the result of poor vetting processes and failure to recognize and take action when necessary.

POLICE SERIAL SEXUAL MURDERERS

Our discussion begins with the worst-case scenario of a law enforcement serial killer in American history—Gerald Schaefer. However, we recognize that DNA analysis has recently revealed that the notorious Golden State Serial Killer and Rapist of the 1970s and 1980s—fifty rapes and at least

123

twelve murders—was a police officer. Further information from this case may eclipse Gerald Schaefer's reign of terror and murder (McNamara, 2018). There is also an unfolding story of a U.S. Custom and Border Patrol agent supervisor who is charged with the serial killing of four women and attempted murder on a fifth (Feis, September 16, 2018). These two cases remind us that unidentified police serial sexual murderers may be present in other U.S. police agencies.

Gerard J. Schaefer Jr.

At the top of any list of sexually motivated serial killer cops is Gerard John Schaefer Jr. The grim reaper could be seen in his eyes, a former lover remarked (Mason, 2008). A psychiatrist opined, "Schaefer is an anti-social personality, which is manifested by sexual deviation and erotic sadism." He killed his victims in pairs and sometimes threes because "doing doubles is far more difficult than doing singles, but on the other hand it also puts one in a position to have twice as much fun" (Mason, 2008).

Schaefer's reign of terror was an act of whore cleansing. Schaefer claimed that he killed his victims to stop them from being whores or to release them from the life of being a whore, as he defined it. Any girl out on the street, especially hitchhikers, was a whore in his twisted logic. That he became a LEO is regrettable, especially when there were good reasons why he should have never put on the badge.

A routine background check would have discovered the red flags and disqualified his application, but it was never done—*no background check was ever done* (Green, 2018). One red flag raised was hard to miss, but it was. Gerard pretended to be a transvestite to avoid the draft during the Vietnam War. He writes that the Society of Friends came to campus and described ways to avoid the draft, a common practice during this unpopular war (Schaefer, 1989). One of the ways mentioned was to seek a one-year deferment for personality disorders. After being drafted, he reported to the army induction center wearing panties, garter belt, and nylons and asked: "Is it gonna be OK to be in the Army if I'm queer?" As expected, he was granted a one-year deferment.

In August 1970, the confused young man got married and received a B.S. degree in geography from Florida Atlantic University. Within a month after his graduation and marriage, the small town Wilton Manor Police Department hired him without undergoing a background check or psychological tests. He completed basic academy training, fulfilled his six-month probationary period, and hit the streets as a sworn, trained certified police officer. There is speculation that the disappearance of a young blonde female driver during his rookie year was his first victim. FBI profilers Ressler and Scachtman (1992) report that he was disciplined for stopping cars driven by young women and then running their licenses for computer checks to learn more about them—a *common technique used by police sexual predators to identify sexual targets* (Barker, 2020).

After two years on the job, Schaefer applied for a position with the Broward County Sheriff's Office, without notifying his current chief. Schaefer failed Broward County's mandatory psychological exam and was disqualified. This information was not shared with any other law enforcement agency. At the time, Florida did not have a certification and decertification system. Two months later he interviewed with the Martin County Sheriff's Department, using a forged letter of recommendation from the Wilton Manor chief of police. He was fired immediately when the Wilton Manor chief learned he interviewed with the Martin County SO, but the sheriff's office hired him.

Gerald John Schaefer was now what is known as a *Gypsy Cop*, moving from department to department under suspicious circumstances (Barker, 2020). Twenty-eight days into his new position, Schaefer's law enforcement career came to an end on July 21, 1972, when he picked up two teenage girls. Nancy Ellen Trotter, age nineteen and Pamela Sue Wells, age nineteen, had hitchhiked from Michigan to Florida for some fun in the sun. Deputy Schaefer, in uniform and driving a police vehicle, picked them up and lectured them on the dangers of hitchhiking. He gave them a ride to the halfway house where they stayed and arranged to meet the next day for a guided tour of the area.

Instead of a tour Schaefer abducted them, took them to remote woods on deserted Hutchinson Island where he bound and gagged them, put a noose around their necks and tied them to trees while threatening to kill them or sell them into prostitution. For some reason, he left the girls handcuffed, gagged, with nooses around their necks tied to a tree leaving them at risk of hanging if they slipped. He told the horrified girls he would be back shortly. Ressler and Shachtman (1992: 142) opine that he left the scene to answer roll call because he returned to the scene two hours later in uniform, but they were gone. One of the girls managed to escape her noose and run to a nearby road where a passing motorist stopped and picked up the urine-soaked survivor and drove to a police station. When Schaefer returned and found the girls missing, he called Sheriff Crowder and confessed that he had done something foolish. He said he played a joke on two girls who were hitchhiking, and he pretended to kidnap and threaten them to scare them out of this risky behavior. Sheriff Crowder ordered him to the station where he was stripped of his badge, fired, and arrested for false imprisonment and aggravated assault.

Schaefer was in jail from July 1972 until September 1972 and then released on his recognizance. The killing spree began. While out on bond, young girls started disappearing. The later investigation revealed Schaefer abducted and slaughtered Susan Place, age seventeen, and Georgia Jessup, age sixteen, during that period. Place's mother last saw the girls leaving with a man named Gerry Shepherd. Suspicious of Shepherd she wrote down the car's license plate number. Later, their mutilated remains were found on Hutchinson Island. Almost a year later the police finally got around to trace the number, but by that time other young girls were butchered, and Schaefer was charged with other murders. Following the disappearance of Jessup and Place, two young girls Mary Briscolina, age fourteen, and Elsie Farmer, age fourteen, disappeared. They were last seen hitchhiking in the Fort Lauderdale area. A piece of Elsie's jewelry would be found in Schaefer's trophy stash, and he would "sort of confess" to killing these young girls.

Schaeffer returned to court on the first kidnap victims in December 1972 and pleaded guilty to picking up Trotter and Wells and taking them to the remote Hutchinson Island. He was sentenced to six months to a year in jail and three years probation after all the charges, except for one count of assault, were dropped. His former status as a cop was taken into consideration in dropping the charges and his light sentencing.

The day before Schaefer was to report to jail to begin serving his six-month sentence Collette Goodenough, age nineteen, and Barbara Wilcox, age nineteen, disappeared while hitchhiking from Sioux City, Iowa to Florida. Some of their personal items were found in Schaefer's trophy stash, but their remains were not found until four years later, well after Schaefer had been convicted of the murders of Susan Place and Georgia Jessup. In April 1973, the decomposing, butchered remains of Place and Jessup were found in shallow graves on Hutchinson Island. The location of their remains was in the same general area where Trotter and Wells were held. The similarities of the abduction to the earlier false imprisonment and aggravated assault cases and the evidence that victims Place and Jessup had been tied to a tree led to a search warrant for Schafer's apartment and mother's house.

Nothing incriminating was found in Schaefer's apartment, but the search of his mother's house produced a mother's lode of evidence, leading to his prosecution for the murders of Place and Jessup, and implicated him in several unsolved disappearances. The police found detailed writings from the killer's perspective describing the torture, rape, and murder of women referred to as whores and sluts. Also found was his stash of victim's trophies—personal belongings such as jewelry, driver's licenses, passports diaries, and teeth from at least eight young women and girls who had gone missing in recent years. It was learned that Schaefer had given Susan Place's purse to his wife.

After a circus of motions to declare him insane failed, Schaefer's trial for the murders of Susan Place and Georgia Jessup began in a packed courtroom on September 17, 1973. A six-member jury with one alternate decided the case. The death penalty was not an option because the murders occurred during a period when the U.S. Supreme Court declared the death penalty unconstitutional. The amount of evidence against him was shocking, scary, brutal, and immense.

Nancy Trotter and Pamela Wells testified about their encounter with Deputy Schaefer and their narrow escape. Their testimony ended with a video presentation enactment of what they had endured, including them reenacting bound and gagged hanging by nooses from trees. The jury was given a copy of one of Schaefer's writings found during the searches. The manuscript titled "How to Go Un-Apprehended in the Perpetration of an Execution-Style Murder" went into gory detail after gory detail explaining how to choose and murder women, even up to selecting victims in pairs. A weak defense followed, and the jury began its deliberation on September 27, 1973. The jury returned a verdict of guilty after several hours of deliberation. On October 4, 1973, the former deputy sheriff was sentenced to life in prison. Twenty appeals were turned down by a variety of courts.

While in prison Schaefer, who had taken several creative writing courses in college, developed what he called a new writing genre called "killer fiction" described as "where the writer takes violence as an artistic medium and instead of glorifying it, makes the reader see it as the cruel and horrid act as it is in reality. I don't represent violence as good or bad, merely as it is" (Mason, 2008). Among his gory stories was a collection of five brief homicidal scenarios titled "Whores—What to *DO* About them." The sadistic and blood-curdling tales describe five whores who were shot, stabbed, hung, and eviscerated with a razor-sharp skinning knife by a serial killer. Schaefer bragged that he killed at least eighty women. On December 3, 1990, an inmate burst into Schaefer's cell and slit his throat and stabbed him in both eyes, claiming he was a "rat" and troublemaker.

Anthony "Jack" Sully—Former Millbrae, California Police Officer

Anthony Sully is one of several former police officers that "left the job" and engaged in serial murders. He, like the other former officers, is suspected of murders while "on the job" and using their police training and experience to facilitate their heinous sexual murders. The evidence suggests that Sully's bizarre sexual habits and drug taking began during his police years, and increased after he quit the police force. The contacts with prostitutes, pimps, and drug dealers made during his police career facilitated his known murders. For these reasons, he is classified as a police serial killer. According to court documents, he told an accomplice in his murders, the "only difference between killing someone now and killing someone as a policeman" was that the police had permission to do it" (*People v. Sully* (1991)).

For eight years Sully served as a police officer for the city of Millbrae, California. There is no information on his police career; however, he left the police department and established an electrical contracting business, operating out of a warehouse in Burlingame, California. The warehouse was where he worked, lived, and tortured and murdered his victims. The former cop also invested in an escort service and began in engaging in hard-core drug use. During a six-month period in 1983, he tortured and murdered six people. Four of his victims were prostitutes, one was a pimp, and one was a drug dealer (*People v. Sully (1991); Sully v. Ayers, August 6, 2013*).

The first murder he was convicted for was particularly brutal. The victim was a prostitute who worked for the escort service he invested in. Another prostitute brought her to the warehouse, and Sully bound and handcuffed her. He hung her from the ceiling and repeatedly raped her, while pausing to freebase cocaine. When she screamed for help, he put a hangman's noose around her neck and tightened it until she went limp. Sully and the prostitute accomplice put her in a car and were driving to dump the body, when they discovered she was still alive. Sully then hacked at the victim with a hatchet until he was certain she was dead. The other five murders he was charged with are equally macabre (*People v. Sully (1991); Sully v. Ayers, August 6, 2013*). Anthony Sully was convicted of all murders and sentenced to death in the gas chamber. He has exhausted all appeals and is on California's Death Row.

David Middleton the Cable Guy Killer

The following narrative is from three sources (Kaye, 2008, *Middleton v. State of Nevada* 114 Nev. Adv. Op. 120—No. 31499, November 25, 1998, and Barker, 2020).

Former police officer David Middleton was first identified as a sexual predator while a working police officer and then continued his sexual depravations after leaving police work (Barker, 2020). He was convicted of two murders and sentenced to death. Both victims where abducted, held captive in a leased storage unit, sexually assaulted, tortured, killed, and their bodies dumped. However, he is suspected of several other murders.

Victim Number 1—Katherine Powell

Katherine Powell, the first-known Nevada victim, was forty-five years old, a third-grade schoolteacher, divorced, and lived alone in Reno, Nevada. She did not report to her teaching position on Monday, February 6, 1995, and was reported missing by school workers who went to her home and could not get an answer to repeated knocks. The police responded and entered the residence but found nothing suspicious. Five days later on Saturday, February 11, Reno

Police received a report that a homeless "dumpster diver" found a body in a dumpster. The police found a yellow plastic bag covering a sleeping bag that contained a naked, bound female body—Katherine Powell. She had been sexually assaulted, tortured, and brutally murdered.

A neighborhood canvass revealed David Middleton, a black "cable guy" technician, in a TCI Cable red truck, was seen in front of Powell's home on Saturday, February 4, 1995. On Sunday, February 5, a male disguising his voice to appear female called a Reno store and ordered a $1,900 piece of stereo equipment using Powell's credit card. A woman, who turned out to be Middleton's long-time live-in girlfriend, picked up the stereo equipment. She drove a red truck with TCI Cable on the side and Colorado plates to the store.

During the investigation, detectives discovered the yellow plastic bags covering the sleeping bag were sold at two local hardware stores. One store sold a box of the 33-gallon bags on Wednesday, February 8—three days before Powell's body was discovered. The description of the purchaser fit David Middleton.

Middleton was interviewed and admitted he made a service call to the Powell house on January 28, 1995, and did own a red truck. He denied knowing anything about the stereo or Powell's credit card. He said he knew nothing about the yellow garbage bags. One of the detectives noticed what looked like keys for a lock that would fit on a storage unit on his key ring, so he asked Middleton if he had a rented storage unit. Middleton said no and walked out of the interview.

On March 5, 1995, an anonymous caller—never identified—informed the detectives that Middleton and his live-in girlfriend had a storage unit and gave its location. The next day the police executed a search warrant on the storage unit and found a "treasure load" of incriminating evidence, including a box of yellow 33-gallon plastic bags with one missing, and the stereo equipment purchased with Powell's credit card. Powell's house and car keys; and her camera, computer, and other personal items were also found.

The search found a refrigerator lying on its back on the floor. Fibers found in the refrigerator matched those found on Powell's body. The refrigerator was modified and served as the "torture chamber" for Powell. According to court transcripts, Powell was stored in the refrigerator, and Middleton would come by and torture her while engaging in vaginal and anal sex. When finished, he would place her back in the refrigerator and come back again until she died. The investigation revealed Powell lived for two days until the air coming in from two holes drilled in the bottom was exhausted, and she suffocated. A foam ball with teeth marks on it was found in the storage unit. This was stuffed in the victim's mouths to muffle their screams while he engaged in his depraved sex acts. A stun gun and rope similar to that used to tie Powell's body was also found.

As the search continued more ominous pieces of evidence were discovered, including orange-handled tension clips containing hair and fiber, black canvas belts with Velcro, black wire ties, handcuffs, condoms, and partial rolls of duct tape. The detectives discovered a second makeshift "torture and storage" container—a large speaker box with a space behind the speaker about 14-inches deep, 30-inches wide, and 36-inches high. The speaker box could hold a small woman or child, raising the distinct possibility of one or more victims. Hair and fibers found in the speaker box confirmed their suspicion. A nearly empty industrialized jug of Clorox bleach found inside the storage unit and the obvious smell of Clorox used to clean up the unit led to the suspicion that someone with police experience who knew that bleach will obliterate DNA was involved.

The detectives discovered that David Middleton was a convicted sex offender and a former police officer. His records revealed Middleton was a Boston PD police cadet for two years before resigning. He then became a police officer with the Miami, Florida PD for eight years before resigning. His resignation date revealed he was a cop when he was arrested for the original charges of kidnapping and sexual assault. His original charges on November 19, 1989, were kidnapping and sexual assault, and he was convicted of the charges of false imprisonment and aggravated battery in June 1990. He was sentenced to two concurrent five-year prison terms and released in 1993 after serving a little more than two years. The Reno detectives speculated that the bad outcome of the first-known kidnapping and rape led him to kill future victims.

The investigators found other possible sexual murder victims. Ex Miami cop David Middleton was listed as a suspect in the disappearance of a Montrose, Colorado eighteen-year-old girl before moving to Reno. The Reno detectives went to Colorado and discovered incriminating evidence, but there was no body or indication of murder. They returned to Reno with the firm belief that Middleton was indeed a serial killer. The Reno detectives flew to Florida to see what they could learn about his eight-year tenure as a Miami-Dade police officer.

What they found solidified their suspicion that David Middleton was a seriously disturbed sexually motivated serial killer and police sexual predator. The Miami prosecutor said he was "a bad cop who was twisted enough to use his badge and uniform to hunt down women and sexually abuse them" (Kaye, 2008: 159). She said that when he was arrested, he had tapes of him having sadomasochistic sex with women, believed to be prostitutes. The women in the tapes were in handcuffs and obviously in pain. The former prosecutor regretted that a bureaucratic mistake prevented her from introducing the tape as evidence that would surely lead to a rape conviction and a long prison sentence. She also admitted that she wanted to file federal charges, but her supervisor stopped her. Officers who worked with Middleton at Miami-Dade described him as obsessed with sex and bragging about having tapes of him having sex with women. All seven of the cops interviewed stated that Middleton had sexually deviant tendencies long before he moved to Reno.

Victim Number 2—Thelma Davila

Two months after Powell's body was found, the body of a second and prior victim who left the hair and fibers in the speaker box in the storage unit was found. On April 9, 1995, a man walking his dog found a skull and human remains and notified the Washoe County Sheriff's Office. Earlier in 1994, the remnants of a sleeping bag had been found with bone fragments strewn nearby.

A dental bridge in the skull was identified as belonging to Thelma Davila, a forty-two-year-old woman who lived with her sister in a one-bedroom apartment in Sparks. She was reported missing on August 10, 1994. A blanket, a black lacy top and other personal items belonging to Davila were found in Middleton's storage unit. Hairs found on duct tape in the storage unit were consistent with Davila's. Knots found in the ropes on Powell and Davila's bodies and remains were the same.

She and Middleton met at a Latin dance club in downtown Reno and had been seen in each other's company numerous times by friends. Middleton had installed the TV cable in her apartment.

David Middleton went on trial in 1997 and was convicted of two counts of first-degree murder, and two counts of first-degree kidnapping. He was sentenced to death. The ex-cop serial murderer is on Nevada's death row and is a "person of interest" in several unsolved murders of women in Colorado, Florida, and Nevada.

RECENT REVELATIONS OF POLICE SERIAL KILLERS

Joseph DeAngelo—Golden State Killer

> James DeAngelo Jr. believes that without law and order there can be no government and without a democratic government there can be no freedom. Law is his career, he says, and his job is serving the community. (*Exeter Sun,* April 22, 1973)

The newspaper article went on to say that DeAngelo, an Exeter police officer (1973–1976) was a Navy veteran who had served in Vietnam. The young officer had an associate of arts degree in police science and a bachelor's degree in criminal justice, specializing in criminal law. The poster child for a professional police officer—veteran and college degree—is also the most prolific police serial killer in U.S. history. In 2018, DeAngelo—now known as the Golden State Killer—was arrested, based on DNA evidence, for at least thirteen murders and more than fifty rapes in the 1970s and 1980s (Nolasco, May 17, 2018). Many of those rapes and murders occurred while he was a working police officer at Exeter or Auburn, California, where he went to work in 1976. He was fired in 1979 for shoplifting.

It is alleged that the masked DeAngelo armed with a gun would break into homes with single women or sleeping couples from 1974 to 1986. His typical MO was to tie the man up, rape the woman, and sometimes kill both. His crimes remained unsolved for decades until he became a suspect—it is not known at this time how he became a suspect. He was put under surveillance. The surveillance team recovered a discarded coke can and ran his DNA against DNA in a genealogical website. There was a match, and he was arrested. He has not gone to trial at this time. When he does go to trial we will learn more about his violent behavior.

Supervisory Border Patrol Agent—Juan David Ortiz

CBP Agent Juan Ortiz is a ten-year veteran Border Patrol agent with a bachelor's and a master's degree. He is also the latest known police serial killer. He has confessed to the murder of four prostitutes and the kidnapping and attempted murder of a fifth victim (Kalmbacher, September 15, 2018). He was part of the U.S. Border Patrol Highway Interdiction team on the U.S. Texas-Mexico Southern border. His fifth kidnap victim escaped before she was killed and reported her abduction to the Sheriff's department (Horton, September 17, 2018).

RAPE PLUS MURDER: KILLER COPS

The sex-related murders described in this category occur when the victim is killed to eliminate a witness, reduce the chances of the sexual aggressor being identified, or the victim resists the sexual aggression. They are situational or instrumental murders (James & Prouix, 2016; Stefanska, Higgs, Carter, & Beech, 2017; Barker, 2019). The murderers are best described as a "rape plus murder" killer who kills to avoid detection (Healey, Beauregard, Beech, & Vettor, 2014). The murder was not a source of sexual stimulation. Killing is an integral source of sexual stimulation for serial sexual killers. However, sexual abuse by an armed aggressor always involves the possibility of murder as an outcome (Higgs, Carter, Stefanska, & Glorney, 2015).

The "killer cops" status as a LEO with ties to respectability exacerbates the likelihood of murder. We expect a particular way of behavior—a way of life—from those who carry a badge. They have a lot to lose by exposure as a sexual predator—a stake in conformity. Furthermore, the person who becomes a LEO is forever defined as a former or ex-LEO. Their behavior will always be judged by the expected behavior for LEOs. Rightly or wrongly, LEOs on- or off-duty, retired or former will still be accepted, rejected, or judged by the pattern of behavior deemed appropriate for the policework occupation. Because of this master status, a rape-murder that follows a sexual assault by police officers or former police officers receives extensive media attention whenever or wherever they occur. Selected examples of this category of law enforcement–caused homicides are presented in the following paragraphs.

California Highway Patrolman: George M. Gwaltney, 1982

The first California Highway Patrol officer charged with an on-duty murder was George M. Gwaltney. He is also the first California police officer to be tried federally for the violation of a person's civil rights under the color of law. Gwaltney, a ten-year highly respected California Highway Patrolman, was at one time the agency's Officer of the Year. Well known in the community for his good deeds and helpfulness, the jovial "officer friendly" had a secret. On-duty, alone, and unsupervised, he was a sexual predator stopping women and young girls to bargain leniency for sex. Give it up or get a ticket or go to jail—Sexual Shakedown. His first-known murder victim was hunted and stopped on a deserted road.

On January 11, 1982, an attractive twenty-three-year-old aspiring actress, Robin Bishop, was driving alone from Los Angeles to her home in Las Vegas (*U.S. v George M. Gwaltney, 1986,* The FBI Files, 2008). It was slightly past 8.30 p.m. on a pitch-dark evening. Unknown to Bishop, Gwaltney spotted her coming out of a fast-food establishment and noticed her Nevada license plate. He guessed the route she would take and began hunting for her. In the high-desert area Northeast of Barstow, California, he saw her car and made his move.

Gwaltney stopped Bishop in a desolate area on Interstate 15 some 30 miles Northeast of Barstow. He encountered an agitated young woman with a problem. Robin Bishop had a terrible driving record. One more speeding ticket would cause her to lose her driver's license. According to the theory of her murder, Robin argued with him to no avail. "The speed limit is what it is for a reason," he sternly countered. Gwaltney took the young victim out of her car, handcuffed her, and put her in the back seat of his police vehicle. He drove to an isolated frontage road just off the interstate and parked, and started taking off his uniform. The investigation revealed that Gwaltney used this same frontage road for other sexual liaisons with other victims.

Secluded from the interstate by brush and darkness, the officer took the handcuffs off the twenty-three-year-old and sexually assaulted her. Again, the theory of the case describes what happened next (*U.S. v. George M. Gwaltney*, 1986). The sexual violation over the distraught victim sat on the ground putting her boots on. At that very moment, a San Bernardino County deputy sheriff drove by on the interstate and flashed his spotlight on the California Highway Patrol car. It was a signal of recognition from a fellow LEO. The theory of the murder is that Miss Bishop probably sensed help would come and said something to the effect of "see they saw you, and now you are going to pay for what you've done to me."

The rattled rapist, fearing job loss and possibly prison, walked up behind the distraught victim and shot her in the back of the head with his .357 caliber service revolver. Gwaltney, voice quivering and short of breath, called in and reported a body, possibly a suicide at the location.

Speculation is that he had intended to let the young girl go, but the passing deputy sheriff caused him to "lose his cool" and murder Robin Bishop—*sexual assault plus murder*. Finding himself in a desperate situation, the veteran officer continued his attempt to conceal the crime. Moving the body and turning it over to locate the bullet, he disturbed the crime scene. The veteran LEO knew a ballistic examination would reveal the bullet was fired from his service revolver. He could not find the bullet. The bullet did not exit Robin's head; instead, it lodged in her jaw.

The detectives called to the scene discovered troubling details. Miss Bishop's car was found about 200 feet from the location of her body. The car was in gear with the keys in the ignition and no evidence of any malfunctions that would cause her to stop where she did. There were visible handcuff marks on her wrist. The autopsy revealed the recovered bullet came from a .357 caliber weapon, the required weapon for the California Highway Patrol. These facts suggested that a police officer or someone pretending to be a police officer was the murderer. Robin Bishop trusted whoever got her to stop. Still, the focus was not on Gwaltney; after all, he found the body, and no one believed he would murder someone. His peer group knew he would hit on a pretty girl like Robin but kill her absolutely not. Not George M. Gwaltney whose brother was also a California Highway Patrol (CHP) officer.

The next move was clear to the investigators. To eliminate officers working the night of the murder, the officers were ordered to turn in their service weapons for ballistic examination. They all did except one—Gwaltney. Investigators and a California Highway Patrol captain went to his house to retrieve his service revolver. He didn't have it; he told them. Incredibly, he explained, it had been stolen in an unreported burglary sometime after his shift ended.

Gwaltney was now a suspect. With his consent, a search was conducted of his home and surrounding area. The stripped-down frame of his service weapon was found in his truck with the barrel missing. Gwaltney made no attempt to explain the missing barrel or how the stolen stripped-down weapon was in his truck. Later, he would claim that someone was trying to frame him.

Investigators canvassed gun shops in the area asking if Gwaltney had attempted to buy a new barrel for the weapon. Why else would he keep the frame? None of the gun shops reported an order for a new barrel. Then three women came forward saying that Gwaltney had stopped them and made sexual advances toward them. Gwaltney was fired, and based on the overwhelming circumstantial evidence arrested for Robin Bishop's murder.

George M. Gwaltney was tried twice by the State of California, and both trials ended in hung juries: 8–4 for acquittal the first time, and 7–5 for acquittal the second time (*U.S. v George M. Gwaltney, 1986,* The FBI Files, 2008). A third trial by the state was ruled out, and the charges were dismissed. He was home free; at least that is what he thought. In the early 1980s, there were not many police-involved shootings drawing the media's attention. No 24/7 TV news shows were repeating the same stories as they filled in the time. However, one agency noticed the murder and the two state hung juries. The Los Angeles FBI office monitored the case from the beginning, primarily because it was an alleged murder committed by an on-duty police officer, a clear civil rights violation if true. Federal authorities decided to try the "clearly" guilty police officer for a civil rights violation on the theory that he had murdered Robin Bishop on-duty and in uniform, thereby depriving her of her civil rights under cover of law. Under the federal microscope, the series of lies told in his first trials started falling apart.

His alibi for the time of the murder was shown to be off by at least 30 minutes, giving him ample time to commit the crime and establish an alibi. Semen found on the victim came from a person who had a reversed vasectomy. Gwaltney had a vasectomy and then had it reversed. A forensic serologist testified that rare anti-sperm antibodies found in the sperm of men who have vasectomies reversed were found on Bishop's clothing and on the back seat of Gwaltney's patrol car. The FBI lab made a match on one of the tools in his garage and the marks on the gun frame, showing the tool had been used to remove the barrel.

FBI agents re-interviewed the gun shop owners. The agents reminded the gun shop owners that it was a felony to lie to a federal agent conducting an investigation. One admitted he lied at both state trials. Gwaltney had asked him to order a new gun barrel for his service weapon. The FBI agents pulled all of Gwaltney's citations for the last year of his employment and interviewed all the females who received tickets. No rape victims were found, but dozens of women revealed that he had solicited sex from them in return for no ticket, thus demonstrating a pattern of sexual coercion. The trial in Federal District Court in Los Angeles lasted six-weeks, and the jury was out for one and a half days. George M. Gwaltney was found guilty of the murder of Robin Bishop, thereby depriving her of her civil rights under cover of law. He was sentenced to ninety years in prison and died twelve years later of a heart attack. At his sentencing, the unruffled Gwaltney said, "I have been thinking of what I should say for the last 40-some odd days. I will stand by my plea of innocence. I killed nobody" (Anon, June 28, 1994). Four years later another California Highway Patrolman would murder another young woman during a sexual encounter.

California Highway Patrolman: Craig Peyer, 1986

The arrest of a veteran CHP officer for murder created a shockwave in the San Diego area. The neighbors and friends of Craig Peyer, the thirteen-year veteran of the CHP and Vietnam veteran, were stunned by his arrest for the murder of Cara Knott, a twenty-year-old college student.

However, the investigation, testimony, and court documents painted a different picture of Peyer (Leaf, December 27, 2014).

The young woman was driving home from her fiancé's house in Escondido to her parent's home in El Cajon on a foggy night, December 27, 1986. The attractive University of San Diego honors student never completed the 33–35 mile trip down Interstate 15, because Craig Peyer, the husband, father, son, and neighbor revered by his friends was also a callous sexual predator with a badge who often trolled for female drivers on the lonely road Cara traveled. According to court testimony, he often stopped his prey and ordered them to pull off the road in deserted dark spaces. He would then detain them for long periods engaging in personal "flirting" conversations.

According to the theory of the case, the feisty young victim was not intimidated by the bullying police office and wanted to continue home. She rebuffed his advances, fought back, and threatened to report him. Her righteous outburst and rage were met by overwhelming force as the lecherous murderer with a badge smashed a flashlight against her skull and strangled her to death—*sexual assault plus murder.*

Facing the problem all murderers encounter—what to do with the body—the CHP's officer put the lifeless body on the hood of his car like a slaughtered deer and drove to a safe place to stash the corpse and evidence. He did not want any trace evidence to be found in his patrol car. However, he was too late; trace evidence was on him and his victim. Prosecutors alleged that Peyer calmly drove to a familiar remote area and threw the body over an abandoned bridge near the isolated Mercy Road off-ramp into the bushes of a dry creek bed 65 feet below. Frantically driving to a nearby service station, he cleaned up and resumed his routine police duties, even writing a traffic ticket to a young man hoping to establish an alibi. The time he wrote on the ticket put Peyer miles away when Cara Knott was murdered.

Cara's sister and brother-in-law found Cara Knott's car at dawn the next day. The passenger door was locked, and the driver's window was half down, the keys still in the ignition. They drove to a payphone and called the San Diego police who found Cara's body in their search of the area.

The discovery set off a wave of terror among women living in the region. In an attempt to ally women's fears, CHP's Officer Craig Peyer appeared on local television giving safety tips to women who traveled alone. He told the women watching, "You never know whom you may meet along the road" and added emphatically, "You could even get killed." The callous murderer appeared on TV complete with fresh scratch marks on his face. His TV appearance prompted several women to call in with unexpected comments. The concerned women reported that the same security-conscious CHP officer on TV had stopped them and kept them for long periods engaging in bizarre behavior such as gently stroking their hair and shoulders, making them feel uncomfortable. As is common in police agencies, his fellow officers were aware of his bizarre antics.

Peyer's known reputation for stopping young female drivers raised the hackles of suspicion among his peers. At roll call several mornings after the murder, one of his fellow officers "jokingly" asked if he had killed Cara Knott, all eyes turned to Peyer, and the room went silent. He did not say a word. Prior complaints against Peyer were dismissed. He was considered a good officer. Known as "hot pencil" he averaged 250 tickets a month. His silly sex peccadillos were overlooked.

Peyer's feeble attempt at an alibi blew up. Investigators checking tickets written on that road the night of the murder discovered a ticket Peyer wrote that had 9.20 p.m. on top of a scratched-out 10.30 p.m. The seventeen-year-old young man said Peyer stopped him at 10 p.m. and wrote 10.30 p.m. on the ticket before changing the time to 9.20 p.m. Investigators sensed a deliberate attempt to create an alibi—the Knott's girl was killed between 9 p.m. and 10 p.m. The 9 to 10 p.m. period for her time of death was established through the habits of a usually cautious young girl who kept her family informed of her whereabouts. Cara Knott had called her family to let them know she was heading home and she stopped at a gas station at 8.27 p.m. to purchase gas and was never seen again.

Two witnesses reported they saw Knott's empty white Volkswagen in the Mercy Road area at 9.45 p.m., three-tenths of a mile from where her body was found. It was painfully obvious who was the "likely" for the murder of Cara Knott—a cop (Barker, 2020). Evidence gathering began. Investigators took Peyer's uniform to the police laboratory and searched his home and locker.

Circumstantial evidence mounted. Tire marks found at the scene came from a law enforcement vehicle. The television footage showing the scratch marks on his face required an explanation. Peyer said the scratch marks resulted from slipping on a gas spill and falling against a CHP parking lot chain-link fence. However, a service station attendant reported that Peyer stopped the night of the murder to get gas, and he "seemed nervous, disheveled, and he had scratches on his face." She said he had come to the station between 9.30 and 9.45 p.m. The scratches were bright and red as if recent. This was hours before he claimed to fall into the fence. CHP officer Craig Peyer was arrested for the murder of Cara Knott and placed in the San Diego County Jail on January 17, 1987.

Following his arrest, bond was set at $1 million. Close friends and family mortgaged their homes and other valuable property to raise the minimum $100,000 cash bond. Although stripped of his LEO powers, he collected his $33,000 a year salary and continued to pay his bills. That ended when he was fired in June 1987. A trial date was set for September 1987. Friends rallied to help him in his time of need.

Even before the murder tail began, Knott's father filed suit against the CHP saying that the law enforcement agency knew that Craig Peyer had the habit of stopping women motorists and had a known drinking problem. In support of the allegations, the complaint cited evidence presented at the April preliminary hearing where several women testified that Peyer had pulled them over and detained them for excessive lengths engaging in uncomfortable conversations and inappropriate touching. His drinking problems supposedly led to outbursts of ungovernable temper (Frammolino, August 14, 1987). This civil suit would not be resolved until after Peyer's trial on criminal charges, resulting in a settlement for a $2.7 million.

Expert witness testimony at the April 1987 preliminary hearing revealed fibers recovered from one of Knott's hands matched fibers from Craig Peyer's CHP jacket. Fibers from Knott's sweat suit were found on his gun belt. Spots of blood matching Peyer's blood type were found on the young victim's sweatshirt. A slam-dunk case for sure.

The trial began on January 18, 1988, with a jury of nine men and three women before a packed courtroom of Peyer supporters. The prosecution called to the stand nearly two-dozen women who testified that Peyer had pulled them over for a variety of minor "chicken crap" violations, including faulty lights. All the stops occurred on or near the isolated Mercy Road off-ramp in 1986 where the body was found. The trace evidence—fibers, blood spots, etc.—was introduced. The abundance of circumstantial evidence was immense. Witnesses who had seen the scratch marks the night of the murder took the stand. Then, reasonable doubt raised its ugly head. The first signal that the case was not a slam dunk came when a San Diego police criminalist testifying for the prosecution said he did not find any traces of blood or skin under Knott's fingernails, calling into question the origin of the scratches on Peyer's face. Further clouding the source of the scratches was testimony from an off-duty San Diego police officer who said he was in the service station when Peyer pulled up and did not see any scratch marks on the CHP officer's face.

On February 17, 1988, the trial ended with closing arguments. Van Orshoven, the prosecutor, often with his voice quivering, described Cara Knott's stop by CHP officer Craig Peyer. The impassioned prosecutor emphasized that the extremely cautious young woman trained in self-defense would not stop for just anyone, but she would stop for a policeman in uniform driving a marked police car. That policeman, he said, was Craig Peyer, a rogue cop with a history of stopping young women on deserted roads. Peyer detained the young woman, the prosecutor continued, until she became anxious and exploded, scratching the face of her assailant in an attempt to getaway. Threatening to report and expose her abductor, the young girl struggled until the assailant in blue, fearing exposure and job loss silenced her. The prosecutor, pointing at Peyer, roared: "He silenced Cara Knott by bashing her skull with his flashlight and then strangling her."

Defense attorney, Robert Grimes, countered by calmly informing the jury there was room for doubt in the state's case. He reminded the jury that reasonable doubt dictated that his client should be acquitted. The defense attorney did not challenge the blood and fiber evidence. He dismissed the supposed evidence as all-circumstantial, again reminding the jurors of reasonable doubt. Jurors began their deliberations.

The prosecution team expected a quick conviction, but it was not forthcoming. The jury became hopelessly deadlocked. Five jurors were unshaken in the belief that the prosecution did not show a clear motive or sufficient evidence that Craig Peyer killed Cara Knott. One juror went so far as to say that even though the CHP officer had a propensity to stop good-looking girls that did not prove anything. He discounted the twenty-something women who testified Peyer stopped them. Fear of exposure was discounted as a motive because some jurors believed a veteran police officer could certainly handle that. He would have just put handcuffs on someone who had an outburst like the prosecutor suggested several jurors put forth. One juror did not give much weight to the blood and fiber evidence because it was not conclusive. After seven days of deliberation, the trial ended with a 7–5 deadlock for conviction. A mistrial was declared. Round two began when the state decided on a retrial.

Former CHP officer Craig Peyer was free on bail for almost a year when his second trial began before a six man, six women jury in May 1988. More than 277 prospective jurors were quizzed over three weeks before arriving at the twelve-member jury. Excessive publicity and strong opinions of guilt and innocence complicated the selection. Deputy district attorney, Paul Plingst, the prosecutor for the state, replaced Deputy DA Joseph Van Orshoven. Defense attorney Grimes was satisfied that the jury looked like "a group of reasonable people" and he was comfortable with their selection. Grimes did suffer a setback when the trial judge limited the defense's fiber expert in the second trial. His testimony had contradicted the prosecution's fiber expert, but his credentials and techniques were criticized.

The second trial had a new and damaging witness. A woman came forward after the first trial ended in a deadlock and said she and her fiancé had seen a CHP car pull over a light-colored Volkswagen occupied by a lone female between 8 and 9 p.m. on I-15 the night Cara Knott has disappeared. The defense could not shake the witnesses' resolve. She saw what she saw. The service station attendant who had seen Peyer with fresh "claw marks oozing blood" on his face when he pulled in to clean up added that Peyer retrieved a flashlight and nightstick from the trunk of his cruiser and cleaned them off with a red grease rag. A supervisor had written an injury report on Peyer's alleged fall against the chain-link fence and said it was inconsistent with a person falling against it. This was not allowed into evidence because the judge ruled it to be hearsay evidence. The judge ruled that if the chain-link fence testimony were to come in Peyer would have to take the stand and give testimony. The defense called twenty-seven witnesses to the stand, including Peyer's wife to rebut the prosecution's witnesses. Craig Peyer did not take the stand. No chain-link fence testimony. No deadlocked jury.

After sixteen hours of deliberation, Craig Peyer was convicted of the on-duty murder of Cara Knott, with the presiding judge stating he was "absolutely convinced to a moral certainty" that "Mr. Peyer killed Cara Knott" (Reza, August 4, 1989). He was sentenced to twenty-five years to life for the murder. At Peyer's sentencing hearing, the judge heaped scorn on the CHP officials who had not acted on prior complaints about Peyer's conduct in stopping female drivers. Newspaper accounts quote the judge as rebuking the CHP agency for allowing the rogue officer "to continue taking young women to the off-ramp, even after receiving complaints" about his bizarre behavior. He emphasized his point by saying if they had acted on the complaints instead of dismissing them "Cara Knott would be alive, and Craig Peyer would not be on his way to state prison" (Reza, August 4, 1989).

The graying grandfather, Inmate number D93018, sits in his prison cell at California Men's Colony in San Luis Obispo, proclaiming his innocence. Peyer lives in the medium-security prison among the general population still maintaining there was nothing wrong with his forced personal chats with young women. He has been denied parole three times, each time telling the parole board, "I have no idea how it happened." He will have another parole hearing in 2027 if he lives that long. He did tell one parole board that he had read the self-help book *Men are from Mars, Women are from Venus*, twice. In 2007, Peyer was given a chance to prove his innocence when the district attorney's office requested a DNA sample (DNA testing was not available at the time of his trial) for the Innocence Project (Barker, 2019). At the time, the DA's office was reexamining old cases to ensure that justice had been served. Peyer declined to provide a sample without explanation.

Florida Highway Patrol Trooper Timothy Scott Harris: 1990

Florida State Highway Patrol Trooper Timothy Scott Harris is the first Florida State Trooper to be arrested for a murder committed while on duty. The eight-year veteran worked for two small Florida police agencies, Sebastian and Melbourne Village, before becoming a trooper. The television crew of *ABC 20/20* discovered what the Florida Highway Patrol (FHP) should have in their background investigation—if one was done—*improper vetting*. While employed with the Melbourne Village PD (MVPD), the future trooper had been suspended once. When he resigned in 1982, Harris had three serious allegations of misconduct pending against him. Timothy Scott Harris was a "Gypsy Cop" allowed to resign in lieu of charges being filed and then moved on to another law enforcement agency. The Melbourne Village director of public safety described his former employee to *20/20* as "totally incompetent" and "not fit to be a policeman." The MVPD wanted to get rid of their problem employee and send him on his way, so he left, as too often happens with a glowing recommendation stating "He is trustworthy, intelligent, and has a high sense of responsibility toward his profession as a police officer." He would be some other agency's problem.

The FHP would not learn until it was too late that Harris had come to them with a well-developed habit of stopping women, taking down their personal information and then pursuing them. He also perfected the technique of sitting along the highways with his car pointed in the direction of oncoming traffic to pick out attractive women to stop. Harris had other disgusting habits, described by his lawyer as referring to women as "sluts" and yelling sexual comments as he drove by them. He flicked his tongue at women, often with other police officers in the car with him. He wrote lewd comments on traffic tickets and hung obscene cartoons in his patrol car. In keeping with the sexual machismo attitude of his colleagues in blue, no one turned him in. A captain with Vero Beach Police Department became disturbed by Trooper Harris's off-duty behavior, such as appearing in public unkempt, and living in parking lots and rest stops, following the breakup of his marriage, and wrote a letter to the FHP. Nothing happened. The inevitable and predictable sad culmination of Harris's bizarre behavior came on March 4, 1990.

A woman traveling south on Interstate 95 in Indian River County at approximately 10.00 a.m. looked up to see an FHP vehicle behind her with his blue lights flashing (Sellers, April 16, 1990). She wondered why she was being stopped—she was not speeding—as she pulled onto the shoulder of the road. The woman sat still as Trooper Tim Harris, age thirty-two, approached her driver's window. The trooper peered in the window and asked to see her license. The woman later recounted that the officer had stared at her very pregnant stomach. The trooper wrote the woman a warning ticket for going 6 miles over the speed limit and sent her on her way. The unborn child in her womb had, in all probability, saved her life. The next woman Harris stopped that day would not be so lucky.

According to court documents, an hour later Lorraine Hendricks, an extremely attractive former model, age forty-three, a devout Catholic and mother of a six-year-old daughter was driving the same Interstate 95 in Indian River County. In a note of irony, Lorraine Hendricks had once appeared as a model in the FHP's Arrive Alive publicity campaign. The hapless victim would soon be raped, tortured, and strangled by a FHP trooper. She would not arrive alive. Speculation is that she saw the FHP vehicle with his lights flashing in her rearview mirror and pulled to the side of the road. The burly 6-foot 3-inch 200-pound dark-haired trooper came to her window.

Lorraine Hendricks disappeared and was never seen again until her badly decomposed nude remains were discovered five days later covered with pine needles in a thick stand of trees and palmettos. Her silver Honda Accord had been found earlier less than a mile away from where the body was found. The car, when found, had no indications of car trouble or a struggle. Her possessions, minus her driver's license, and car registration were in the abandoned car. Investigators immediately sensed she had stopped for someone she trusted like a police officer or someone pretending to be a police officer.

Trooper Harris was brought in for questioning and admitted running radar in the area where the abandoned car was found. After sustained questioning, he admitted he stopped Lorraine Hendricks and took her to a secluded stand of pines where they had consensual sex. The questioning continued, and finally, a calm but teary-eyed Timothy Harris admitted he had raped, tortured, and slowly strangled the resisting woman as she pleaded for her life. He blamed the murder on his mental breakdown from being estranged from his wife. Harris pleaded no contest to the charge of first-degree murder in exchange for a life sentence carrying a mandatory term of twenty-five years. Technically, he will be eligible for parole after serving twenty-five years, but there is little chance of parole.

Josh Griffin-Monroe, North Carolina PD (MPD): Sexual Killer Cop, 1997

In 1997, the Monroe, North Carolina Police Department had a reputation for its officers stopping females for sexual reasons—trolling for sex. One of these officers was Joshua Patrick Griffin, a twenty-four-year-old cop known for being a "skirt chaser" (AP. July 21, 2005).

On March 29, 1997, about 2 a.m., Griffin was off-duty but in uniform and driving his marked cruiser with lights and siren. The sex predator in blue was trolling for a victim. He saw her coming down the dark highway (AP. July 21, 2005). Twenty-six-year-old Kim Medlin, a cocktail waitress at a Charlotte strip club was off work and heading home. There is evidence Griffin knew her and had remarked that she "looked good" on a previous encounter. Whether or not he was waiting for her is not known, but she was driving a very recognizable red Jeep, so it is likely he knew who was in that car and whom he was going to stop at this early morning hour. He was not out running traffic; he was a man with a purpose.

Officer Josh Griffin "lit her up," and she stopped. The horrible nightmare with a tragic ending began. In his confession, four years after his conviction for murdering Medlin, he gave the details of the encounter. He pulled Medlin over, had her produce her driver's license, and made her get in his patrol car, routine police work. This fits the crime scene found later. Medlin's car was found at 4 a.m. on the side of the road with the engine running and the lights burning. Her purse and cash were on the seat, but Medlin and her driver's license were missing. To a police investigator that screams out—it was a cop who stopped her, someone pretending to be a cop or someone she knew. Griffin confessed he took her to a deserted cul-de-sac and demanded sex. She refused and ridiculed him, infuriating the horny sex predator. He hit the screaming woman, knocking her down, and then he choked her into semi-consciousness. In a rage, he began stomping the woman who just insulted him. His footprint was left on the sweater she wore, a piece of evidence that would help convict him. He left the discarded battered body lying on the ground like some discarded trash and drove off. Kim Medlin's body was found the next day with a broken neck and a broken back. Following a contentious trial, Joshua Patrick Griffin was found guilty and sentenced to life in prison. The Killer Cop is alive and still in prison.

Amarillo, Texas Rookie Police Officer, Jim Vanderbilt Dies on Death Row

Former Amarillo, Texas police officer Jim Vanderbilt died of pneumonia on October 17, 2002, in a prison hospital waiting for execution for the kidnapping and sexual murder of the daughter of a Texas State Representative (AP. October 28, 2002). The vicious Killer Cop waited in prison for his state-ordered death twenty-five years, ten months, and sixteen days, nine years longer than his sixteen-year-old victim enjoyed her brief life. The Killer Cop at his trial was described as being very impulsive likely to act "without thinking or without being aware of the consequences of his behavior." The examining state forensic psychiatrist concluded that Vanderbilt had "no conscience" or "feelings of wrongness" for what he did. This description fits the actions of most of the Killer Cops examined.

The public record of Jim Vanderbilt's sordid life begins on October 1, 1974, when he was hired by the Amarillo, Texas Police Department. There is little information about his behavior during his brief tenure at APD, but four fellow officers testified at trial that he had a bad reputation in the community, leading to the unanswered question: Why was he hired?

On the evening of March 27, 1975, a young woman walked to her car in a shopping mall after her workday ended. She made the same walk many times with no worries; however, this night was different. She took her keys out, opened the door, not noticing the man coming up the side of her car with a gun in his hand. She closed the car door; it was jerked opened; a gun was stuck in her face. She was ordered to move over. It happened so fast she did not have time to do anything but move over. Then, the man told her to stick her hands out, and he handcuffed her. According to court testimony, the frightened young woman's brain went into high gear trying to put it all together, "Is he a cop? Am I under arrest? Is he going to steal my car? Is he going to rape me? Is he going to kill me?" He drove in silence, as she felt too sick to talk. One block, a second block, and then a dark construction site came into view. He drove into a dark corner, stopped, pulled her from the car, and threw her into the back seat, pulled her dress up, pulled her panties down, and quickly penetrated her. It was over as fast as it started. She struggled to put her panties back on with the handcuffs on her wrists. The man just forcibly violated her; she was not about to ask for his help.

They got back in the front seat. The man driving retraced the route. He stopped and took the handcuffs off and drove into the shopping center parking lot. Once in the lot, he stopped again, got out, and left her there, scared, puzzled, and thankful to be alive. The woman sat there for some time, going over the surreal events. Finally, the shaking victim burst into tears, drove home, threw away her clothes, took a shower, and called the police. From a law enforcement perspective, she did everything wrong, but a list of what to do if raped are not listed as safety factors in cars.

Vanderbilt's next victim did not survive her random encounter with this vicious Killer Cop. Sixteen-year-old Katina Moyer drove to the school where her schoolteacher mother worked. As she waited for her mother to come out, Vanderbilt repeated his actions from the first sexual assault. He jerked the driver's side door open, stuck a gun into the face of his stunned victim, and told her to move over. He clamped a set of stainless steel restraints on her wrists as she cried and begged him not to hurt her. He told her to shut up and drove off. Vanderbilt's next move insured Katina would die. He drove to his home and dragged the young victim into the living room. He later said he noticed her looking around the room as if she was trying to remember what she saw. He knew he had made a mistake. Katina had to die. Vanderbilt confessed he drove to a secluded area, put the .357 pistol to her head, and pulled the trigger as the crying teenager pleaded and promised she would not tell on him. The badge packer with "no conscience" killed his last victim.

CONCLUSION

The existence of *police serial sexual* killers and *rape plus murder* killers cannot be dismissed as bad apples in an honorable "profession." Their presence in any law enforcement agency demands answers to several questions: (1) Could there be something wrong with the agency's vetting process? There were vetting problems in some agencies examined. However, simple silver bullet solutions like requiring a college degree are not the answer—witness Schaefer, DeAngelo, and Ortiz. (2) Is there something amiss with the internal discipline system? There is enough evidence to suggest this is a factor. (3) Are there other unidentified factors? We need answers to all these questions, because, up to now most police professionals were loath to admit that *Sexually Motivated Killer Cops* existed. Furthermore, academic research on this topic is nonexistent.

SOURCES

Anon. (June 26, 1994). Ex-CHP officer gets 90 years. *Daily Breeze.*

AP. (July 21, 2005). Josh Griffin serving a life sentence for murder in the 1997 death of a Cocktail waitress he'd pulled over in his police cruiser in 1997. AP.

Barker, T. (2020). *Aggressors in Blue: Exposing Police Sexual Abuse.* Palgrave.

Feis, A. (September 16, 2018). This is the "serial killer" US border agent accused of slaying prostitutes. *New York Post.*

Frammolino, R. (August 14, 1987). Agency "know of problems": Peyer, CHP sued by victim's father. *Los Angeles Times.*

Gorman, T. (June 23, 1988). Peyer neighbors react with shock and relief. *Los Angeles Times.*

Gorman, T. (January 12, 1996). Trooper charged with rape kills himself. *Los Angeles Times.*

Gorman, T. & Reza, H.G. (January 21, 1987). Craig Peyer's neighbors rally "round" Start relief fund to help accused CHP officer's family survive. *Los Angeles Times.*

Green, R. (2018). *Killer Cop: The Deviant Deputy Who Kidnapped, Raped and Killed.* Lexington, KY: Ryan Green.

Healey, J., Beauregard, E., Beech, A., & Vettor, S. (2014). Is the sexual murderer a unique type of offender? A typology of violent sexual offenders using crime scene behaviors. *Sexual Abuse.* 28 (6): 512–533.

Higgs, T., Carter, A.J., Stefanska, E.B., & Clorney, E. (2015). Toward identification of the sexual killer: A comparison of sexual killers engaging in post-mortem sexual interference and non-homicide sexual aggressors. *Sexual Abuse.* 29: 472–499.

Horton, A. (September 17, 2008). A woman's daring escape from a Border Patrol agent helped reveal a 'serial killer,' police say. *The Washington Post.*

James, J. & Prouix, J. (2016). The modus operandi of serial and nonserial sexual murderers: A systematic review. *Aggression and Violent Behavior.* 31: 105–118.

Kalmbacher, C. (September 15, 2018). Border agent confesses to being serial killer who targeted sex workers. *Lawandcrime.com.*

Kaye, J. (2008). *Beware of the Cable Guy: From Cop to Serial Killer.* Palm Springs, CA: Polimedia Books.

Leaf, A. (December 27, 2014). The tragic story of Cara Knott murdered by CHP Officer Peyer in San Diego. *United Against Police Terror.*

Mason, Y. (2008). *Silent Scream.* Dressing Your Book.

McNamara, M. (2018). *I'll Be Gone in the Dark: One Woman's Obsessive Search for the Golden State Killer.* New York: Harper's Collins.

Nolasco, S. (May 7, 2018). Golden State Killer investigator talks suspect's strange behavior, launching true crime podcast 'Murder Squad.' *Fox News.*

People V. Sully (199!). No, S004721. Crim. No. 25590.

Puskar, S. & Li, D.K. (January 17, 2019). 3 Chicago officers acquitted of covering up for colleague who shot Laquan McDonald. *NBCnews.com.*

Ressler, R.H. & Shactman, T. (1992). *Whoever Fights Monsters: My Twenty Years Tracking Serial Killers for the FBI.* New York: St. Martin's Paperback.

Reza, H.G. (August 4, 1989). An emotional judge gives Peyer 25 years for killing Cara Knotts. *Los Angeles Times.*

Schaefer, G.J. as told to Sondra London. (1989). *Killer Fiction.* Los Angeles: Feral House.

Sellers, L. (April 16, 1990). A woman is slain, a trooper confesses, a fear festers. *Orlando Sentinel.*

Stefanska, E. B, Higgs, T., Carter, A.J., & Beech, A.R. (2017). When is a murder a sexual murder? Understanding the sexual element in the classification of sexual killer. *Journal of Criminal Justice.* 50: 53–61.

Sully v. Ayers. (2013). *Sully v. Ayers.* United States Court of Appeals for the Ninth Circuit. No 08-99011. DC. No. 3-92-C.V.-00829-WHA.Punta.

The FBI Files. (2008). *Above the Law.* DVR-The First Season: Discovery Channel.

U.S. v. George W. Gwaltney, 790 F. 2d 1378 (9th Cir. 1986).

Warren, J. (May 31, 1987). Family, boyfriend describe search for Knott the night she disappeared. *Los Angeles Times.*

Warren, J. (April 20, 1988). Judge, attorneys question 20 as picking of Peyer, jury inches on. *Los Angeles Times.*

Chapter 10

Domestic Violence Homicides

Killer Cops

INTRODUCTION

The Killer Cops discussed in this chapter kill those who share a personal, emotional, and/or sexual relationship with them. By definition, this is domestic violence; however, the deaths are premeditated murders of intimate partners—significant others, mistresses, lovers, wives, and husbands. The deaths occur because the police perpetrator intended to murder, not batter or abuse the victim; he or she wanted to cause death, not pain or injury. Murder is the objective, not the result of a pattern of abuse. These Killer Cops kill to conceal some secret, exact revenge, or they are motivated by greed, sex, jealousy, and other typical murder motives.

Many domestic partners entering into the relationships with Killer Cops are doomed from the beginning. The victims do not know it, but in many cases, they should have. The victim's road to the grave is slow at first but picks up speed to the eventual end—death. Most victims go to their deaths without a struggle, frozen by shock and disbelief. The murders may appear random and senseless without motive. Not true. There is always a motive; even no motive is a motive. Some people are mean without a soul. Cops know that. Unfortunately, some of these mean persons carry a badge. We begin our discussion with the first female U.S. state trooper killed in the line of duty.

DOMESTIC VIOLENCE KILLER COPS

Joe Cecil Duncan: Alabama State Trooper: Killer Cop Who Killed Another Cop (October 11, 1987), Motivated by Greed

Joe Duncan is not the first U.S. Killer Cop to kill a fellow cop. Louisville, Kentucky, police officer Claude T. Downs is the first recorded domestic violence Killer Cop (Wilbanks, 2000). Downs was off-duty on May 16, 1977, when he called dispatch and asked for his on-duty wife to meet him at a Whites Castle restaurant. When twenty-five-year-old African American Louisville Detective Gwendolyn Downs and her partner arrived in the restaurant parking lot, they spotted her husband waiting in his car. Earlier that day, she complained to Internal Affairs about her husband, but they dismissed her complaint, saying they could do nothing because he had broken no laws or department regulations.

Claude Downs signaled her to come over to his car. She went despite her partner's caution not to. They talked for about 15 minutes, and the two married cops started loudly arguing, then he shot his wife four times. Detective Downs's partner ran to the car with his gun drawn, but before he reached the scene, Claude Downs shot himself in the head.

Joe Duncan's case is different from the one described above; rather than a "heat of passion" murder during a domestic disturbance, Duncan planned and executed his fiancée to collect on her insurance. I knew Joe Duncan and his victim Trooper Elizabeth Cobb. Growing up in the mean streets of a large urban Southern city, I knew several murderers and their victims; however, this was my first experience—but not the last—of a cop killing another cop.

When I first met Joe Duncan in the 1980s, he was the deputy chief of the two-person police department (Chief and him) of Ohatchee, Alabama, a small town of about 800 people in Western Calhoun County close to Neely Henry Lake. On my way to or from fishing, I sometimes stopped at the police department to kibitz with the chief. His new deputy chief, a wet behind the ears neophyte who had not received any training, was in the office on some occasions. I always felt unease around Joe; he was so pumped up about being a deputy chief. He was not even a certified officer yet, but his ego screamed power and authority. The chief thought his "piss and vinegar gung-ho" attitude was amusing. I did not agree; he had trouble written all over him. Deputy Chief Joe Duncan did not look you in the eye when he talked. However, I never suspected he would be a Killer Cop.

As was the custom, then in Alabama, an untrained police officer in most rural agencies could "police" for up to a year before attending the police academy. Deputy Chief Duncan attended the Northeast Alabama Police Academy in Brewer Hall on the campus of Jacksonville State University in

Jacksonville, Alabama. I was a specialized instructor instructing the entry and advanced classes in the academy. As I recall, his aloof attitude did not go over well with the others in his class. I heard Duncan went to work with another small police department in the area after he graduated from the academy and then went to work with Alabama State Troopers in 1985.

I heard nothing from him or about him until October 15, 1987, at the funeral of his fiancée, Elizabeth "Liz" Sue Cobb, an Alabama State Trooper. An unknown assailant had shot Trooper Cobb in the head. Trooper Joe Cecil Duncan drove the family to the funeral and sat with them, crying and consoling them. His loss was as great as theirs. At least that was what he was acting out. Duncan, in full uniform, presented the flag from her casket to the grieving mother. She cried and said, "Thank You, Joe." He merely nodded. After all, it was show time for him (Wilbanks, 2000).

Five-feet five-inch, 115-pound, brown-haired, pleasing and pretty Elizabeth Cobb was in excellent physical shape, running every day and winning medals in races and marathons. She did volunteer work at her church and was an Airman 1st Class in the Air National Guard. A very busy rookie—eight months on the job when her boyfriend, some say fiancée, and fellow trooper blew her brains out in their "secret meeting place" behind a rural church near Selma, Alabama. A death of a fellow officer always tears the heart out of the brothers and sisters in Blue, but Liz was different.

She was well known in the Alabama law enforcement community (Wilbanks, 2000). The perky, courteous young woman worked as a stenographer in the Alabama Department of Public Safety offices in both Birmingham and Montgomery for ten years (1976–1986) until she fulfilled her lifetime ambition of becoming an Alabama State Trooper. Ultimately, she wanted to become an investigator with the elite Alabama Bureau of Investigation (ABI), but she had to work with the Division of Highway Patrol—Alabama State Troopers—for two years. These brave men and women like almost all U.S. highway patrol or state police work by themselves with little available backup. Liz Cobb was working by herself on that dreadful night of Sunday, October 11, 1987.

She reported to work for her 3 p.m.–11 p.m. shift at the Craig Field trooper station in Selma and began "rolling and patrolling." She came back to the station at 7.36 p.m. for about 35 minutes and left again for routine patrol. That was the last time anyone saw her alive. When she did not report off-duty at midnight, the dispatcher called her home. No answer. The dispatcher called Duncan, and the line was busy. A state trooper went to her house. Nothing. The trooper went to Duncan's residence. Duncan claimed he had not heard from her since 7 p.m. A search began with all agencies in the area joining in. Trooper Elizabeth Cobb's body was found at 9.38 a.m. Monday morning sitting in her marked patrol car with the window down behind a church on a country road. She sat in the driver's seat with three .22 caliber bullet holes in her head. Her car keys, service revolver, and ticket book were gone. The state forensic pathologist estimated the time of death at between 7.00 p.m. and 9.00 p.m. on October 11, 1987. The crime scene was processed; the patrol car dusted for prints, casts made of the tire impressions; alerts for information were broadcast; and a $10,000 reward was posted. The ABI went to work.

Puzzling and possibly incriminating information surfaced. Duncan was at his house with two female staff workers playing cards the night Cobb was killed after the estimated time of death. One of the women, knowing he was reportedly engaged to Liz Cobb, asked him what she would say if she came in after she got off work. He emphatically replied, "She won't" (Wilbanks, 2000). The woman testified later that his response was peculiar. He appeared convinced Liz Cobb was not coming. He knew she would not show up. The ABI investigators uncovered a bombshell piece of evidence. Joe Duncan took out a $350,000 life insurance policy on Elizabeth Cobb with him as the beneficiary three months before her murder.

Furthermore, he recently called the insurance company and asked if the policy paid double indemnity for a line of duty deaths—obviously, that warranted examination of his finances. Duncan was drowning in debt and behind on support payments to two ex-wives and four children. He had a net worth of zero. The motive screamed out to the seasoned investigators: murder for financial gain.

Four days after Trooper Elizabeth Cobb's funeral on October 19, 1987, Joe Duncan was brought in for questioning. At first, he maintained his innocence and said that being a beneficiary on her insurance policy was not all that unusual. She was the beneficiary on a similar policy for him. Then he followed the well-worn path of those who consent to talk to law enforcement authorities without "lawyering" up. He talked himself on death row.

Duncan fell apart on continued questioning from the seasoned investigators and spun an unbelievable tale. The experienced interrogators sat there with their expressionless masks on their faces and let Duncan spew out his incriminating blather. They did not take any notes or make any movements to interrupt him. The videotape and the person or persons on the other side of the two-way mirror would take copious notes. Surprising, to the interrogators that Duncan was such a "stupid son of a bitch." According to the investigators, Duncan started slowly as if he was thinking his comments out, "I was there but only to meet with her." He took a deep breath and slowly continued, breathing normally.

"I parked behind her car, and then I snuck up on the car. I was going to scare her." According to court testimony and the video, his eyes darted around the room, and his breaths came in short spurts. "The window was down, and when I looked, I knew she was dead, blood was everywhere, and I smelled gunpowder. I panicked. I was scared. I didn't even have a gun on me. The killers could still be around, and I would be next." Another pause, as Duncan searched for what to say next. Duncan stood, and it was clear that his emotions were now in charge of his brain and mouth. "Man, I was scared shiftless. I could be next." The investigators listened without saying a word, knowing that at a time like this, suspects have to say anything, however ridiculous it sounds.

Lying under pressure is hard, but it is very hard when you have murdered someone. "I ran back to my car and left in a hurry. What in the hell would you expect me to do? I'm off duty without a gun." Realizing he was standing up and waving his arms and the two stoic ABI agents were staring at him, he sat down. He took a breath and paused again, probably trying to explain why he kept everything silent because he had to realize it was a huge mistake to leave and not report the murder of a fellow trooper. He looked at the ceiling and blurted out, "I left because I was afraid I might be a suspect." That part of his ridiculous tale was true.

Nowhere in the fairy tale did he blurt out or show any concern or feeling for Trooper Liz Cobb. He never said he loved her or missed her. The interrogation was over at this point. Once the interrogation results were conveyed up the chain of command, Duncan was immediately fired for "cowardice" for leaving the murder scene. He was then arrested and charged with Trooper Cobb's ambush murder.

The first trial lasted twelve days ending on March 21, 1988. It was largely a circumstantial evidence trial as many trials are. The murder weapon was never found. The tire prints left at the scene did not match Duncan's car or his patrol car. The footprints at the scene did not match any of his shoes. Duncan's fingerprints were found on the passenger's door, and some of the paperwork found in Cobb's patrol car. His debt level and listing as a beneficiary on the insurance policy and bizarre explanation of being on the scene were presented to the jury. The state's expert testified that the aroma of gunpowder only lasts a minute or two, so if Duncan smelled it at the scene, he would have seen whoever shot Elizabeth Cobb at such close range. Duncan's statement to the female's playing cards with him was presented. The jury deliberated for three hours, finding Duncan guilty of capital murder.

The jury's sentencing deliberation was contentious and split 10–2 for life imprisonment without parole. On April 12, 1988, the presiding judge overturned the life imprisonment sentence and imposed the death penalty, saying the killing of Elizabeth Cobb was a "premeditated, diabolic, planned execution." The case was not over. On September 18, 1992, the Alabama Court of Appeals overturned the verdict on a technicality and called for a new trial. The second trial began on June 12, 1995, and ended on June 21.

Jury deliberation ran into difficulty nine hours into a bitter debate and a 6–6 deadlock. The prosecution, fearing a loss offered a plea deal to non-capital murder and a sentence of twenty-five years. Duncan admitted to the murder and accepted a sentence of twenty-five years and eligibility for parole. He went up for parole three times, once advocating the most-offered reason at parole hearings—he was a born again Christian and accepted Christ as his savior. No one accepted his crocodile tears, and his "saved" proclamation; he was denied each time. Duncan served out his sentence and was released from prison on October 14, 2012. No one knows where he is.

Pikeville, Kentucky: FBI Special Agent Mark Putnam, 1990, FBI Killer Cop

FBI Special Agent Mark Putnam admitted murdering an informant in June 1989. The informant Susan Daniels Smith was his sex partner who threatened to make the tryst public (Jones, 1992; Sharkey, 1993 & 2017). "Supposedly" consensual sex between LEOs and vulnerable partners often has disastrous consequences (Barker, 2020). Police rules and regulations prohibit this behavior. Proscribed Law Enforcement Ethical standards strongly condemn sexual actions between LEOs and informants at all levels of government. Putnam acknowledged he was aware of the prohibitions against intimate relationships with informants. However, forbidden sex was not the only reward Putnam received. The vulnerable victim provided information to Putnam on criminal activity by her crooked friends, resulting in adulation from his supervisors and recognition as a rising FBI star.

The future tragic events were set in motion by Putnam's first posting. The "rookie" agent's first assignment fresh out of the FBI Academy was a remote two-person office in a rural mining country in Pikeville, Kentucky (Jones, 1992; Sharkey, 1993 & 2017). Local police authorities in an attempt to help introduced Putnam to a female informant, Susan Daniels Smith, who could identify criminals working in the Pikeville area. However, they advised that she should be handled carefully. Susan Smith operated as a well-known police informant for years. The paid snitch was streetwise, and he could find himself in her clutches if he were not careful; they advised. The neophyte federal investigator should have listened.

The female informant, Susan Smith, was an attractive dirt-poor coal miner's daughter with the reputation of being a "loose" woman and a consistent liar. She received $9,000 for her snitch work. She turned in criminal friends and relatives for money. Smith continually romanticized about meeting her Prince Charming, who would take her away from the squalor she lived into living in luxury. The young married father of two, Mark Putnam, was her ticket out of Eastern Kentucky into her dream world.

Shortly after their first meeting, Smith and Putnam began having sex in his FBI car in deserted coalmine sites. The encounters intensified. The other FBI agent in the two-person office observed the two lovebirds hugging and kissing in the office. Then, the assignations moved to a small low-rent "no-tell" motel directly across from the Pikeville Kentucky State Police Post. Whenever his wife made trips back east, Putnam and Smith spent the nights in his house. Following these intense sexual encounters, Susan Smith gave her sister lurid accounts of the affairs, and Putnam's promises to leave his wife and marry her. The Susan Smith–Mark Putman romance took an unexpected turn.

Smith increased their sexual liaisons in the hopes she would become pregnant, forcing Putnam to leave his wife and marry her. She did become pregnant, but the result was not what she expected. Putnam, based on his successes from the information supplied by Smith, was transferred to the more desirable assignment in the Miami, Florida FBI Office. The move enraged his spurned informant and sex plaything. Putnam wanted to put the affair in the past, but the now pregnant Susan Smith threatened to go public unless he made good on his promise to marry her. Putnam was scheduled to return to Pikeville to testify in a criminal case, and they made plans to meet and resolve the issue.

According to his later confession, they met in Pikeville and drove to a secluded site to discuss the options. She threatened to tell the FBI, his family, and the newspapers about the baby (Jones, 1992; Sharkey, 1993 & 2017). He agreed to adopt the baby but not leave his wife. The enraged spurned lover began pummeling him with blows and scratching his face. In a desperate attempt to stop the assault, he claims he accidentally strangled her. Putnam then placed her lifeless body in the trunk of his rental car and drove off. He had a real problem. What to do with the body, and how to explain the cracked windshield resulting from the wild altercation? He drove around with the body in his trunk for two days before deciding to drive out to a desolate and abandoned strip mine site. He threw the body down a 19-foot ravine near an old cold-mining road nine miles north of Pikeville. He cleaned the blood out of the rental car and returned it asking for another because of the cracked windshield. He claimed flying gravel from the ubiquitous coal trucks traveling the roadways, a common occurrence in coal country, broke the windshield.

The strangling "may" have been a crime of passion, but the dumping of the body and getting rid of the car and evidence reveal a calculating Killer Cop attempting to conceal his crime. The decomposing body lay hidden for a year as the suspicion of her murder by FBI Special Agent Mark Putnam intensified. The cries for justice came from the Smith family, who believed Putnam killed her to conceal the affair and pregnancy. Two weeks after her disappearance, the family reported their suspicions that Putnam had murdered Susan Smith. The FBI and Putnam thwarted repeated attempts to interview and polygraph Putnam by Kentucky State authorities. Finally, an FBI special investigating team became involved to put the allegations to rest. Putnam gave contradictory and disturbing answers to the FBI interviewers, leading them to suspect he killed Susan Smith. He failed a polygraph examination, confirming their suspicions.

Realizing that continued denials were useless, and it was only a matter of time before the body would be found, and a murder charge laid, Putnam and his lawyer entered into plea negotiations with the Commonwealth's Attorney. After weeks of negotiation, they agreed on a guilty plea to a lesser charge of first-degree manslaughter instead of murder and a sixteen-year prison sentence. The indictment said Putnam killed Smith "while under extreme emotional duress." He confessed to "acting in extreme rage," and reaching across the car and "grabbed her by the throat with both hands and straddled her by actually sitting on top of her in the seat. I started choking her and telling her to shut up" (Jones, 1992). When he checked for a pulse two minutes later, she was dead. The Smith family was outraged but was finally convinced that Putnam could not be prosecuted without a body and direct evidence of a crime. The outcome was not what the Commonwealth wanted, but it was the best they could get. Putnam confessed and led the authorities to the badly decomposed body. He claimed he only had sex with Smith four or five times and only in his car: a dubious claim disputed by others. In 2000, Mark Putnam, a model prisoner, was released from prison after serving ten years of his sixteen-year sentence (Gentile, September 29, 2000). Two years before his release, his wife, who stood by him during the scandal and prison sentence, died of organ failure brought on by excessive drinking.

Denton, Texas Police Department Detective Robert "Bobby" Lozano Kills His Wife and Almost Gets Away with It

Detective Bobby Lozano, a seventeen-year police veteran, killed his wife Virginia "Viki," an elementary schoolteacher and mother of his eleven-month baby boy, on July 2002, and was indicted for her murder in December 2002. The indictment was dismissed in July 2004. In October 2008, Bobby Lozano was again indicted for Viki's murder. He was convicted of the murder in 2009. Seven years for justice. Why? The macabre long journey to justice is stranger than fiction. The reconstructed events leading to the murder and seven-year odyssey to justice is described by the husband and wife team of Denton County Assistant District Attorneys writing in *Prosecutor: The Journal of the National District Attorneys Association* and the book *Ladykiller* by Donna Fielder (Piel & Piel, November 2009; Fielder, 2012). Fielder is an award-winning journalist whose articles brought about the eventual trial and conviction of Bobby Lozano.

Typical for Killer Cops, Lozano was a cop with baggage. Detective Bobby Lozano was a narcissistic skirt-chasing problem police officer who would sooner or later disgrace the badge and the department. His disturbing sexual behavior practices and violations of police department policies, procedures, and rules were ignored, covered-up, and facilitated by police peers. At the time of his wife's suspicious death, the "pussy hound" was having an eighteen-month affair with a female Denton detective.

Bobby Lozano, a poster child for police sexual predators, used his law enforcement position to initiate and commit sexual acts with crime victims, witnesses, police interns, and fellow female officers (Fielder, 2012). His law enforcement role provided ample opportunity for illicit sex. His police status and peer group support—overt and latent—provided cover for his sexual indiscretions.

According to investigators, Lozano had "many, many, many" affairs during his sixteen-year marriage to Viki Lozano. The majority of the sexual liaisons were job-related. Two rape victims came to him to investigate their crimes and ended up as sexual partners; one miscarried his child. Other job-related throwaway sex toys included a female crime suspect and a witness. He traded sex for dropping cases—sexual extortion. His most disturbing sex partner was a young female police intern—a real "no-no" in police work (Barker, 2019). Lozano carried on a three-year affair with her. Being married never seemed to bother Lozano, his sexual conquests, or his police peers. Lozano felt so comfortable in sexual misconduct acts that he did not try to keep them secret. He sent his sex partners gifts, text messages, and took them to public places, leaving an easy trail for investigators.

The police intern worked for his best friend in the department. The intern's supervising police officer half-heartedly tried to prevent the violation of the law and police regulations and rules. He warned the young girl that Bobby was married and a known "skirt chaser." The fellow officer also cautioned Bobby Lozano not to engage in a clear violation of police rules. The fellow cop relented and gave his blessing. He said he would not have a problem with Lozano dating the intern. And he would keep his silence (Fielder, 2012).

Detective Lozano had one line for each gullible woman. "I love you and want to marry you. But, I can't leave my wife. She controls the money." Two of the naive paramours testified at trial—seven years delayed—they believed they were heading to the altar, but Lozano kept postponing leaving his wife. He groomed his victims with false promises of love and affection. However, things changed with his last sex toy. At the time of his wife's death, Lozano was no longer worried about money; he had a million-dollar life insurance policy on Viki—a clear motive for murder. Four months before his wife's death, Lozano sent the Denton PD female detective a prophetic love card addressing her as "My wife, soon to be, but not soon enough." Seven years later, the jury gasped when this was read in court (Fielder, 2012).

THE MURDER EVENTS

At 9.05 p.m. on July 6, 2002, Bobby Lozano claimed to have returned from an "emergency" tanning session and found his wife lying on their bed amid gun cleaning gear shot in the chest. He called 911, saying she was not breathing, and he would begin CPR until the paramedics arrived. At approximately 9.09 p.m., the paramedics arrived to find the immaculately dressed Bobby Lozano at the front door without a hair out of place, holding the couple's eleven-month son, Monty. Bobby was not out of breath as he should be after administering CPR. There was no visible blood on him, his clothing, or the child as would be expected from giving CPR to a gunshot victim. The paramedics proceeded to the master bedroom and found the victim lying on her back on the side of the bed with her right foot hanging off touching the floor. No lifesaving measures were attempted. One paramedic said it was apparent she was "dead-dead." Her skin was cold to the touch, she was pale, and her right foot and ankle had obvious lividity—a telltale clue of death. Lividity begins within thirty minutes of death and lasts about six hours. The lividity in her right foot and ankle—the lowest part of her body and touching the floor—indicated she was dead and had been dead at least an hour or ninety minutes. That was undoubtedly longer than the 30–45 minutes Lozano claimed he had been at the tanning salon. The suspicious paramedics left without the body.

On the bed with Viki was an open gun cleaning kit, two sheets of newspaper, cleaning supplies, and Bobby Lozano's 9-mm Glock service weapon covered in oil. Bobby claimed he was cleaning his service weapon when he decided to get an "emergency" tanning, leaving the gun on the bed. Who cleans a pistol on the bed? Furthermore, then leaves everything as it is to get an emergency tanning, leaving his wife in the same bed. Bobby Lozano does, and he has an explanation, no matter how implausible it sounds. "Viki must have decided to clean the weapon, and it accidentally discharged, or maybe she committed suicide," he told cops, family and friends alike—anyone and everyone who would listen (Piel & Piel, November 2009).

According to the eventual prosecutors, a series of mistakes were made at the crime scene, and the initial investigation as responding officers attempted to be sensitive to the feelings of a fellow officer who just lost his wife to accident or suicide. They failed to follow standard death investigation protocols. None of the officers at the scene wanted to believe a fellow officer would kill his wife.

There are standard police protocols to follow in sudden death investigations until the death is ruled a homicide, suicide, accident, or natural causes. The first rule is to secure the scene and remove all non-essential persons. Friends and family flooded into the house to support Bobby and offer their condolences, resulting in only the master bedroom being a protected crime scene—a serious error. In a dwelling, the entire area is a crime scene until it is determined that the death occurred where the body is found, and there is no incriminating evidence elsewhere. Forced entry must be ruled out. A thorough search should be conducted of the entire premises. Of course, this is unsettling to those present, especially friends and relatives, probably the reason why Bobby's fellow cops ignored this rule. However, homicide investigators learn early in their training that they are Advocates for the Dead, not the living. The rest of the house was not searched, leaving the possibility that evidence would not be found.

The mistakes piled up. Lozano's car was not searched, obviously a concession to a fellow officer. No one drove the route to the tanning salon to time the travel and confirm his alibi. Viki's hands were tested for gunshot residue, but the kit was out of date, nullifying the results. Out of deference to Bobby Lozano, no gunshot residue tests were taken, and he was not brought to headquarters for questioning or interviewed at the scene.

Two hours after the 911 call, the crime scene team began taking pictures. Their sloppy work led to an unfathomable error. The ejected shell casing was not found on the bed, so after the body was removed, the investigators moved the cleaning kit, the newspaper sheets, and the other cleaning materials to the foot of the bed to search for the missing casing. They did not photograph the item's original position before moving them (Piel & Piel, November 2009). The missing casing was found in one of the blanket folds, photographed, bagged, and placed into evidence. What was the casings' exact location before everything was moved? That question was an issue seven years later.

Bobby's behavior at the scene was disturbing. He attempted to appear crying, but no one saw tears. Walking from person to person, he repeated his alibi without prompting. *He protested too much*, many thought but held their tongue. He was not responsible was the point of his comments (Fielder, 2012). His behavior was totally out of character for a grieving husband after the sudden and tragic death of his "dear" wife. He wanted to know if anyone knew who cremated bodies. "Viki wanted to be cremated," he told one of his police colleagues. *What a damn thing to be thinking about with your wife's body sprawled out on the bed*, his police buddy thought but kept his mouth shut. His behavior was especially suspicious to those who knew he continually cheated on his dear wife. His sister knew and even came upon him and a lover in his wife's bed previously. He told his sister that he had sex with another woman the day before he married Viki and the day after the wedding.

Years later, his cop buddies in the house admitted knowing of his philandering and being troubled by his behavior at the scene. According to later trial testimony, Bobby stopped the medical examiner's stretcher as Viki's body was being removed and asked to see her one last time—a reasonable request. The body bag was unzipped, and his last comment of "take care" shocked those present—a never heard last comment (Fielder, 2012). His best friend and the department chaplain remarked at trial seven years later, "For someone to say 'take care' and walk back inside as if nothing happened, I thought that was being really cold."

The scientific evidence from the medical examiner's office added to the confusion and a strange set of events, prolonging the road to justice. The medical examiner ruled the cause of death was a gunshot wound to the chest, but the manner of death was undetermined. He could not conclusively say if the death was homicide, suicide, or accident. From the location of the body and angle of the wound, he could not determine if she pulled the trigger or someone else did. The gunshot residue test was of no use because it was contaminated.

Even more disturbing was the lab findings three weeks later. Small fragments of popcorn husks were found stuck to her body and in her mouth. *Viki Lozano was eating popcorn when she was shot.* Who cleans an oily pistol while eating popcorn? However, no popcorn was found at the crime scene or anywhere in the house. Why? No one searched the house, and it was clear that the bedroom had been vacuumed. Bobby Lozano claimed he vacuumed the room that day. No doubt, he did, but when? No container of popcorn was found at the death scene. Why? Someone removed it, and it was not Viki. Then who? The answers to these questions, along with other disturbing evidence and a million-dollar motive, pointed at Bobby Lozano. Bobby Lozano resigned from the police department three weeks after his wife's death, casting further doubts on his account of the events of that night. No longer a police department employee, he could not face an Internal Affairs review. He had to be arrested and Mirandized for any further questioning. Then, the female police paramour confessed to her supervisors that she was having an affair with the "grieving" widower. Bobby Lozano was arrested and indicted for his wife's murder. The strange journey to justice had begun.

Disturbed by the inconclusive findings from the original medical examiner, the District Attorney's office sought a second opinion on the manner of death. A chief medical examiner from Cooke County, Illinois, was in Dallas at a conference, and the original prosecutors met him at this hotel. They had the original files and photographs of the crime scene. The Illinois medical examiner reviewed these documents and supposedly concluded—he later denied this—there was insufficient evidence to conclusively establish the manner of death between suicide, homicide, and accident (Fielder, 2012). Once again,

Bobby Lozano was granted a "pass" for murder. The original indictment of December 12, 2002, was dismissed on July 14, 2004, due to insufficient evidence to establish a prima facie case. Lozano and his former police mistress resumed their affair, and he put the murder in his past. He was home free, or that was what he thought. An investigative reporter for the *Denton Record-Chronicle* took up the quest for justice for Viki Lozano.

The reporter Donna Felder's dogged efforts to receive information for the Denton Police Department through open records request finally led to a series of articles in September 2008. She raised the question: Did Bobby Lozano get away with the murder of his wife? She certainly thought so and convinced a large portion of her readers. Another change occurred that sealed Bobby Lozano's fate.

A new district attorney was elected since the dismissal of the indictment. The new team spurred on by Felder's revelations met to determine if the case should be reopened. Following a review of the boxes of case files, the team was unanimous—Bobby Lozano had indeed gotten away with murder (Piel & Piel, November 2009). The review found the "smoking gun," the missing ejected shell casing had been found under the cleaning kit. It could not have rolled under the heavy box. Someone had to have put it there. Who? A seventeen-year police veteran—Bobby Lozano—had staged the crime scene, and he had done a perfect job. It was apparent he put the cleaning kit on the bed after he shot Viki. There was no other possible explanation.

The missing popcorn husks buttressed the conclusion that Bobby Lozano staged the crime scene. Viki had popcorn husks down the front of her shirt and on her side. They were stuck to the blood on her shirt. However, no popcorn, a container for the popcorn, a napkin or paper towel was in the crime scene. They had been removed after she was shot. The reexamined evidence led to the conclusion that the body had been moved after she was shot.

The new evidence was introduced at trial along with his numerous affairs and the insurance policies—a few months before the murder, Bobby had talked Viki into getting a million-dollar life policy. Seven years and twenty days after Viki Lozano's death, the jury took only five hours to convict Bobby Lozano of her death. He was sentenced to forty-five years in prison.

Columbia, Missouri: Officer Stephen Rios Murders His Gay Lover

In this premeditated murder, the Killer Cop, Columbia, Missouri Police Officer Stephen Rios, used his badge for same-sex opportunities with a male victim and killed him in an attempt to conceal his homosexual affair. The prosecutor at trial said, "[Rios] used his badge for sex and then used his knife to forever close the mouth of his secret lover" (Ryan, May 23, 2005).

Officer Steven Rios's victim, a twenty-three-year-old gay male, was a vulnerable victim with creditability problems, making him a "perfect victim" for a police sexual predator (Barker, 2020). The openly gay University of Missouri-Columbia junior had a history of promiscuous homosexual contacts with gay males, making no effort to conceal his gay lifestyle. Officer Rios exploited this for his sexual purposes. Officer Steven Rios was married with a year-old child, outwardly an unlikely gay sexual predator. However, the murder investigation revealed the three-year veteran officer with the 144-person police department was a sexual predator of both males and females he encountered during his police duties. Allegations of "hitting on" female motorists for sex surfaced after his first murder trial.

Rios's creditability problems could have been known, or knowable, to the Columbia Police Department before his employment. Columbia is the county seat of Boone County, Missouri, and Rios was fired from the Boone County jail for renting a storage space under another officer's name. Rios was a known liar.

A routine background check should have revealed he was fired from the jail for lying. Why this was ignored is not explained? However, at trial, he was described as a compulsive liar by the prosecution. Rios's deceptive practices surfaced again and again in the seven-week homosexual relationship that ended in murder. There is no answer to the question: Why was he hired as a police officer when he was a known liar? Improper vetting is a contributory factor in many of the Killer Cops described in this book. The illicit and fatal relationship between the victim and the Killer Cop began with a routine disturbance call (Ryan, May 23, 2005, *Missouri v Rios*-Appellant, 2007).

The short journey to murder started in the early morning hours of April 18, 2004, with three separate disturbance calls—loud party—to an off-campus apartment. On the third call, Officer Stephen Rios was one of the three Columbia responding police officers. Two of the partiers, Jesse Valencia, and an unnamed male, refused to leave and were taken into custody. Rios issued Valencia a summons to appear in court for obstructing a police operation and released, but not before the arresting officer, and the arrestee made arrangements to meet again. Later the same day, Valencia told friends his handsome arresting officer was going to pick him up after he finished his shift at the Campus Inn. The friends reacted in stunned disbelief. Not a cop, especially one who has just arrested you, they responded to Valencia's boast. It was bizarre but true. Rios picked Valencia up in his private vehicle and was seen dropping off Valencia at his apartment. The relationship progressed and became visible to the gay community.

On May 8, a female acquaintance of Valencia stayed at his apartment because she was too drunk to drive. She responded to a 3 a.m. knock on the door. She opened the door and was shocked to see the arresting officer in civilian clothes looking for Valencia. She recognized him from the April 18 disturbance call. He wanted to know why she was there and where was Valencia. She explained that her friend let her stay because she was too drunk to drive and he was not there. The perplexed woman did not ask the obvious question: Why are you here? Officer Rios offered to drive her home. She refused his offer, and he left. The next encounter is surreal and provides direct evidence of the sexual nature of Officer Rios and Valencia's relationship.

About 1:30 a.m. on May 14, 2004, Jesse Valencia and a male friend went to his apartment after a date. They were engaged in sexual activity about 3:00 a.m. when Officer Rios, in uniform, knocked on the door. Jesse let him in, and he followed Valencia into the bedroom. Once in the bedroom, Rios told the men to resume their sex, and he would join them. Officer Rios stripped out of his uniform and jumped into the bed, and they became a "threesome." When their sexual acts were finished, Rios refused to tell the third man his name and cautioned that the liaison must remain a secret. The relationship would not remain secret long in the Columbia gay community. Officer Rios received a dispatch call, and he told Valencia he would see him again. Officer Rios put his uniform back on and left. The predictable disclosure and tragic events were set in motion. The "secret" sexual affair unraveled because of the original arrest.

Mr. Valencia appeared in court on the "obstructing a government operation" charge on May 20, 2004, and the original summons was amended to read "obstructing a government operation by physical interference." The amended charges appeared ominous and more serious, disturbing Valencia. He pleaded not guilty, and the case was set for a pretrial conference on June 28, 2004. Jesse Valencia would be dead before that pretrial conference occurred. Leaving the courtroom, Valencia was having serious doubts about his relationship with a cop he barely knew. Valencia told friends he was concerned by the relationship with his arresting officer and a new lover. He was going to break it off. Valencia revealed he did not know if his new sex partner was married; Rios would not directly answer the question when asked. Jesse promised his friends if the officer was married, he was going to break off the relationship, "Because if he's married, I don't want to be involved in a relationship with a married man."

Valencia was disturbed by the charges he faced and determined to have them dropped, or he would tell the police chief his officer's dirty secret. Valencia vowed to present this ultimatum to Rios the next time they met. Officer Steven Rios, trapped in the web he wove, decided that murder was his way out.

Jesse Valencia's battered and mutilated body was found at about 2:00 p.m. on June 5, 2004, between two houses, several blocks from his residence. It was a brutal crime scene of up close, personal, and vicious murder. The police speculated that someone he knew killed Valencia. Valencia was lying on his back in an awkward position with his throat slit and flies buzzing around the open wound. He had been there for several hours. Dried blood ran down his neck and over his shoulders. Blood had pooled under his upper body. His body was bagged, tagged, and transported to the medical examiner's office for evidence collection and autopsy.

The autopsy revealed the deep neck wound severed Mr. Valencia's jugular veins and muscles on the side of his neck and nicked his spine, an indication of rage by his slayer. He was nearly decapitated. The nature of the wound and the body's location indicated Jesse Valencia was unconscious and lying down when his throat was cut. The wound suggested to the medical examiner that the weapon was a serrated knife. Additional wounds on the body revealed Valencia was severely beaten before he was rendered unconscious, another indication of rage and hatred by someone he knew. Valencia had an injury to his lip, contusions along his jawline, a bad bruise to his left ear, and contusions and abrasions on his arms, abdomen, hips, and knees. His eyes and larynx showed petechial hemorrhaging (pinpoint round spots on the skin as a result of bleeding). This hemorrhaging is consistent with being rendered unconscious. The absence of defensive wounds on the hands or arms buttressed the conclusion that Jesse Valencia was unconscious when his throat was viciously slashed. The investigation took an unexpected turn through a series of strange behaviors by Officer Rios.

Officer Rios reported to his shift between 6:00 and 6:30 p.m. on the day—June 5, 2004—Jesse Valencia's body was found. He approached the shift supervisor and remarked that he heard there was a murder on his beat. The sergeant said he thought the victim was a young male named Jesse Valencia. Rios said he had arrested Jesse Valencia before, and he could confirm his identity if needed. The sergeant took him up on that offer. The sergeant drove Rios to the scene, and Rios identified a photo of the body as the Jesse Valencia he arrested previously. This was strange but not an implicating development by itself. In an ironic twist to the murder, Rios, the murderer, was assigned as one of the officers protecting the crime scene of his victim as the investigation proceeded. What happened next is an incredibly reckless action by any murderer, let alone a Killer Cop who should have known better.

On June 6, 2004, two days after the murder, the police department received a Crime Stoppers Tip that Jesse Valencia was having an affair with a married Columbia PD officer. The tip was routinely disregarded by the police department, as are most phoned-in tips. Someone was trying to besmirch the Columbia PD was the conclusion. Then, Officer Rios made his reckless move. On June 8, Officer Rios approached a sergeant in his office and told him he had learned of the Crime Stoppers Tip and wanted to assure the sergeant that he was not having a sexual affair with Jesse Valencia; however, he thought the tip was about him. The stunned sergeant responded by saying no one had considered him to be the subject of the tip; however, Rios needed to talk to the investigating detectives. The sergeant left and returned with a detective working the murder. Rios was now the prime suspect. Columbia Police Officer Stephen Rios had just talked his way into prison.

Rios denied having any sexual contact with Jesse Valencia. However, the detectives had already interviewed many of Valencia's friends who gave statements about Valencia's affair with an unidentified Columbia police officer. Confronted with these statements, Rios tearfully revealed the homosexual liaisons but denied the murder. Rios claimed he was at a police "Choir Practice" (police after-shift drinking and BS session) when the murder was committed. Other evidence surfaced. DNA was found under Valencia's fingernails and on his chest, adding additional evidence of a recent sexual encounter. The DNA came from Rios. Valencia's friends revealed the police lover had given Valencia and them a false name. The detectives discovered the false name belonged to a Columbia police officer whose breast pocket nametag had been stolen. Recall that Rios had been fired from the Boone County jail for using another jailer's name in renting a storage space. Rios was now in deep trouble. The State's theory of the murder became clear.

The next step was to establish a timeline of Valencia's movements. The last person to see Jesse Valencia alive was a neighbor who saw him walking by at 3:45 a.m. on the morning of June 4, 2004, the day he was murdered. He waved at Valencia, and Jesse said he was going home to go to sleep. The man living in the apartment next to Valencia reported that about 3:00 a.m. on the night of the murder, loud bumping on the walls between the two apartments awakened him. He yelled for the noise to stop, and it did. When he got up to go to work, he noticed the door to Valencia's apartment was halfway open. It appeared to the detectives that Valencia and his assailant fought in the apartment and left in a hurry without shutting the door. The investigators concluded Valencia fled the apartment in fear and was chased by the crazed killer.

The next step in the investigation was to construct a timeline on the main suspect, Officer Rios, for the morning of the murder. Rios admitted to the affair but claimed not to have seen Valencia for six days before the murder, disputing this statement was his DNA under Valencia's fingernails and on Valencia's chest. Rios's alibi of being at the police Choir Practice when the murder occurred had to be debunked. Statements from other Columbia officers revealed that the morning of the murder, Rios and three other officers met on the Columbia PD's garage roof after their shift ended at 3:00 a.m. and began drinking and socializing. A police officer present during the Choir Practice said Rios left at approximately 4:47 a.m. (Eder & Larmer, July 20, 2008). Rios's wife, supporting his alibi, estimated that he arrived home between 5:15 a.m. and 5:25 a.m.. A short window existed between the last time the officers saw Rios and when his wife claimed he returned home, and enough to commit the murder. Investigators drove and timed the route from the garage to the murder scene and his residence. At that time of the early morning with no or little traffic, Rios could leave the other officers, murder Valencia, and return home within the timeline. A murder theory emerged and presented at trial by the State.

The State's murder theory was clear. Officer Rios, after leaving the drinking session, stopped at Valencia's apartment. The two men engaged in a heated argument with Valencia threatening to expose the relationship. Rios became enraged and began beating Valencia—the bumping noises heard by the neighbor (*Missouri v Rios*-Appellant, 2007). Valencia, to stop the assault, fled the apartment pursued by Rios. When Rios caught Valencia between the houses, he rendered Valencia unconscious using a police defensive technique known as a "unilateral vascular neck restraint" taught in the police academy. While Valencia was lying on his back on the ground Officer Rios slit his throat with a serrated knife, he was known to carry. Rios calmly left the scene and drove home.

This State's theory was presented at trial on September 1, 2004. Following a week long trial, Rios was convicted and sentenced to life imprisonment without parole plus a consecutive ten-year sentence for armed criminal action. This conviction was reversed on procedural errors. Rios was retried again in December 2008 and convicted once more (AP, December 6, 2008). He received the same punishment and is currently in prison proclaiming his innocence and asking for a third trial, claiming inadequate representation by his lawyers. No one is listening. Twenty-four people have already said he murdered Jesse Valencia.

Drew Walter Peterson, Sergeant Bolingbrook, Ill. PD: The Epitome of a Killer Cop

In 2010, Stacy Dittrich, a former police officer, and author, published a popular market nonfiction book—*Murder Behind the Badge: True Stories of COPS WHO KILL* (Dittrich, 2010). The book opened up with a chapter on Sergeant Drew Peterson and the media circus surrounding the allegations that Peterson murdered one or more of his wives. Dittrich speculated that Peterson was at the center of the most profiled murder-by-cop mystery of this century. Parts of this mystery have been solved. According to Dittrich, Peterson clowned around and announced that "No Body No Crime." He was wrong. Killer Cop Drew Peterson is serving thirty-eight years in prison for the murder of his third wife and an additional forty years for solicitation of murder and soliciting a murder for hire. The last sentence resulted from

Peterson's attempt to have the county prosecutor responsible for his murder conviction assassinated (Walberg, July 29, 2016). The following discussion relies on three primary sources: Hosey, J. (2008). *Fatal Vows: The Tragic Wives of Sergeant Drew Peterson*, Smith, C. (2010). *Cold as Ice*, and *People v. Peterson, 2012 IL APP (3d) 100514-B.*

Peterson was married four times, and each marriage was marked by abuse, serial infidelity, and threats to kill his spouses and escape punishment. He allegedly claimed because he was a cop, he knew how to commit murders and get away with them. Peterson was a serial adulterer throughout his marriages and well known in the police department as a skirt chaser. His blatant sex acts had no bounds of decency or fear of exposure. He was married to his first wife for six years until she found out he was cheating on her and divorced him. He and his second wife were married for ten years until she learned he was carrying on an affair with his soon to be third wife. The third marriage broke up because he was having sex with his eventual fourth wife. He had sex with his soon to be the fourth wife when she was a minor in the basement of his home while the third wife slept upstairs with their two children.

His first two wives are lucky. They are still alive. They divorced him and only suffered abuse, regrets, and the humiliation of his extramarital affairs. His last two wives were not so fortunate; they ended up dead or missing. The third wife "accidentally" drowned in the bathtub. The fourth wife suspiciously disappeared, creating a sensationalized reexamination of the "accidental" drowning of his third wife and sending Peterson to prison.

The investigation leading to the murder charges erupted into a social media circus. The story had all the necessary elements for media exploitation—dead wife, a missing wife, both married to the same veteran police officer. Before the media brouhaha ran its course, Peterson appeared on the Greta Van Susteren's Fox Cable News show *On the Record* twenty-nine times and twenty times on Nancy Grace's CNN Headline News. Jon Gibson on Fox, Dan Abrams on MSNBC, Matt Lauer on the Today Show, and Diane Sawyer on Good Morning America also interviewed him. Stories appeared in *Newsweek*, *Peoples Magazine*, and of course, the *National Enquirer*. The *Chicago Tribune* published an e-book of all the articles that appeared in their newspaper. Fox News paid for the world-famous Dr. William Baden to perform an autopsy that was filmed and shown on TV sans shots of the body. Three nonfiction books have been published. Sorting through the court records, media interviews, and published materials reveals a convoluted set of events.

The strange odyssey began on March 1, 2004. Forty-year-old Kathleen Savio, Peterson's third wife, was found dead in the bathtub of her home in Bolingbrook, Illinois. The house was supposedly locked, and there did not appear to be evidence of a struggle to the first investigators. There was no water in the tub, leading to the conjecture that the water had seeped out from the time of death and the discovery of the body. There was an inch-long deep gash in the back of her head; leading to the conjecture that she had fallen in the tub knocked herself unconscious, and she drowned. Contusions and bruises were found on her back and attributed to normal activity. Accidental death by drowning was the conclusion drawn by all those who witnessed the scene, including the investigators.

Cops know accidental deaths such as falling in bathrooms and drowning in a bathtub happen all too frequently. However, accidental bathtub deaths are sometimes staged homicides. Trained and experienced homicide investigators know this (personal knowledge). Trained and experienced cops who would stage a crime scene know this. Sergeant Drew Peterson knew this from the crime scene investigation courses he had taken during his twenty-seven years of police service. Court records indicated Drew Peterson was at one time a certified evidence technician. However, standard police protocol is that all deaths not attended by a physician are to be approached as a possible homicide until proven otherwise (personal knowledge). Drew Peterson and Kathleen Savio were going through a bifurcated divorce proceeding when she "drowned." The marriage was dissolved, but the two combatants were scheduled for a property division with pension and child support issues remaining—a motive for murder.

Sergeant Drew Peterson's behavior was suspicious. He became engaged to the minor, Stacy, whom he was seducing while married to his third wife. He married her while the bifurcated divorce proceeding was in progress and bought a house three blocks down from his third wife. The engagement and marriage created a public scandal, causing the police department to ask the state's attorney if the sexual relationship between a seventeen-year-old and a forty-seven-year-old police sergeant violated any sexual-abuse statutes. According to Joseph Hosey, the author of *Fatal Vows: The Tragic Wives of Sergeant Drew Peterson*, the state's attorney said Peterson was not doing anything wrong. Stacy was seventeen—the age of consent in Illinois.

Because Peterson was a sergeant with the Bolingbrook police department, the Illinois State Police (ISP) was called in to investigate the third wife's death—Kathleen Savio— to avoid any conflict of interest accusations. This was a smart move on the part of the Bolingbrook PD, but it did not prevent undue influence on the investigation. According to Carlton Smith, the author of *Cold as Ice*, the lead ISP investigator of Savio's death freely admitted that he let Peterson have fellow officers special treatment during the investigation of his third wife's death. That special treatment included letting him sit in on the interview of Peterson's alibi witness, his fourth wife, Stacy Peterson. This was the first time and only time the ISP investigator had violated this accepted police practice. Stacy was the minor Peterson was having sex with while he was married to the "accidentally" drowned third wife. Letting a third party, especially one with a close relationship, sit in on an interview of a witness is a no-no in police work unless the witness is a minor or juvenile (personal knowledge).

Furthermore, the ISP investigating officer—who would be banned from investigating crimes in the county—was not qualified to investigate homicides and was only on the scene for 15 to 20 minutes. Newspaper sources reveal this was the ISP investigator's first homicide investigation other than those involving motor vehicle accidents. Assuming the house was locked was a questionable conclusion. Court documents show that the investigator checked the outside doors to see if they locked but did not examine the basement windows or check for fingerprints (Hosey, 2008). This calls into question the conclusion that the house was locked when the body was discovered. An assailant could have come in the basement window or been in the house previously. It is possible that an assailant in the house before the murder could have exited and pushed the lock button on the doorknob when leaving. Supporting this conclusion is the finding that the double lock on the front door was not locked when neighbors made entry to the house and found the body. The outcome of this death investigation was predictable as the participants in the sham inquiry fell lockstep in line.

The pathologist who performed the autopsy concluded Savio had drowned but did not determine the manner of death—natural causes, suicide, accident, homicide, or undetermined. An inquest was held, and the coroner's jury listed the cause of death as accidental. The state investigator who processed the crime scene did not appear at the inquest. He was on vacation. His supervisor, who had not been to the scene or interviewed anyone, read from the investigator's report. After all, in the minds of those involved, the drowning was a slam-dunk accident. A police sergeant with twenty-plus years would not kill his wife. It just was not possible. No charges were filed. Savio's family vigorously opposed the lack of a complete investigation at the inquest. They based their objections on Drew Peterson's abuse and threats to kill Savio and escape prosecution. They were ignored. The ISP investigator never talked to them.

The vindicated Sergeant Drew Peterson retained his pension, financial assets and collected on his wife's life insurance policies—one that went to him for $100,000 and another for $1 million split between their two sons. Peterson went back to his normal routine until October 2007.

Drew Peterson and his fourth wife, Stacy, were going through a contentious divorce when she mysteriously disappeared. She was last seen at her home on October 28, 2007, approximately three and a half years after the "accidental" drowning of his third wife. Stacy Peterson was the alibi witness for Drew Peterson during the "accidental" drowning investigation, a dangerous liability for the former paramour. Peterson began his pattern of abuse and threats soon after they were married. Stacy told friends and relatives that

Drew had threatened her and claimed he could kill her and get away with it because he was a cop. She even told a neighbor, if she disappeared, Drew would be responsible for her disappearance. Drew was cheating on her just as he had with his other wives. Stacy learned there is a short jump from cheating with to being cheating on. In the nasty divorce, Stacy was going after his pension and other financial assets.

Stacy's disappearance was suspicious. However, Peterson was not charged with any crimes. There was no body and no proof someone was killed. However, the cops believed he was implicated in the disappearance. The dots were there, but without evidence and a body, they could not be connected. Nevertheless, the state police had another option. Go after Drew Peterson for the murder of his third wife. The case was cold, but it was not closed. This time the i's would be all dotted, and the t's would be crossed. Within two weeks of Stacy's disappearance, ISP ruled the disappearance a "potential homicide" and designated Drew Peterson a suspect. On the same day following that announcement, the county prosecutor issued a court order to exhume the body of Peterson's third wife, Kathleen Savio. Drew Peterson's secret life and public lies would be closely scrutinized.

The body was exhumed, and two autopsies were performed. According to court records, the state's forensic pathologist, Dr. Larry Blum, who performed the second autopsy for the state, reviewed the reports and photographs, and went to the Savio house and viewed the bathroom and tub in which the body was found. Following the autopsy, Dr. Blum concluded that Kathleen Savio had drowned, and her death was a homicide (Glasgow, February 21, 2008). He found from the reports that no drugs and alcohol were in her system and that none of the factors for accidental drowning or suicide were present. The pattern of injuries was not consistent with an accidental fall. Dr. Blum stated there was an absence of injuries on the body's backside that would have been present in an accidental fall. He also opined that the dry rivulets of blood on Savio's face would not have formed if there had been water in the tub when her head was bleeding. Dr. Michael Baden, a paid consultant for Fox National News, also testified as an expert witness in forensic pathology. He performed a second autopsy at the behest of Kathleen Savio's family. He opined that the death was a homicide and not an accident. In May 2009, Drew Peterson was charged with the first-degree murder of his third wife, Kathleen Savio.

Peterson's trial began on July 2012. The trial lasted six weeks. The trial was based on a combination of circumstantial evidence and hearsay testimony. There was no physical evidence or eyewitnesses to put Drew Peterson at the scene of the crime. The allowed hearsay evidence was damaging to the defendant portraying him as violent and threatening (Curry, September 2, 2012). Susan Doman, Kathleen's sister, testified Kathleen had told her

Peterson had held a knife to her throat and said he could kill her and make it look like an accident. Another witness confirmed this incident. A former boarder in the Savio basement testified Kathleen told her Peterson had broken into her house dressed in an all-black SWAT clothes and held a knife to her throat and threatened to kill her and make it look like an accident. A third witness provided the same corroborating testimony.

A pastor testified that Stacy Peterson told him a story that contradicted the alibi version she gave the police in the original investigation. According to the pastor, Savio said she woke up in the middle of the night the "accidental drowning" occurred and Drew was not in bed with her. She searched the house and could not find him. She called his cell phone and got no answer. Then sometime in the early morning hours, she saw Drew standing by the washer and dryer dressed in all black and carrying a bag. Stacy saw Drew undress and take the contents of the bag and put it all into the washer. She walked over to the washer and saw women's clothing that did not belong to her. Later Drew told her that police would want to interview her, and he spent hours telling her what to say. The following testimony was even more damaging. Drew Peterson learned a lesson from his police experience that should have taught him—a shut mouth gets in no trouble. An old saw known by defense attorneys and cops alike is, "He who doesn't talk, walks [personal knowledge]."

A friend testified that he went on a police ride-along with Peterson, who told him that his third wife was causing him trouble (Smith, 2010). Drew asked him if he knew someone who could take care of the problem for him. Peterson allegedly offered $25,000 for the murder. Peterson said if he could find someone else who would do it for less, he could keep the difference. In a later ride-along, Sergeant Peterson told him to forget about the previous conversation because his third wife was found dead in the bathtub.

In a dramatic turn in the courtroom drama, a real Perry Mason moment, the lead defense attorney over the loud objections of his fellow defense attorneys called Stacy Peterson's divorce attorney to the stand. On the stand, the divorce lawyer testified that Savio had asked if she could get more money from Peterson if she told the truth about her alibi statement. This testimony introduced the primary motivation for her murder. It was clear to the court and jury that Drew Peterson killed Kathleen Savio, and Stacy Peterson's disappearance was in all probability related to her threat to reveal his alibi as a lie and cause his financial ruin.

The state's theory presented to the jury was that Drew Peterson entered the house in an unknown manner as he had before and put Kathleen Savio in a police sleeper hold, causing unconsciousness. He then unclothed her and put her in a tub full of water, leading to her death. He then struck her in the back of the head with some instrument, probably a police baton to simulate a fall in the tub. He then returned to his home, where Stacy Peterson saw him undressing and washing his clothes and those of the woman he just murdered. The jury believed this theory after two days of deliberation.

On September 6, 2012, Drew Peterson was found guilty of Kathleen Savio's premeditated murder and sentenced to thirty-eight years. Justice was finally achieved when it was not expected. Drew Peterson is in prison, but Stacy Peterson is still missing.

LAPD Detective Stephanie Lazarus, 2009: Justice a Long Time Coming, Female Killer Cop

The Drew Peterson case and this one share similar characteristics; both investigation created a media outburst involving a love triangle, a cold murder case, and alleged preferential treatment for a Killer Cop. The present case adds a woman scorned killing for rage and jealousy. The first crime scene investigation in both cases was bungled; suspicious facts were ignored, leading to allegations of a police cover-up. In both cases, the preferential treatment was given over the vociferous objections of the victim's family. Lastly, a second Cold Case examination in each led to conviction and justice. *Justice was a Long Time Coming.* The following discussion is based on the following sources: (1) Transcription of a tape-recorded interview of Stephanie Lazurus, by [LAPD] Detective D. Jaramillo and Detective G. Stearnes, June 22, 2009; (2) M. Mcgough, M. (June 2011). The Lazarus File. *Atlantic*; (3) Mikulan, S. (September 1, 2012). In Plain Sight. *LAMagazine*; and, *California Vs. Stephanie Lazarus.* Los Angeles County Superior Court. Case No: HA357423. APPELLANT'S OPENING BRIEF).

On February 24, 1986, Sherri Rasmussen, a bride of three months, was found brutally murdered. Her husband, John Ruetten, found her body in the couple's posh three-story townhouse in Van Nuys, California. The townhouse had three levels with two bedrooms on the third level, a kitchen and dining room on the second; according to the crime scene description, the entrance to the two-car garage was on this level. The lowest level contained the living room and entrance foyer. Therefore, there were two entrances to the townhouse—first and second levels. According to court documents, Ruetten left the townhouse for work and returned each time using the second-level entrance. On this date, he did not activate the security alarm on leaving, as was his routine. There is no evidence that he locked this door or the front door. As a result, the front door and the garage door may have been unlocked and the alarm off, allowing for entry without the wife's knowledge who was in bed on the third level when he left for work. Sherrie Rasmussen was supposed to be at work but called in for a sick day that morning. Ruetten was supposedly the only person that knew Sherrie was at home alone.

Two possible scenarios, separated by twenty-three years, were used to explain the entry and murder of Sherrie. The first scenario by the LAPD detectives investigating the murder theorized that one or more burglars entered the unlocked front door and were ransacking the house when Sherrie Rasmussen came down from the third level and surprised them on the second level. Stereo equipment was stacked ready to be taken away when the burglars were surprised by Sherrie. An all too common happening, homeowner alone surprises burglars and is killed. Several weeks later, two male burglars surprised a woman in her nearby townhouse. These burglar's actions fit the modus operandi of the Rasmussen burglary. Detectives opined that a vicious struggle ensued, and Sherrie ran to the first level where she was beaten and shot to death. The burglars searched Sherrie's purse, ignoring a wallet filled with cash, stealing her Marriage License?, and the keys to her car a new BMW parked in the garage. They exited the house through the door on the second level leading to the garage, taking the BMW as they fled.

Autopsy results revealed that Sherrie was shot three times in the chest; each shot was a fatal wound. One wound was a direct contact wound—an unusual wound for a surprised burglar, firing a weapon directly into the victim's chest at that close range. The crime scene was processed, including a swab of a bite mark on Sherrie's left arm. The time of death could not be determined. The forensic evidence, according to court records, included two broken fingernails, and multiple fingerprints, a bloody fingerprint and palm print on the stereo equipment, fingerprints on the banister to the garage, blood samples on the wall in the stairwell. This evidence, except for the DNA swap and blood evidence, was put in the secure LAPD evidence locker and forgotten. No suspects were identified, and no arrests made. The case went cold.

The official murder theory was unquestioned by the authorities, even though the murdered woman's family vigorously objected for twenty-three years to the original findings and suggested a good "likely" for the murder— an unnamed jilted LAPD female police officer, who had been stalking and harassing their murdered daughter. The detectives never mentioned the jilted girlfriend as a possible suspect or made any attempt to match her fingerprints to those found at the crime scene. Court records indicate the husband told the detectives about the jilted LAPD girlfriend officer. Ruetten disclosed that the jilted lover made threatening visits to the home and the deceased woman's workplace. Why she was not interviewed is a curious omission by experienced homicide investigators. Experienced homicide detectives would have pursued this possible lead. Jilted lovers are always on their checklist of possible subjects right below the husband. There were other curious actions by LAPD members.

The police department up to the chief of police met the murdered girl's family's repeated requests for a complete investigation with scorn and indifference. Why? Could it be that no member of the LAPD was going to recognize that a female LAPD officer was the possible murderer? The question arose again in 2004 when Cold Case Homicide Detectives who were routinely examining unsolved murders surreptitiously reexamined the Rasmussen case.

Cold Case detectives uncovered some shocking details. Their first startling discovery, the evidence gathered at the Rasmussen crime scene, was missing. The forensic evidence that was taken at the original crime scene—hair, fiber, and blood samples, mysteriously disappeared in 1996. According to Alexander (2011), an LAPD detective, giving a false name, appeared at the property room and checked out all the forensic evidence for the Rasmussen case and never returned it. However, one piece of evidence was still available. The deep bite, almost to the bone, on Sherrie Rasmussen's arm, left a DNA sample. The DNA evidence was safe because it was stored in the coroner's freezer, not the police evidence locker, all those years. The DNA testing "blew up" and discredited the original investigation scenario—the DNA came from a woman. The murder was a woman-on-woman murder and not the result of surprised male burglars.

Then, the Cold Case detectives found a "Nuclear Bomb" in the *Murder Book* a three-ringed loose-leaf binder containing the case file is kept on all LAPD murders. The *Murder Book* is necessary because murder cases take time, and detectives retire or die with cases unsolved. The discovery sent seismic waves throughout the law enforcement community. An entry in the *Murder Book* with the source unidentified, a violation of LAPD police procedure, read, "Verified S. Lazarus is the former girlfriend. P.O." The quizzical detectives searched for answers. There was nothing in the *Murder Book* about girlfriends, and what did "P.O." mean? Did it mean parole officer or? Their thoughts ran together stopping at—did it mean police officer? That could not be it the stunned detectives thought, but they had to check. Lazarus is not a common last name, and searching the files of LAPD officers, they found one. Stephanie Lazarus, Detective II assigned to the Commercial Crimes Division, Art Theft Detail. She worked in the office right across the hall from them. Now, what the hell do you, they asked themselves? It they accuse her and are wrong, they will have sullied her reputation, and they will all be walking a lonely beat if they are not fired. If they do nothing, she escapes punishment for murder and remains a police officer. They moved on with the investigation, anticipating the worst possible outcome—a Killer Cop. Their next move was necessary and predictable.

The lead investigator knew they were looking into the possibility of an LAPD officer murdering without notifying anyone at the head shed in Parker Center, a serious breach of department protocol and a firing offense. He decided to kick it upstairs. He called his commanding officer at home and broke the news, "Boss, one of our detectives may have committed one of our murders [Cold Case murder]." After a stunned silence, the response was, "What evidence do you have to support that statement?" The investigator provided the supporting evidence, and the commander replied, "Keep the investigation going. I will notify the chief, and you do not tell anyone what is going on without telling me. Keep this shit quiet?" There was one way of determining if Stephanie Lazarus, LAPD Detective II, was the killer. Compare her DNA to the sample.

LAPD Police Chief William Bratton, a well-known police reformer, permitted a deep cover surveillance team out of headquarters to follow Lazarus until they collected a DNA sample. One day Lazarus, after finishing her lunch in a mall food court, threw away her drink cup and straw, leaving a sample of her saliva. The surveillance team immediately retrieved the discarded items. The cup and straw were taken immediately to the crime lab, bypassing the evidence locker. Usually, DNA testing takes days or weeks; however, the results were back in 24 hours, with the statement every investigator hopes for, "You have a match." The match was such that no other person on earth could match the DNA profile but Stephanie Lazarus. Lazarus's upcoming arrest presented dangerous problems and had to be handled carefully.

Lazarus was married to an LAPD officer and had a young daughter; therefore, Chief Bratton said the arrest should not be made at her home but downtown at her worksite in Parker Center. The possibility of an armed shootout and traumatic effects on the child was just too high. A safe and straightforward plan was devised. June 5, 2009, about eight o'clock a detective from the Cold Case squad walked across the hall and approached Detective Lazarus and said, "Hi, we have a subject down in the interview room who says he has information on some art thefts. Will you come down and talk to him?" "Sure, let me get my notepad and follow you down there?" The interview room is in the basement inside the jail, so both detectives had to surrender their weapons to enter. No shootout now.

Inside the interview room were two special investigation officers and no suspect. After several moments of benign chitchat, the special investigators began asking the stunned Art Theft detective questions about the murder of Sherrie Rasmussen and Lazarus's relationship with the deceased woman's husband. Lazarus became increasingly agitated about the questions, and then the detectives asked if she would provide a DNA sample. She said it is time for me to get a lawyer and stood up to leave. As she approached the exit door, she was confronted by two other detectives who announced, "You are under arrest for the murder of Sherrie Rae Rasmussen." They read her the Miranda Warning. Lazarus had repeated the same procedure numerous times in her police career, but the shocked detective supposedly looked as if she could not comprehend what had just happened. The full realization of these events would sink in later when she was placed in her drab, windowless cell. That was her last day as a free person. The freedom to make good and bad decisions was over. She was handcuffed, searched, and given prisoner clothing and placed in a cell. Her bail was set at $10 million because she was a flight risk. She remained in jail until her trial.

Former LAPD Stephanie Lazarus Detective II remained in jail for two and a half years before her trial began on February 6, 2012. She sat stoic, expressionless, and impassive throughout the whole trail. It was as if she knew the outcome. The death penalty was taken off the table. She knew she would probably never get out of prison. Her lawyer would argue that the DNA sample, the primary evidence against her had degraded or been mishandled in the decades it sat in the coroner's freezer. That is possible, but she knew and the prosecutor told the jury, "DNA may degrade, but it does not turn into someone else's DNA." The evidence from fifty-one state witnesses piled up, revealing a cold calculated murder from a jealous and jilted lover who carried a badge. According to court records, the executive director of the Forensic Behavioral Services, an expert in the analysis of violent crimes—how and why they occur—testified the homicide did not occur during a burglary or attempted burglary. He opined that the initial attack occurred in the breakfast nook area. Rasmussen broke away, pursued by the attacker, and reengaged in the entryway and moved into the living room where the attacker smashed a vase to Rasmussen's head, knocking her unconscious. The perpetrator wrapped a quilt around the gun to muffle the sound and fired three shots into Rasmussen's chest. The final witness, an FBI profiler, was called on February 24, 2012. He testified that someone with police experience had staged the burglary scene and that someone was Stephanie Lazarus. The trail ended that day, the twenty-fifth anniversary of the death of Sherrie Rae Rasmussen. After a day of deliberation, the jury found Rasmussen guilty of second-degree murder.

LAPD Chief of Police Charley Beck issued a written statement expressing the sense of betrayal the department felt with the murderer being one of their own. He apologized for the long time coming for justice. On May 11, 2012, Lazarus was sentenced to twenty-five years-to-life, plus another two years for the firearms enhancement. She will die in prison.

Metropolitan DC Police Department (MPD) Richmond Phillips, 2011: Killed Mistress and "Cooked" Their Baby

The callous murders and tortures of Killer Cop serial murderers in an earlier chapter were horrifying; however, the odious behavior of Metro DC Detective Richmond Phillips, a member of the MPD's narcotics unit, is equally shocking and disturbing. Detective Richmond Phillips, a married officer—thirteen years— with a twelve-year-old daughter, killed one of his two mistresses, threw her body in the woods of a Prince George County park, and then drove her car up a hill to another location and abandoned it. Inside the abandoned car was their love child, an eleven-month old baby girl, still in her car seat. The child was left to "cook" in the 125-degree heat. *Why?* He did not want the affair to become known, and he did not want to pay child support (*Daily Mail Reporter* & AP, January 14, 2013).

Phillips and his former mistress, Wynetta Wright, were set to appear in court for a paternity hearing the day before the woman and her eleven-month old baby girl, Jaylin, disappeared. The hearing was to determine if he was the little girl's father, how much child support he would pay, and force him to pay the child's insurance. Wright's mother knew she met with Phillips the night before, but she did not return from the meeting. Supposedly, the estranged former lovers were to discuss the little girl's future. The mother reported Wynetta and Jaylin missing. The callous Phillips showed up for the meeting as if nothing happened, but the mother and child did not appear. They were dead, and he knew it.

Three days later, Wynetta's body, rapidly decomposing in the scorching mid-week heat, was found in the park's wooded area dead from a single small-caliber bullet to the head. The body's discovery prompted a feverish search for Wynetta's missing car and the baby. The missing car was found a mile away in an apartment complex parking lot. The police attached a GPS device and watched it for several hours, not knowing the baby's body was inside. After waiting for someone to come to the car, a police officer made a grisly discovery (Zapotsky, January 15, 2013). The baby was in the car seat of the abandoned car. She was dead, with no visible signs of trauma, although it was clear that blood had come from her nose. The autopsy would reveal what the investigating officer had feared. Baby Jaylin "cooked" to death from the extreme heat in the car—a horrible, slow death. The crying police officers at the scene of this unspeakable tragedy believed the tinted car windows made it impossible for anyone passing by to see the distressed child as she slowly succumbed to the heat. The officer who found the little girl's body cried on the stand describing his terrible discovery.

The police department moved quickly and arrested Detective Phillips for first-degree murder. It did not take the abilities of Sherlock Holmes to identify Phillips as a suspect. He bungled the initial interview. During the initial interview, Richmond Phillips, a member of the department since 2003, lied his way into prison. His answers to the investigator's questions revealed that his eight years of police work taught him nothing—he should have lawyered up, or the investigators considering him to be a suspect surprised him.

At first, Phillips told the Prince George detective looking for the missing mistress and baby that he had not spoken to Wynetta in a year. When confronted with phone records revealing at least forty calls, he admitted they sent text messages, but he had not met at any time. Phillips was not prepared for what came next. The park had surveillance cameras. The officer showed the tapes to Phillip's and asked, "Is that you sitting next to Wynetta on the bench? The stunned Phillips replied after several seconds, "Yeah, but I left her there on the bench and drove off" (Zapotsky, January 15, 2013).

The Prince George County District Attorney in her opening statement said, "He [Richmond Phillips] was either going to talk her [Wynetta Wright] out of the paternity suit, or he was going to kill her" and she added, "he allowed Jaylin [the eleven-month baby] to cook in that car" (Zapotsky, Jan 15, 2013). Wynetta was shot with a small .22 caliber bullet, but the weapon was never found. Another mistress, an administrative assistant for the MPD who did not know the philandering Phillips was married, testified at trial. She said she saw a "small caliber" gun strapped to Phillips's left ankle when she was naked with him in a hotel room (Crimesider Staff, January 16, 2013). Phillip's wife testified that the night of the murder, he did not come home until the next morning. She tried to call him thirty-five to forty times without success. Phillips's DNA was found in Wynette's car, and several witnesses testified that Philips had told them he was going to meet with Wynetta "to work this thing out." The defense admitted Phillips met with Wynetta, but he did not kill her or abandon the baby. He, they also admitted, was a liar and adulterer, but that did not make him a murderer. The jury was not sympathetic to the defense arguments. The jury deliberated for two hours and found Richmond Phillips guilty of two counts of first-degree murder.

CONCLUSION

The incidents discussed are illustrative, not exhaustive, examples of *Officer Domestic Violence Perpetrated Homicides—Killer Cops*. The examples are U.S. Killer Cops, even though the author knows Killer Cops exist in other countries. For example, a police sergeant from the UK's Greater Manchester Police Force has been charged with the murder of his wife, a detective with the same police force (Jones, October 12, 2017). There are other examples of Killer Cops from the UK and other countries, but that topic is beyond the scope of this book. The author will address that issue—Killer Cops worldwide—in a subsequent book. However, there are a number of U.S. officer caused domestic violence homicides not included in this chapter such as a Mansfield, Ohio officer who killed his teenage "police groupie" lover because she was pregnant with his child, and she was going to reveal it; a Charleston, South Carolina officer who molested his stepdaughter and then killed his wife.

He has been on the run for fifteen years. A Florida deputy sheriff killed his wife and her lover, who was also a police officer, and there is a Texas police sitting on death row for the contract murder of his wife during a contentious custody battle. A Baltimore police officer killed his former girlfriend and her new boyfriend—a Baltimore firefighter-before committing suicide. There are numerous murder-suicides where police officers killed their spouses and then committed suicides.

The examples presented were chosen to show that Killer Cops, who commit murders, come from all parts of the county and size of the department. Killer Cops and their victims are males, females, and the same sex. They are a small minority of police officers. The LAPD case is noteworthy because it again shows the value of DNA analysis. Technological assists have impacted policework immensely. However, Killer Cops are a real problem in police work and deserve more attention from the scholarly and professional community.

SOURCES

Alexander, P. (2011). *Murdered.* New York: Rosetta Books.

AP. (December 6, 2008). Retrial: Married Mizzou cop convicted for murder of lover. *Associated Press.*

Crimesider Staff. (January 16, 2013). Richmond Phillips trial: Second mistress testifies in murder trial for D.C. cop accused in 2 deaths. *CBS News.*

Curry, C. (September 7, 2012). Drew Peterson Jury says hearsay evidence convinced them to convict. *ABC News.*

Daily Mail Reporter & AP. (January 14, 2013). Cop shot dead mistress and left their baby to die in boiling car—because he didn't want to pay child support. *Daily Mail.*

Dittrich, S. (2010). *Murder Behind the Badge: True Stories of Cops Who Kill.* Amherst, New York: Prometheus.

Eder, A. & Larmer, S. (July 20, 2008). Police seize items from Rios' home. *Columbia Missourian.*

Fielder, D. (2012). *Lady Killer.* New York: Berkeley Publishing Group.

Gentile, O.F. (September 29, 2000). Agent who killed lover ends sentence. *Courant.*

Glasgow. (February 21, 2008). James W. Glasgow—States attorney of will county press release. Pathologist declares Kathleen Savio's death a homicide.

Hosey, J. (2008). *Fatal Vows: The Tragic Wives of Sergeant Drew Peterson.* Beverly Hills, CA: Phoenix Books.

Jones, A. (1992). *FBI Killer.* New York: Pinnacle Books.

Jones, H. (October 2, 2017). Police sergeant charged with murder of his detective wife. *The Guardian.*

Missouri v. Rios—Appellant. Case No. WD65708. 27/4/2007. Missouri Court of Appeals Western District.

People v. Peterson, 2012 IL APP (3d) 100514-B.

Piel, C. & Piel, S.C. (November 2009). He almost got away with murder. *Prosecutor.* 39(6): 28–40.

Ryan, H. (May 23, 2005). Police officer convicted of killing his gay lover. *Court TV.*

Sharkey, J. (1993 & 2017). *Above Suspicion.* New York: Open Road.

Smith, C. (2010). *Cold as Ice.* New York: St. Martins.

Walberg, M. (July 29, 2016). Drew Peterson gets 40 years for plot to kill prosecutor. *Chicago Tribune.*

Wilbanks, W. (2000). *True Heroines: Police Women Killed in the Line of Duty Throughout the United States 1916–1999.* Paducah, KY: Turner Publishing CO.

Zapotski, M. (January 15, 2013). Officer who found dead girl testifies in murder trial. *The Washington Post.*

Chapter 11

Rogue Killer Cops

Two Categories

INTRODUCTION

Barker's *Continuum of Officers in Corrupt Police Departments* identified Rouge Police Officers at the far end of a deviant police officers scale. Rogue police officers were defined as a "[police officer] who is thoroughly corrupt and considered an aberration even by *meat-eaters* [officers who seek out opportunities for corruption]" (Barker, 2011: 87). A modified and expanded Rouge Police Officer category includes two categories of LEO Killer Cops: (1) LEOs who murder because of ties to organized crime or (2) cops who murder with premeditated intent under the circumstances outside the range of deviant behaviors of even corrupt or criminal cops (Barker, 2018). The latter category is a "bad to the bone" Killer Cop's pattern of behavior.

Rogue Killer Cops with Ties to Organized Crime

Barker (2011) supplied two examples of *Rouge Killer Cops with ties to organized criminal activities* in the earlier publication. The first example was a New Orleans PD officer Len Davis, who is currently on Louisiana's death row for arranging the murder of a woman who filed a brutality complaint against him (Barker, 2011: 87). The murder came as a direct result of Davis's ties to organized crime groups. Davis operated a police drug trafficking protection ring and feared that the complaint would expose his organized criminal activities. The second example was a Harlan County, Kentucky Deputy Sheriff and drug trafficker who pleaded guilty to facilitating the murder of a man running for sheriff. The deputy feared that the sheriff candidate would fire him if elected because of his involvement in criminal behavior.

Barker (2011, 2018) alluded to police officers who are criminals and join police departments to continue their criminal behavior, singularly or in an organized network of other police criminals—police gang. Murder is always a possibility in these organized criminal activities. An example of this behavior was an NYPD officer who was a member of a violent, including murder, gang that robbed drug dealers in Queens, Manhattan, and Philadelphia. The NYPD officer supplied the gang with NYPD raid jackets, bulletproof vests, badges, and guns. He participated in one hundred robberies, and an unknown number of murders.

Bad to the Bone Rogue Killer Cops

In addition to Rogue Killer Cops *with ties to criminal organizations*, there are Rogue Killer Cops who commit "outlandish" murders not related to sexual motivations, domestic partnerships, or known ties to criminal organizations— Bad to the Bone Rogue Killer Cops. The "typical" murder motives of Killer Cops in this category are greed, anger, jealousy, revenge, or money. Although some may argue that the following example should be included in domestic partnership homicides, it is included here because it is the murder of an adulterer, not the domestic partner.

A U.S. Border agent suspecting that his wife was engaged in an affair tied her up in their Corpus Christy, Texas home, and forced her to give the name of her lover (AP, January 3, 2014). He then drove 160 miles to the southern Texas Gulf Coast near the town of Hondo. He killed the lover and then led Medina County Sheriff's deputies on a wild chase until they forced him off the road. He pleaded guilty to murder and was sentenced to thirty years in prison. A second example of Rouge Killer Cops who commit premeditated murders not related to organized crime is Michael Harold Chapel currently serving life in prison in Georgia.

The Chapel information comes from the transcript of his appeal to the Georgia Supreme Court (*Chapel v. the State, 1998*). The facts, as outlined in the court documents, are as follows. On April 3, 1993, a fifty-three-year-old woman reported a burglary to the Gwinnett County Georgia police, and Officer Michael H. Chapel answered the call. The woman who lived in a trailer with her son said that she had $14,000 in cash hidden in a secret place, and someone had stolen $7,000. The officer said he suspected her son, who had previously stolen $300 from her. The woman agreed and declined to press charges. According to court documents, the officer who was in serious financial difficulty and facing IRS difficulty decided to rob the woman of the remaining money. The lady told several friends that the officer was going to help her recover her money. She went on to say that he wanted to meet with her and compare the serial numbers of bills in his possession to the remaining money. The meeting took place on April 25, 1993, outside a muffler shop. Court testimony revealed that Chapel shot the woman twice and took the remaining money.

The evidence against Chapel was circumstantial but damning. DNA evidence showed that blood in Chapel's police vehicle matched the slain women. Eyewitnesses saw Chapel riding in the area the night and time of the murder. Chapel was seen spending $100 bills, and his wife had a lot of money. As to motive, Chapel was facing an IRS audit with the potential of $4,000 additional tax liability. A jury found him guilty of malice murder, armed robbery, and possession of a firearm in the commission of a felony and sentenced him to life imprisonment. His appeal was not successful.

ROGUE KILLER COPS WITH TIES TO ORGANIZED CRIME

Cops banding together for criminal behavior is a historical phenomenon that is all too common in the United States (Barker, 2011). Police criminal gangs have been exposed in small towns and large cities, like Chicago, Los Angeles, Baltimore, Miami, New Orleans, and New York City for years (Barker, 2011). Police adult criminal gangs have engaged in burglaries, robberies, drug trafficking, and other organized crime activities (Barker, 2020). In 1999, thirty West New York officers were charged with organized drug trafficking and other crimes. In court, the West New York chief of police admitted that the department was a racketeering gang that was involved in accepting bribes and kickbacks to protect prostitutes and illegal gambling operations (Anon, 1999). Barker (2011) cited numerous examples of police gangs engaged in organized criminal behavior. In 2010, three Prince George County, Maryland officers and six civilians were charged with corruption, drug trafficking, and firearms violations. The next year two Laredo, Texas police officers were charged with escorting drug traffickers through the city. Killer Cops, with ties to criminal groups or criminal enterprises use their police powers to conduct, support, facilitate, and protect criminal behavior.

In recent years, police criminal gangs have become more "common" as groups of "rotten apples" come together in gangs to commit burglaries, robberies, and traffic in drugs, often using violence, including murder, to effect or facilitate their crimes. The New York City Knapp Commission and its revelations of "meat eaters"—aggressive, premeditated criminals in blue—demonstrated that there is no limit to the crimes criminal cops will commit. William S. Phillips, a star witness of the Knapp Commission, was convicted of murdering a witness and served thirty-two years in prison. At the time, Phillips was the epitome of a Killer Cop with ties to criminal groups or criminal enterprises. Following the findings of the Mollen Commission of the NYPD in the early 1990s, then NYPD Police Commissioner, William Bratton, is quoted as saying, "we have criminals in blue uniforms who are more vicious than some of the criminals they are supposedly policing." He was alluding to police criminals as individuals and groups. The Mollen commission concluded that "the corrupt acts were the result of small groups of rotten apples and not systematic corruption within the department" (Mollen Committee, 1994). Among the criminal police, groups are Killer Cops acting as enforcers or protectors for criminal enterprises, and this is an American historical tradition.

Selected Examples of Killer Cops with Ties to Organized Crime

NYPD Lieutenant Charles Becker-1912—Lt. Becker was the first-known American police officer to be executed for an on-duty murder in support of organized crime activities (Root, 1961; Cohen, 2006; Dash, 2007). Although some claim Becker was wrongly arrested, tried, and convicted, the available evidence discounts this theory. Becker was the first of several police officers to be called the most corrupt NYC police officer in history. This was an interesting appellation at a time when police corruption was the norm for American urban police agencies. He did not act alone. Becker in conjunction with politicians and gangsters oversaw a police protection ring in the city's notorious Tenderloin District. A victim of his extortion racket, Herman "Beansie" Rosenthal went to the newspapers and publicly exposed Becker. Four members of the Jewish Lennox Avenue shot Rosenthal to death in a public place—Hotel Metropole. Becker's bagman who collected the "tribute" from the gamblers and other gangsters gave Becker up and identified the four gunmen. All five defendants were arrested, tried, convicted, and executed.

Phenix City, Alabama Chief Deputy Albert Fuller, 1954—As a teenager growing up in Alabama, I was aware of what the then secretary of war called the "wickedest city in America." However, most Alabamians just called Phenix City, Alabama's "Sin City." I recall the day when the Alabama State attorney-elect Albert Patterson was murdered in 1954. Years later, I would come to know his son James Patterson as Governor Patterson. I would also come to know others who were there when the assassination occurred or who were involved in the investigation, arrest, trial, and conviction of the Killer Cop, Chief Deputy Albert Fuller. The backstory of this murder is still a black mark in Alabama history.

The sordid history of "Sin City" Alabama is one of crime, police corruption, organized crime, and murder (Grady, 2003; Mosely, December 10, 2005; Barnes, 2012). For the first half of the twentieth century, Phenix City,

Alabama, was the home of organized crime in the form of gambling, prostitution, bootlegging, drugs, white slavery, theft, and murder supported and protected by the "good citizens" and the police. There was even a black market baby adoption racket. The local police, the sheriff, judges, and the county prosecutor shared the protection graft.

The city located on the banks of the Chattahoochee River separating Alabama and Georgia had been the pit of corruption and "sin" for decades. During World War I, Phenix City had the nation's highest venereal disease rate. In 1918, the U.S. government built Fort Benning Army just across the river in Georgia and increased the opportunities for sin and corruption. During Prohibition, "Sin City" was a mecca for illegal booze. When the depression occurred, and the city fathers faced bankruptcy, the solution was to authorize gambling illegally and collect revenue by licensing the liquor, gambling, and prostitution houses. Raids were conducted to resemble a semblance of control; however, the gangsters were notified in advance. It was in this sordid atmosphere that a local "betterment" society decided to run a candidate for statewide office to clean up the city and the county. The person chosen to run for State Attorney General was a local attorney Albert Patterson.

Albert Patterson ran on a campaign to clean up Phenix City and break the hold of the gangsters. The gangsters decided to prevent the gambling and vice cleanup by murdering Albert Patterson. His murder had the opposite effect. The governor declared martial law and sent the National Guard to Phenix City. The Colonel in charge of the Alabama National Guard unit sent in to clean the city up was a Birmingham, Alabama Police Captain. That same captain would swear me in as a BPD officer eleven years later. The National Guard raided the gambling and vice dens and ousted many corrupt officials, including the police chief and the sheriff. Three men were indicted, but only Chief Deputy Albert Fuller was tried and convicted of the murder of Albert Patterson. He was sentenced to life in prison but only served ten years. Albert Fuller was the first-known Alabama Killer Cop in modern Alabama history; however, he was not the only one (personal knowledge).

NYPD DETECTIVES LOUIS EPPOLITO AND STEVEN CARACAPA, THE 1980S TO EARLY 1990S: MAFIA COPS

For over a decade, these two Killer Cops, known as the Mafia Cops, acted as agents of the New York Mafia crime families and murdered at least nine people. In 2009, the two Killer Cops with a combined forty-four years on the NYPD were found guilty of participating in eight murders, two attempted murders and one murder conspiracy, witness tampering, witness retaliation, obstruction of justice, money laundering, and drug charges (Stephens, March

6, 2009). They were sentenced to life in prison without parole. Court testimony revealed that the Mafia paid them $4,000 a month. They were paid an additional $65, 000 by a Mafia crime boss to kill another mobster during a phony traffic stop.

WILLOW SPRINGS, ILLINOIS PD
CHIEF MICHAEL CORBITT, 1989

The bizarre story of Killer Cop Michael Corbitt is described in a popular market book. The New York Times bestseller, Michael Corbitt with Sam Giancana, *Double Deal: The Inside Story of Murder, Unbridled Corruption, and the Cop Who Was a Mobster*, is Corbitt's memoir written with the son of the Chicago Outfit mobster who recruited him into policework and the life of crime. As a young man, Corbitt did favors for members of the Chicago Outfit, such as storing hijacked trucks in a gas station he bought with Outfit money (Flood & McGough, October 20, 1997; Corbitt & Giancana, 2003). The Chicago crime boss Sam Giancana offered him a police officer's position in Willow Spring, Illinois. After he was sworn in, Giancana instructed him to remember who his friends were. At the time, Willow Springs was entirely under the control of the Outfit. Corbittt soon became the bagman for the Outfit. He was soon collecting a "street tax" from other criminals and vice operators in the city and passing along the money to the gangsters. In 1982, he and two other gangsters engaged in a hit for hire. They were tried and convicted of murder, and he was sentenced to twenty years in prison and died from lung cancer in 2004.

FBI SPECIAL AGENT PAUL RICO, BOSTON, 1980S

It is alleged that Rico acted as an associate of the notorious Boston Winter Hill Gang run by James "Whitey" Bulger and Stephen "The Riflemen" Flemmi. He was indicted for a 1981 murder in 2003 but died before trial. In 2003, Rico was indicted for the 1981 murder of World Jai Alai owner Roger Wheeler in Oklahoma (Murphy, January 18, 2004). At the time of the murder, the retired FBI agent was head of security for the World Jai Alai organization. The allegations are that the Boston Winter Hill run by FBI informants, "Whitey" Bulger and Stephen "The Rifleman" Flemmi, was skimming money from World Jai Lai. According to the two gangsters charged with the slaying, Bulger and Flemmi ordered the murder, and Rico facilitated the homicide. There was no trial to settle the allegations. Rico died two days after pleading not guilty. This was the first time an FBI agent had been charged with conspiracy to commit murder; however, there was evidence to support the allegations. There was also another FBI agent connected to the murder of Roger Wheeler. Moreover, he was alive and well.

FBI Special Agent Joseph John Connolly: Member of the Gang

At his 2009 murder trial in Miami, the prosecutor described Connolly as "just another member of the gang" (Anon, September 15, 2008, see also Lehr & O'Neill, 2000; Ranalli, 2001). The gang was the Boston Winter Hill Gang run by James "Whitey" Bulger and Stephen "The Riflemen" Flemmi. Before his 2009 murder trial, Connolly was charged with alerting Bulger and Flemmi to on-going investigations and accepting bribes. He was convicted of these and other racketeering offenses in 2002 and sentenced to ten years in prison. The 2009 murder trial in Miami accused Connolly of alerting the Boston gangsters that a Miami businessman was acting as a government informer in the Oklahoma murder that Agent Paul Rico was charged with. Connolly was convicted and sentenced to forty years in prison.

LEO Double Agent: DEA Agent and Member of a Violent Drug Trafficking Agent, 2018

For eight years, DEA Agent Fernando Gomez, former U.S. Marine, worked for the Evanston, Illinois Police Department (IPD). His last IPD assignment was an assignment to the tactical unit, assisting with drug and gang investigations (Meisner & Kellman, December 12, 2018). It is alleged in a federal indictment that during his time as an IPD member, he obtained firearms from drug dealers and gave them to Jose Martinez, the founder and leader of the Organizacion de Narcotraficntes Unidos—United Organization of Drug Traffickers. The United Organization of Drug Traffickers was a gang of drug traffickers based in Puerto Rico. The criminal organization was responsible for importing large shipments of cocaine into New York and Puerto Rico from the Dominican Republic. The gang was violent and committed at least eight murders since 2005.

It is alleged that his friend, the leader of the drug trafficking gang, persuaded Gomez to leave the police department and become a DEA—Drug Enforcement Administration—agent to make the drug cartel "unstoppable" (Meadows, December 20, 2018). The Drug Trafficking Organization (DTO) was successful until the federal indictment was unsealed in Chicago in 2018. Gomez and the leader of the United Organization of Drug Traffickers and numerous members are awaiting trial in New York. At this time, we do not know how many murders the former DEA Killer Cop was involved in or facilitated.

BAD TO THE BONE ROGUE KILLER COPS

As stated, in addition to Rogue Killer Cops *with ties to criminal organizations*, there are *Bad to the Bone Rogue Killer Cops* who commit "outlandish" murders not related to sexual motivations, domestic partnerships, or known ties to criminal organizations. The "typical" murder motives in this category are greed, anger, jealousy, revenge, or money. We gave several examples: A U.S. Border Agent cuckold who killed his wife's lover. A second example was a Georgia Killer Cops who is serving life in prison for murdering an elderly woman during a robbery. There are numerous other examples of U.S. Bad to the Bone Killer Cops dating back to LEOs in the settling of the West; however, we will provide selected illustrative, not exhaustive examples from the 1990s forward.

Selected Examples of Bad to the Bone Killer Cops

LAPD William Leasure, 1991

Leasure is a convicted murderer who has the dubious honor of being known as the most corrupt LAPD police officer in LAPD history. According to court testimony, Leasure spent his seventeen years as an LAPD officer while engaged in criminal activities that varied from running a multi-million dollar yacht theft ring to arranging and participating in three contact murders (Humes, October 27, 1991). Complicating the arrest and charges against Leasure was the work status of his wife. She was a Los Angeles assistant city attorney and had once headed up the elite criminal prosecution. Following the execution of search warrants, the immense amount of stolen property convinced the authorities that she had to be aware of her husband's yacht thefts (Harris, December 27, 1987). She was fired but never charged.

Following Leasure's arrest on the yacht theft ring charges, a hitman came forward and said he was the triggerman for three murders arranged by Leasure. He said that Leasure was the wheelman in the murders. The alleged hitman was given immunity for testifying against Leasure. The first trial ended in a mistrial after the jury deadlocked. Leasure pleaded no contest to two counts of second-degree murder before his second trial began. His charges were reduced from first-degree murder, and the felony charges for yacht theft, car theft, and insurance fraud were dismissed (Serrano, November 2, 1991). He received two 15 years to life sentences.

Harris County, Texas Deputy Sheriff Joseph K. McGowen, 1992

In 2016, former Harris County deputy sheriff Joseph McGowen, who was described by the prosecutor as a "rogue cop," was convicted for the second time for the murder of a woman in 1992. He was sentenced to twenty years in prison (Lezon, August 10, 2016). An earlier 1994 conviction was overturned because the presiding judge did not allow McGowen's attorney to make an opening sentence. McGowen had arrested the victim's son before the murder, and she claimed that his arrest occurred because she had resisted his sexual advances. McGowen patrolled the area she lived in and had made numerous stops and made sexual advances. She rebuffed them. The victim had complained to friends and a captain with the sheriff's department, who advised her to file a formal complaint—she did not. McGowen had the known reputation in the sheriff's department as a skirt chaser, often bragging about his on-duty sexual contacts. The "rogue cop's" questionable background and complaints in two previous police agencies should have precluded his hiring for a law enforcement position.

The facts as reported in court testimony are that on August 25, 1992, at or around midnight, Susan White a forty-two-year-old mother of a fifteen-year-old son, was alone in her residence. She was awakened by three Harris County Texas deputies banging on doors and windows demanding entrance. The deputies were executing a "fictitious" felony retaliation arrest warrant on White for threatening a police informant related to the arrest of her son. The U.S. Fifth Circuit Court of Appeals would later say that Deputy McGowen had embellished "White's statements [threats] to the point of fabrication" (*Jason Aguillard v. Joseph K. McGown; et al.*). Instead of letting the officers in, White called 911 and relayed the following:

Operator: 9-1-1 County: What's your emergency?
White: There's a (unintelligible) here at my door. I've filed several complaints with him for sexual harassment and I need some help immediately . . . So you can get McGowan away from my house. Get McGowan away from my house!

Source: McVicker, January 12, 1995.

White's fears became real as McGowen got permission from an on-duty sergeant to break into her house. He and the other deputies entered the house and according to court testimony McGowen entered White's bedroom while she was on the phone with 911. According to forensic reconstruction, White turned her head, and the first bullet fired by McGowen struck her in the nose and lodged in the headboard. As she fell back across the bed, she was struck in the chest by a second bullet. A third bullet entered the back of her right arm, traveled through her arm, and then entered her chest (McVicker, January 12, 1995). Deputy McGowen was the only officer in the room at the time of the shooting. He claimed that White had a gun in her right hand, pointed it at him, and would not drop it. Court testimony revealed that Susan White was left-handed. A twenty-five automatic was found on the bed, but

White's fingerprints were not on the gun. According to one source, the most damning testimony came from an unexpected source—fellow police officers (McVicker, January 12, 1995). Numerous officers he worked with in several police departments gave unsolicited condemning testimony in contradiction to the "supposed" blue wall of silence. One officer who had worked with McGowen told the grand jury that "This is the first time I ever had fear of reprisal for my testimony. I think the boy's crazy. He's very much capable of retaliating against witnesses . . . go out there and look at the poor woman who's dead and tell me you don't think he's dangerous to witnesses. If he'd kill her, he'd kill me" (McVicker, January 12, 1995). One former police sergeant testified that McGowen was always a problem and added that he was an asshole. In sum, his fellow officers considered him a rogue officer capable of murder. A conclusion shared by the two juries that convicted him of murder.

Reginald Jones: Washington, D.C., Police Officer, 2011

In 2011, a Washington, D.C., police officer, Reginald Jones, was sentenced to fifteen years in prison for a 2009 murder that occurred during his involvement in an attempted robbery of a drug dealer (Alexander, October 21, 2011). The on-duty officer was a six-year police veteran when he agreed to park his police vehicle in a manner to scare away witnesses as five other men robbed the drug dealer. The victim resisted and tried to fight off the robbers. The victim's girlfriend ran to the marked police car, and Jones sped off. During the struggle, one of the robbers accidentally shot and killed another robber. The Rogue Killer Cop pleaded guilty to second-degree murder and conspiracy to commit robbery (Alexander, October 21, 2011).

New Orleans PD: Antoinette Frank: Rogue Killer Cop Poster Child

Considered the evilest female Killer Cop, New Orleans PD Officer Antoinette Frank killed an off-duty cop and two others during a robbery with her gangbanger boyfriend and lover. After she was convicted of the murders and sentenced to death, the body of her missing father was found buried under her house with a bullet hole in his head. She admitted the killing but was not charged in his death. Why try her for this murder when she was already sitting on death row along with NOPD officer Len Davis another Killer Cop? Sadly, she should never have become a police officer. According to a retired ATF special agent and author, she lied several times on her employment application (Hustmyre, 2004). She did not divulge past psychiatric problems for which she received treatment. During the application process, she failed two standard personality evaluations. The psychologist who reviewed her scores gave her the lowest score possible—poor. The psychiatrist who interviewed found her unacceptable in integrity, forthrightness, and willingness to accept responsibility. He finished his evaluation by saying that she was not suitable for police work. Giving this poor evaluation, why was she hired? The answer appears to be, in part, the result of the NOPD relaxed recruitment and hiring practices in effect at the time. In the 1990s, NOPD was in the throes of a severe police officer shortage and relaxed their hiring standards in an attempt to employ more minorities. The city had been described as the Murder Capital of the United States in 1994, adding pressure to do something—relaxing employment was part of the answer.

Unintended Consequences of Relaxed Hiring Standards

Relaxing employment standards has been disastrous for several U.S. police agencies. Needing police officers and under pressure to hire minority group members, police agencies find themselves in a no-win situation. Politicians and interest groups often see increasing minority group members as the silver bullet for police-community relations problems. Increased minority group representation is a laudable goal for all police agencies, but using relaxed hiring standards to accomplish that goal often has unintended consequences. An egregious example of the debilitating effects of this hiring practice occurred in the Miami, Florida Police Department. In the early 1980s, Miami PD under pressure to hire police officers and increase minority members adopted a policy that 200 new police officers be hired immediately. The policy dictated that 8 percent of the new applicants were to come from the minority community (Barker, 2011). A combination of poor or no background checks, inadequate training, and negligent supervision led to a third of those hired being terminated. Twelve Rogue Killer Cops, known as the "River Cops" were convicted of crimes ranging from drug trafficking to murder. The investigation and court testimony would reveal that in July 1985, a gang of six Miami police officers calling themselves "The Enterprise" stormed a drug trafficking boat with 9 million dollars of cocaine on it. Six drug traffickers on the boat heard one of the officer's shout "kill them," and the men jumped overboard. Three bodies were found the next day (Miller, May 20, 2009). The following investigation led to over 200 hundred cops being arrested and 20 cops convicted of major felonies, including several Rogue Killer Cops. Many of the Rogue Killer River Cops had joined the Miami PD. to engage in drug trafficking. The disastrous unintended consequences of relaxed recruitment and hiring practices occurred in the New Orleans Police Department.

MURDER EVENTS

In 1995 Antoinette Frank, a black female New Orleans Police Department officer, walked into a Vietnamese restaurant at about 1 a.m. with an eighteen-year-old gangbanger to rob the establishment and murdered three people—an off-duty New Orleans cop working as security and two employees. Frank knew the owners distrusted banks and hid the day's proceeds in the restaurant. The evidence showed beyond a reasonable doubt that the three murders were premeditated and malicious (Sanz, October 2, 1995; Hustmyre, 2004). She and her lover—an eighth-grade dropout and small-time drug dealer—intended to murder all five people present in the restaurant. However, two of those marked for execution were able to hide in a cooler when her robbery intent became clear and before the shooting started. Frank was well-known by the victims. The off-duty police officer working as security worked out of the same district and had ridden together on patrol. On occasion, Frank worked as security in the restaurant. He had to die. Frank's gangbanger lover came up behind him and shot the officer in the back of the head and then two more times as he lay on the floor. The gangbanger took the officer's gun and then stole his wallet. The "brain dead" gangbanger, when he left the scene, used the dead officer's credit card to pay for gas almost immediately after the robbery-murder.

At the scene of the massacre, Frank forced two family members of the owners to reveal the money's hiding place. She then executed them as they were on their knees, praying and begging for their lives. When Frank left the slaughter scene, she went to a nearby police precinct and reported the robbery-murder and convinced the desk sergeant to let her have a marked police vehicle to return to the scene. The theory is that she wanted to return to the scene and murder the other witnesses. Her plans collapsed because one of the surviving witnesses had already called 911. Two plainclothes detectives were close when the call went out and arrived at the scene before she did. They were interviewing the surviving witnesses—also family members, when Frank arrived. One of the survivors identified Frank as the murderer, and she was arrested. At trial, it only took the jury 22 minutes to convict her of three counts of first-degree murder (Sanz, October 2, 1995). The next day, the jury took 45 minutes to recommend the death penalty as punishment.

Frank was the fourth NOPD member to be convicted of murder within the preceding twelve months, according to Sanz (October 2, 1995). In the period October 1994 to October 1995, thirty-one NOPD officers had been arrested for crime, including rape, homicide, and drug trafficking. Lax hiring standards, low salaries, corruption, and police violence were blamed for NOPD problems. Her accomplice was also convicted and sentenced to death. She sits on death row along with another New Orleans Police Department officer, awaiting execution.

CONCLUSIONS

The examples presented of Rogue Killer Cops are not the only ones we are aware of at this time. However, they make the point that the only way to prevent or control police-perpetrated homicides is to recognize the types that exist in the real world. Unfortunately, there is no one "silver bullet" solution to police homicides. Once more, we see that several factors are present in unjustified police-perpetrated homicides—inadequate vetting procedures, early warning systems to identify problem officers, and failure to take appropriate when known problem behaviors occur. The interactions of these factors combined with a Rouge Police Officer who believes that murder is a low-risk behavior when they carry a badge, and the result is a Rogue Killer Cop.

SOURCES

Alexander, K. (October 21, 2011). Former D.C. police officer sentenced to 15 years in '09 murder, robbery. *The Washington Post.*

Anon. (1999). Ex-chief tells of widespread police corruption. *The New York Times.*

A.P. (January 3, 2014). Border Patrol agent accused in fatal shooting. *Associated Press.*

Barker, T. (2011). *Police Ethics: Crisis in Law Enforcement.* Springfield, LL: Charles C. Thomas.

Barker, T. (2018). Killer cops: Policework's deadly secret. Paper Presented at The Annual ACJS Meeting in New Orleans—February 14–18, 2018.

Barker, T. (2019). *North American Adult Criminal Gangs.* 3rd edition. Durham, North Carolina: Carolina Academic Press.

Barnes, M.A. (2012). *The Tragedy and the Triumph of Phenix City, Alabama.* 5th Edition. Macon, Georgia: Mercer University Press.

Chapel v. the State, 1998. Supreme Court of Georgia. *CHAPEL V. THE STATE.* No. S98A0976. Decided November 16, 1998.

Cohen, S. (2006). *The Execution of Officer Becker: The Murder of a Gambler, the Trial of a Cop, and the Birth of Organized Crime.* New York: Carroll & Graff.

Corbitt, M.J. & Giancana, S. (2003). *Double Deal: The Inside Story of Murder, Unbridled Corruption, and the Cop Who Was a Mobster.* New York: Avon Books.

Dash, M. (2007). *Satan's Circus: Murder, Vice, Police Corruption, and New York's Trial of the Century.* New York: Three Rivers Press.

Flood, J.L. & McGough, J. (October 20, 1997). Jailed suburban chief reveals how he became a mobster. www.ispn.org

Grady, A. (2003). *When Good Men do Nothing: The Assassination of Albert Patterson.* Tuscaloosa, Alabama: The University of Alabama Press.

Harris, M.D. (December 27, 1987). Veteran cop, his prosecutor wife, suspects in crime spree. *UPI Archives.*

Hume, E. (October 21, 1991). Is bill leasure the most corrupt cop in L.A.? *L.A. Times.*

Hustmyre, C. (2004). *Killer with a Badge*. New York: Berkley Books.

Jason Aguillard v. Joseph K. McGowan., et al. U.S. Court of appeals for the fifth circuit. N. 97-20039.

Lehr, D. & O'Neill, G. (2000). *Black Mass: The True Story of an Unholy Alliance between the FBI and the Irish Mob*. New York: Perennial.

Lezon, D. (August 10, 2016). 'Rogue cop' gets 20 years in killing. *Houston Chronicle.*

McVicker, S. (January 12, 1995). Killer behind the badge. *Houston Press.*

Meadows, J. (December 20, 2018). Ex-Evanston cop charged with drug, gun conspiracy to remain held. *Patch.*

Meisner, J. & Kellman, J. (December 12, 2018). DEA agent in Chicago charged with conspiring to traffic guns and drug with international gang. *Chicago Tribune.*

Mollen Commission. (1994). *The City of New York Commission to Investigate Allegations of Police Corruption and the Anti-Corruption Procedures of the Police Department: Commission Report*. New York: City of New York.

Mosley, B. (December 12, 2015). Tullahoma man witnessed famous shooting. *Times- Gazette.*

Murphy, S. (January 18, 2004). Former FBI agent Rico dies in hospital. *The Boston Globe.*

Ranalli, R. (2001). *Deadly Alliance: The FBI's Secret Partnership with the Mob*. New York: HarperTorch.

Root, J. (1961). *The Life and Bad Times of Charles Becker*. London: Seeker & Warburg.

Sanz, C. (October 2, 1995). A killer in blue. *People.com.*

Seranno, R.A. (November 2, 1991). Leasure pleads no contest to murder counts. *Los Angeles Times.*

Stephens, C. (March 6, 2009). NYPD's notorious "Mafia Cops" sentenced to life. *Cnn.com.*

Chapter 12

Into the Future

INTRODUCTION

Our discussion focused on the social justice issue of LEO-perpetrated homicides. The police professional community has historically emphasized police homicides with LEOs as victims, while ignoring LEOs as perpetrators of deadly violence. Whenever a LEO homicide was deemed unjustified, the agency and the "blue brotherhood" was quick to close ranks and condemn the rotten apples. After all, the powerful law enforcement community was able to receive, investigate, and adjudicate all complaints against members and the agency. In our fragmented law enforcement system with local, state, and federal agencies there are no national standards or official statistics on the use of force by U.S. law enforcement agencies. There was little in the way of transparency or accountability for police-caused homicides.

The academic community for the most part failed to address deaths caused by LEOs. The lack of data and access to police agencies was the primary cause of this lack of academic interest. This myopic view changed dramatically with the social unrest that followed the 2014 police shooting death of a black man by a white officer in Ferguson, Missouri. A spate of similar shootings followed raising police-perpetrated shooting deaths to a Moral Panic fueled by the social media and special interest groups. However, as laudable as this new interest in police-caused deaths, it has revealed serious gaps in what is known about police-perpetrated homicides. This work attempts to fill those gaps and suggest a new approach to law enforcement–perpetrated homicides.

NEW APPROACH

The understanding of police-perpetrated homicides rests on the empirical foundation that a range of police-caused homicide patterns exist in the real world. The author knew that from his "on the job" experiences and over forty years of research on police misconduct and police criminal behavior. If we seek to prevent, control, and assist the professional community in their reform efforts and conduct research on this social justice problem, we must demystify this complex issue—the police use of deadly force. The first step toward the demystifying goal is the development of a typology of LEO-perpetrated homicides. The types or patterns identified and discussed in this book ranged from accidental homicides to intentional murders.

The typology of LEO-perpetrated homicides developed demonstrates that the issue is a complex problem with no "silver bullet" solutions where one fix will work on all types. Police officers at all levels of government cause these deaths. The victims of police-caused homicides are domestic partners, strangers, family members, fellow officers, criminals, adults, children, males, females, transgender, whites, blacks, other people of color, and the list goes on. In other words, under some circumstances, any person can be a victim of a police-perpetrated homicide. The presence of mentally ill persons and inmates in custody in the large pool of vulnerable victims strongly suggests a reexamination of police training, protocols, and the use of non-lethal weapons. Equally disturbing is the criminal misuse of non-lethal or less than lethal weapons such as the Taser. The examples presented indicate that technological assists, such as surveillance cameras, body cameras, and DNA, can be a part of the police reform effort.

The lack of reliable data on police-perpetrated homicides is the greatest obstacle to a better understanding of law enforcement–perpetrated homicides. However, as pointed out, data collection is improving with the use of several data sets supplemented with open-source data. I am optimistic that researchers and professionals can use the typology as a heuristic device to examine and provide useful solutions to *law enforcement–perpetrated homicides.*

Index

Page numbers in *italics* indicate figures and tables.

About the Author

Dr. Tom Barker has lived the life as an "on the job" police officer, police trainer, and long-time researcher of police crime and misconduct. He is a former ACJS president and recipient of numerous awards. Dr. Barker has published extensively and is recognized as a national and international expert on police issues.

www.ingramcontent.com/pod-product-compliance
Lightning Source LLC
Chambersburg PA
CBHW050648280326
41932CB00015B/2823